'Mad Mike' Hoare: The Legend

Books authored by Mike Hoare

Congo Mercenary
Congo Warriors
The Road to Kalamata
The Seychelles Affair
Three Years with 'Sylvia'
Mike Hoare's Adventures in Africa
Mokoro – A cry for help!
The Last Days of the Cathars

'Mad Mike' Hoare: The Legend

Chris Hoare (signature)

Chris Hoare

Partners in Publishing
Durban, South Africa

First Edition
First published in July 2018 by
Partners in Publishing
PO Box 201191, Durban North, 4016, South Africa

Website: www.madmikehoare.com

ISBN 978-0-620-79861-7

Cover photo: Bob Houcke
Cover: Apple Pie Graphics
Maps (not to scale): Flying Ant Designs
Printed by Pinetown Printers

Dedication:
To my wife Terry, for her abiding patience, kindness and support

Contents

viii

Author's Note

I have always been surprised at the response I usually get when someone finds out that the famous 'Mad Mike' is my father. 'Whaaaat?' they say. 'No way! Wow! That man is a legend, an absolute legend.'

And I have always been fascinated by the inaccuracy of reports about Mike in the media and on the internet. In *The Economist* of 16 February 2002, Mike is described as 'an ex-paratrooper', and at one time Wikipedia said, 'He served in <u>North Africa</u> .... during World War II, and achieved the rank of <u>Captain</u>.'

Mike came to hate publicity and to 'loathe the press – all they are interested in is sensationalism'. And one can sympathise; in 1986 a newspaper serialised Mike's book on the Seychelles affair under the massive headline: The Dogs of Hoare. The writer of the headline was no doubt applauded by his peers, but Mike would have felt castigated. On another occasion he explained, 'It is my <u>private</u> life. I don't want to share it with Tom, Dick and Harry.'

It must be said, of course, that the nature of his activities was sometimes such that he and the media were in opposing camps.

He gave few interviews post-Congo (apart from his tour of America to promote the film *The Wild Geese*), and in his later years turned down scores of requests from documentary filmmakers, journalists and even serious writers and historians. As a result, and in fairness to the media, little reliable information about his life has been available, except what is recorded in his published books. And even then, some of Mike's writings are not accurate, as we shall see.

I started discussing this biography with Mike in the 1980s, and indeed in a letter to me dated 20 August 1985, he refers to me as his biographer. Nevertheless, for decades it was a touchy subject with Mike. I conducted recorded interviews with him in 1985, and again in 2006 by which time he had given proper blessing to the concept of this biography and was prepared to speak more openly.

Mike has not read any of the manuscript.

I have covered the military aspects of his life in full, while also revealing the other sides of his adventurous life. I believe I have painted a true and balanced portrait of Mike as I know him, and I have presented it in the only way I can.

For what it is worth, Mike said of me in *Three Years with 'Sylvia'*, albeit in another context, 'I knew I could rely on him, he has never been known to exaggerate.' And certainly in this case there is no need to exaggerate – the facts are sensation enough.

In writing this book I conducted interviews with people who knew him. I drew on short stories he wrote and sent me; our correspondence over the years including his prison letters, and probably hundreds of emails; newspaper and magazine cuttings, archives, a detailed diary written in 1958, various documents among his papers, speeches he gave and which I recorded, and video material in my possession. And, not least of all, I drew on my own lifetime (69 years plus) of experience as his eldest son.

I have also drawn from his seven published non-fiction works (*Congo Mercenary, The Road to Kalamata, Congo Warriors, The Seychelles Affair, Three Years with 'Sylvia', Mokoro – A cry for help!*, and *Mike Hoare's Adventures in Africa*) and a historical novel (*The Last Days of the Cathars*).

For convenience, I have used the place names and other terms that were in use at the time the events took place.

Round brackets are mine; square brackets are used when the brackets already existed in a quote.

Researching and writing this biography took about 12 years, working between times, and it became my passion. Overall, it was an immensely enjoyable if somewhat solitary experience.

Chris Hoare, Durban

x

Mike Hoare Family Tree

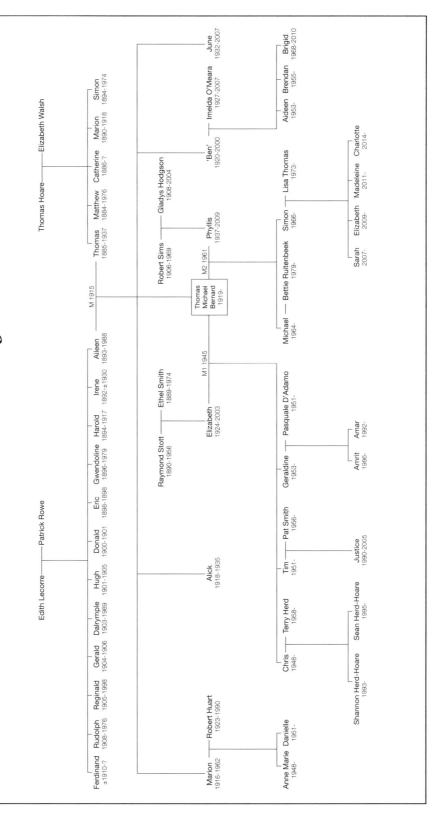

Introduction

Not everyone agreed with the usual description of Mike Hoare – an officer and a gentleman. Some said there was a bit of pirate thrown in. A few said he was mad. One of his officers said he was ruthless.

But everyone agreed he was that rare breed, someone who 'got off his backside and did something about what he believed in'. He believed that the communists were going to take over the Congo and then the countries to the south, including his adopted country, South Africa. He wasn't going to have his children and grandchildren growing up speaking Russian, no sir, so he took the fight to the Reds …

Although he was also called a 'gentleman adventurer', Mike described himself as 'a genuine adventurer', saying adventure had motivated nearly everything he had done. He identified with Sir Francis Drake, and relished the idea of bringing Spanish booty back for the queen who would make you a knight. 'You were respectable – even though you were a thief,' he said.

He had got off to a good start during World War 2 when he was called 'the best bloody soldier in the British Army'; after the war, he embraced the then popular philosophy that you get more out of life by living dangerously. This enigmatic and sometimes sentimental swashbuckler was, by contrast, also a literary man who loved words, paper, writing, books and Shakespeare.

He found relevance in the lines from George Bernard Shaw's *Man and Superman* where Mendoza says in Act III: 'Sir, I will be frank with you. Brigandage is abnormal. Abnormal professions attract two classes: those who are not good enough for ordinary bourgeois life and those who are too good for it. We are dregs and scum sir, the dregs very filthy, the scum very superior.'

Was he mad, or just adventurous, or both? Was he 'dregs very filthy', or 'scum very superior'?

1. The Youngster

'Given his childhood, it's a miracle he is not even more peculiar!' –
First wife, Betty.

When I was a teenager, I remember my mother often saying, 'Your father is peculiar, but given his childhood it is a miracle that he is not even more peculiar!' And now, in retrospect, it seems obvious that it was Mike's peculiar childhood that equipped him so well for the adventures and horrors that were to be his lot in later life.

His male forebears came from the port of Rush, County Dublin, Ireland. Back in the day, it was a tough little place which produced adventurous sailors and indeed Mike's father, grandfather and great-grandfather had all been captains on sailing ships. Many Rush men in days gone by, apparently, were privateers and the family tree describes one Christopher Sheridan, born circa 1720, as a 'smuggler/privateer'.

A family story refers to a time when Mike's grandfather was beating down the Bristol Channel homeward bound. A full-rigged ship was approaching him to starboard, running before the wind, carrying an extravagant amount of sail. He peered at it through his telescope. 'What blithering idiot is in command of that?' he asked. The mate read the name on the ship's transom as she thundered by. 'Your son, captain.'

Mike's father, Thomas, went to sea at the age of 17, doing a five-year apprenticeship on the 3000-ton four-masted steel barque

Fingal, a square-rigged sailing ship owned by Palgrave Murphy, out of Dublin. *Fingal*'s run was to San Francisco and Vancouver via the dreaded Cape Horn, and also across the Pacific to Yokohama, Japan. It would have been a gruelling round trip of many months.

Thomas joined the Port Commissioners in Calcutta Harbour, India, in 1914. Initially, he piloted steamships up the Hooghly River, but by 1916 he was the Assistant Harbour Master, and in 1934 he became Dock Master.[1]

Mike said his father would regularly bring home the officers from the ships he piloted, and they would flatten a few bottles of whisky together. He described his father as a 'tough little character' who was a 'superb pilot', a 'great Bible reader' and a 'reader of history'. He was also a great entertainer who loved museums and all things historical.

Mike's mother was Aileen Muriel Hoare (née Rowe), one of 12 children, and of Irish and French descent. As a young woman, she was a talented musician and a trained singer. Later she was spoken of as a high flyer, and in polite family circles she was described as eccentric; in less polite family circles, she was described less politely.

Mike was born Thomas Michael Bernard in Calcutta. Luck of the Irish, it was St Patrick's Day, 17 March 1919. Not only that, but he was born with a caul membrane surrounding his head – reputed by some to bring luck. And indeed, many is the time that Mike reflected on the luck he had during his life.

He was the middle child of five: Marion, Alick, Matthew (known as Ben) and June.

Mike's early childhood home was at Budge Budge in the south-western suburbs of Calcutta on the banks of the Hooghly River. It was the kind of home where children were to be seen and not heard.

At the age of about four, Mike started going to the Loreto Convent in Calcutta and apparently used to get a lot of mileage out of saying to the nuns, 'Can I have a kiss, then?'[2]

In 1926, the whole family sailed from Calcutta to Plymouth, and thence to Ireland. Soon Mickey, as he was called in the family for many years, was sent with his older brother Alick to Cannock

House, a boarding school in Eltham, Kent; this signalled the end of family life for Mike, then about 8 years of age. Further, he was to see his father during only two patches during the next eight years, when his father got a year's leave from duty in Calcutta every three years and would spend most of that time in Ireland.

Then the boys went to a superior private boarding school, Margate College, in Margate, Kent. Ben joined the school when he was about 14 and later said that his 'very selfish mother simply dumped' Mike and Alick at the school – which was 'run by a colonel like a military school'.

Mike, who often came first in class, became a keen member of the debating society, captain of games (but hated distance runs) and a school prefect – but was the shortest boy in his grade.

Mike, who was later to be most successful in business in South Africa, showed talent with money at a young age. Ben would tell how he and Mike used to get £1 a term in pocket money; after a few weeks, Ben had none left, and Mike had turned a profit by trading in items like sweets that his schoolmates needed.

During the holidays, as their parents were in India, Mike and Alick usually stayed at the school in the care of a Sergeant Badcock, the PT instructor. Badcock, a man of some 55-60 years, had fought in the Anglo-Boer War in South Africa a mere 30 years previously. Mike remembered Badcock as a wiry Cockney who had served in the Middlesex regiment in Natal. Mike and Alick spent long hours with Badcock down at the seaside or in Dane Park, listening to his stories about soldiering; Mike loved the stories and got to know the names of all the towns and battles.

Plainly, Badcock had loved his time in the army, and told his stories with gusto. They sounded 'adventurous, marvellous', Mike said. They 'overflowed into' him, stories about the battle at Spioenkop (1900), where Badcock had actually fought and which he mispronounced 'Spy-on Kop', and other famous battles. Mike got well and truly infected with military fervour and an adventurous heart. This developed into a passion for soldiering.

In the 6th form Mike had an excellent current-affairs teacher who sparked his interest in politics, and the war that was looming with Germany. And it was here that he started reading the *Daily Telegraph* newspaper; it became a lifelong habit.

Mike also developed a love of words and reading at the school, and was influenced by the books of Livingstone, Burton, Speke, Grant and Stanley which had been the companions of his boyhood, as well as characters like Scott of the Antarctic and General Charles Gordon.

Meanwhile, Thomas and Aileen's marriage was foundering. It would appear that Aileen had left Thomas in the late 1920s, returned in the early 1930s, and left again some time after the birth of June in 1932. In 1935, Aileen settled in Spain, taking a house in Palma, Majorca, the largest of the Balearic islands in the Mediterranean. In December 1935, however, tragedy struck. Mike had done the London University matriculation in June 1935[3] and finished school, but was still at Margate College; he wanted more than anything to become an officer in the army, and he was studying for the entrance examination to Sandhurst, the British Army's officer training college. Alick was hoping to go to university. They were waiting for instructions from India.

Suddenly, Alick was taken ill with pneumonia and sent to St Thomas's Hospital in London. His mother was called from Majorca, but Alick died on 17 December before she could get there, with Mike holding his hand. Mike said this heart-breaking event had affected him his whole life.

After a few weeks together as a family in a rented villa at Son Matet, Palma, Marion and Mike returned to London to stay with an aunt, as the stay with their mother had been a disaster.

Then in 1936 the Spanish civil war broke out and all British subjects had to be evacuated. The story goes that Aileen and June had to leave everything behind – including the Cadillac and Spanish 'chauffeur'; they were taken to Portsmouth on a British warship. Later the Foreign Office sent Aileen a note, asking her to kindly call on them, which she did. They then presented her with a bill for the evacuation, which she kindly paid. She then returned to Calcutta.

Now, Mike's unusual childhood was effectively over, but many useful elements were already in place: Irish fighting spirit, military fervour, an adventurous heart, a love of current affairs, entrepreneurial skill, and an unemotional demeanour.

In February 1936, Mike found himself a job in the smalls of the *Daily* with a company of chartered accountants, Brown Fleming & Murray, at 4b Fredericks Place, Old Jewry, London EC4. The wages were £1 a week and Mike would describe it as 'the worst year of my life; all I did was add up figures'.

Then, a second tragedy in just over a year: Mike received the devastating news that his father, aged 52, had drowned (in late January 1937) in a type of reservoir or dam in Calcutta. The cause of death was always a dark secret in the family, but in his old age Mike confided his father had been on his way to visit a ship one night when he was 'robbed and murdered'. No one was ever held accountable.

Then Aileen bought a house at 16 The Ridgeway, Stanmore, in north-west London. The family was re-united and at first harmony prevailed. Marion was apprenticed to a hairdresser in Bond Street and Ben was doing what he wanted: studying to be a wireless operator at sea. June was still a small girl.

Mike, however, was without the means to go to Sandhurst because of his father's death. In April 1937, his mother paid 150 guineas for him to be articled to John M Winter & Sons[4], chartered accountants, at 39 St James's St, London SW1. Mike hated it, but it was at this time that he started doing cryptic crosswords on the commuter train – he got great satisfaction from completing the crossword before the train arrived at his destination. It was the beginning of another lifelong pursuit.

That year (1937), Mike joined the posh Stanmore Cricket Club as a spin bowler, later being more of a batsman. Once a year, his club had the privilege of playing at the prestigious Lord's cricket ground in London. In 1939 Mike played there in the end-of-season match. The opposing team were the ground staff – including the Compton brothers Denis and Leslie, and Bill Edrich.

Back at the Stanmore family home in 1937, life was rosy ...... but in July 1938 it became an 'impossible situation' and Mike and Ben, having to support themselves, went to live in a bedsit in Bayswater.

Mike was now a good-looking 20-year-old, of slight build, with light brown hair, thin nose and, dare I say, almost blowtorch-blue eyes. His front teeth were decidedly irregular, but he was never self-conscious about what he called his 'fangs'. He had a sharp mind and quick wits, was conscientious and well organised. With a developed sense of decorum, and an interest in poetry, literature and classical music, he would soon qualify as cultured. With a double dose of charm and a ready sense of humour, Mike was on his way up.

However, in March 1939 the senior partner at the accountancy practice called all the staff together. He told them that a war was looming, and that each man was to do his bit by enlisting for military service. A short while later, he called another meeting to see who had signed up. Mike was the only one who had responded: on 17 April he had enlisted in the Territorial Army (TA, a reserve force). According to his war service record, his height was 5'7" (1,7 metres) and he weighed 133 pounds (60 kg) at this time. His complexion is given as 'Irish' and his religious denomination as Church of England.[5] His number in the TA was 7014567.

Meanwhile, he had to do a certain number of drills with the London Irish Rifles and attended a 15-day camp at New Forest in August 1939, making some friends in the process. 'Then,' Mike recalls, 'a great and marvellous light appeared in my life – the imminence of war.' However, one-third of his sixth-form class did not come back from the war, and perhaps for this reason he always marked Remembrance Day with a sombre mood.

2. *The Soldier*

Mike was the 'best bloody soldier in the British Army'. – Company commander Paddy Brett

On Friday 1 September 1939, the Territorials were embodied into the British Army. The *Evening News* that day said that key members of the reserves were being called to their units at once. Mike always had an astounding memory for amounts of money he paid or received, and in this case he remembered that a bounty of £5 was payable on embodiment; the impoverished articled clerk called it a 'king's ransom'.

All that week he had been doing a solo audit, something of a promotion for him. At 5 pm he went back to his offices in St James's Street to collect his wages: 35 shillings a week. His principal was concerned only with the following week's audit programme, and Mike began 'to worry that peace might break out'. However, he did not see that office again for seven years.

Mike had been living at his mother's again at Stanmore, and that is where he now went. He later wrote: 'I was a bag of mixed emotions. I was sorry to leave home but happy to be going to war. Little did I know that adventure and war as I was going to find it were two very different things. I dressed slowly in my ill-fitting battledress uniform and hung my city clothes in a wardrobe for the last time. I made my way on the underground to Sloane Square en route for the Duke of York's Headquarters in the King's Road, Chelsea. It was pitch dark when I arrived at the wrought-iron gates, my kit bag on my shoulder. Blackout had descended on London hand in hand with a strange anticipation of we knew not what. I groped my way to a chink of light. A notice on a door said '2 LIR report here'. Inside the candle-lit hut I joined a silent apprehensive queue, all stripped to the waist. When my turn came a Quarter Master Sergeant handed me a book and told me to raise my right hand and recite after him the Oath of Allegiance to the King.

'But Quarter Master,' I said, when I'd been sworn in, 'that's not a Bible, that's a dictionary! I've got one just like it at home.'

'All right sunshine, so you're the only one wot knows. Keep your bleeding trap shut, see. If it's good enough for the other 300, it's good enough for you, i'n it? Over there, MO will look at you.'

'The medical officer, a harassed individual in shirtsleeves with a stethoscope round his neck, examined me perfunctorily. Eyes open and breathing was the minimum standard. Twenty seconds later I was passed fit, a fully fledged rifleman in the infantry.'

Mike was now a Rifleman in E Company in the 2nd Battalion of the London Irish Rifles, The Royal Ulster Rifles.

Finding an orderly sergeant, Mike asked where he would find blankets.

OS: We have no blankets.

MH: But how am I going to sleep without blankets?

OS: You are going to learn, aren't you!

'I joined a group of familiar Irish faces – the brothers Danny and Johnny Long from Kilkenny, little Jimmy Sullivan from Cork, Tommy Clifford from Nenagh, Co. Tip, Paddy Fraser from Limerick, shure hadn't we the gaiety – all destined to be killed or severely wounded in Tunisia fighting alongside the Americans in 1943. God rest their souls. We went to the Nag's Head in Sloane Square for a last civilian or first army drink, wondering when the air raids would begin.

'When the pubs shut we made our way to number 25 Eaton Square where we were to be billeted. It was an empty Victorian mansion. The rooms were dusty and bare. There were no blankets and no lights. We slept on the bare boards, my kit bag making a pillow of sorts. The booze kept me warm. Just after midnight a torch flashed briefly round the walls and a fruity voice breathed o'er Eden, 'Good show chaps. All nice and comfortable, what?' It was one of our officers. He must have been reading Man Management and Leadership. But he waited not for an answer, which, in the circumstances, was just as well.'[6]

On 3 September 1939, Britain declared war on Germany. Mike often referred to this as the happiest day of his life. He always joked that it was because he knew he was now going to get three meals a day, but it seems more likely that he knew his day as a soldier had finally come. In later years, he would invariably write to me on 3 September, recalling those days.

Mike remembers the first morning at the Duke of York's HQ. 'The cookhouse was using fires with stones, camp kettles and so on. Reveille was at 6, breakfast was at 7. We rushed there with our dixies (mess tins) and were served porridge, egg and bacon, bread and hot tea. Even so, some blokes were moaning that their wives served better breakfasts, and so on.' Mike could not believe their attitude – for him, this was luxury.

After about two months at the Duke of York's HQ, his unit moved to Gifford House, Putney where his company was. The training they were getting was 'very basic' as there were 'no arms to speak of'. Mike once said he was issued with a Lee Enfield .303 rifle, and had become a crack shot; when it came to target shooting on the range, he always ranked in the top three in his regiment of 780 men, he said.

He was promoted lance corporal on 1 November 1939 [7], but many believed the war would be over by Christmas. 'This was my greatest fear. The thought of going back to that bloody office was too much for me.'

Late in 1939, Mike got some leave and visited his uncle Simon and other Irish relatives in Rush and this became his preference when on leave during the war. He always remembered how they used to tell him, 'You are not going back to England, you know. You are one of us. You don't owe them anything.' But Mike would have none of it; he was living his dream.

He captained his regiment's soccer team in 1939 and 1940, and

remembered playing, at inside right, in a match against a professional side on his 21st birthday, 17 March 1940. Apparently,
the manager of the other side had made it known that he would
be watching Mike's performance, with a view to signing him on.
However, Mike said he had German measles and a high temperature
that day, and it had all come to nought.

By April 1940, his unit had finally come to rest after being shunted
around the Midlands, but garrison life was getting him down. He
wanted some sort of action. 'One day, Brett sends for me. He says
the officers have had a meeting and the colonel has my name down
to be sent to Sandhurst, and do I want to go? Now, we had formed
groups, the men, and we would go drinking in pubs and so on. I was
particularly enjoying the native Irish – I loved them all. They were
very ordinary blokes, painters, tradesmen, navvies, but real men. I
said I would think about it. Brett said the alternative was the Small
Arms School at Hythe where there were brand new barracks and so
on. If I took that option, then I would not be able to go to Sandhurst,
I would have to return to the unit and train them for a year.'

In 2004 and for the first time, Mike told me that he had had a
good rapport with Capt Brett, who was a regular army officer, and
that Brett had once told him he was 'the best bloody soldier in the
British Army'.

Mike loved small arms and everything about them – he had to go
to Hythe. As it happened, he had been singled out as the only man
from the entire regiment to go to the school. On arrival, in April
1940, Mike realised what an honour his selection had been – all the
other trainees were sergeants and warrant officers, whereas he was
just a lance corporal. He was thus made an honorary sergeant, he
said.[8]

'This was the happiest time of my army life. The course was
beautifully organised and cemented my love of soldiering. I could
see how things could be done.'

Brett once told me how he could still remember Mike's eagerness
in training, and cites it as the primary reason for selecting a lance
corporal to attend an advanced school primarily intended for senior
NCOs and junior officers.

'Mike's real strength at that time was that he was anxious to do something, not just be part of the herd on the sidelines,' he said. 'I sent Mike to Hythe to see if he could take months of what was really a vicious and horrible course, a battle school where you went everywhere at the double, you learned small arms intimately. When you finish at Hythe, there's the beginnings of a bloke who is not going to lose his head.'

Mike, on the other hand, remembered the course as 'marvellous' and 'a turning point in my life as it opened my eyes to a new vision'. 'It taught not so much the mechanics of the weapons, but how to teach. It is an important thing with soldiers, that every trainer teaches exactly the same thing, you don't deviate, and you don't teach too much; they are ordinary blokes, after all.' The weapons training covered various side arms, the Bren light machine gun and the Lee Enfield rifle, Mk III.

Hythe was Mike's first brush with regular soldiers. 'They were back from Afghanistan, Barbados, all over the empire. We had dormitories; it was my first time in a properly organised barracks. I loved that form of soldiering. It was so right. Marvellous. We would hear about the fighting in France on the radio. One day we heard that German panzer divisions had broken through at Sedan and we looked at a map. I remember a hard-bitten bugger starting to cry. He was saying, "I'm here. My regiment is there. I've got to get there." All his mates were getting killed. I have always remembered that scene. It conveyed to me his loyalty to his regiment and showed me that soldiering is more than saluting and drills, it is comradeship of people together. It made a tremendous impression on me.'

Until this time, Mike had been something of a boxer[9] and represented his unit on occasion[10], but this didn't last, he later said, because his uneven teeth caused his top lip to bleed profusely after a blow – and then it would turn septic.

It was marching that Mike really came to love, and later he would say, 'In my day, I could outmarch anybody. March discipline was something I got to know all about in the infantry in the first years of our war. A man who could march 15 to 20 miles in a day in battle order and go to a dance the same evening was my idea of a real soldier. I loved the camaraderie which sprang from those long route marches. I suppose their main purpose was to promote physical fitness, seeing that the army was becoming very largely mechanised, but discipline and the small unit spirit were fostered at the same time, and there are not many ways of doing that. Hardship shared is one of the best ways; another is to face a common fear. Cold fear, as I have found out since, is the greatest leveller and uniter of men, and knows no distinctions of class, race or colour.'[11]

On 30 July 1940, Mike was promoted corporal. Most likely he now spent some months with his unit at Malvern, and, after the Germans had bombed Coventry to destruction in November 1940, he participated in the clean-up effort.[12]

In January 1941, a report by Captain Brett states that Mike is of 'above average intelligence and of good character; keen in every way. Always keen to do any extra training. Clean turn out.' He also noted Mike had played soccer and cricket in the battalion team. Brett now sent Mike from Malvern to the 170 (MG) Officer Cadet Training Unit (OCTU) at Droitwich.[13]

Here, Mike was regarded as a weapons expert, and he got to love the Vickers machine gun. 'The Vickers did not play a big part in World War 2, in which mobility of troops was restored. World War 1 was a ghastly affair, and I put it down to stupidity between the politicians and the generals of that time. Can you imagine Passchendaele? Hundreds of thousands of casualties in one long battle! Unbelievable! Lines over 100 miles long firing barrages for 30 hours. Can you imagine what that was like?'

Each cadet had to deliver a formal address on a subject of their choice during their spell at Droitwich. It is notable that Mike spoke on 'Iron Discipline', lauding the Germans in this regard. He said, however, that his address had not been that well received higher up, because it was felt the German attitude to discipline, while militarily effective, was also destructive of soldiers.

Two cadets got an A rating at the end of the OCTU course; Mike was one of them. The company commander's report on Mike is worth repeating in full:

'1st month: Has personality and a sense of humour. Is a very good
Bren LMG instructor, has been used as such. Both practical and
theoretical work good. Will make a good officer.
2nd month: Keen and capable. Shows many qualities of leadership.
3rd month: Has worked very well and is developing satisfactorily.
4th month: Has all the qualities of a good platoon commander and
should do extremely well.
5th and 6th months combined: A forceful and aggressive type who
should make a first class leader in battle and would undoubtedly
be the inspiration of his platoon. Has worked extremely well
throughout and has a very sound theoretical knowledge.'[14]
The commanding officer's remarks on 26 May 1941 are:
'Category A: This cadet is outstanding and has done excellent
work throughout. He will make a sound and reliable officer and
should go a long way.'[15]

On 31 May 1941 Mike was commissioned second lieutenant. It
had taken him longer than usual to become an officer, but he was
also now an authority on small arms, which was 'invaluable'. He
went home to Stanmore on leave, and thence to Rush.[16]

In June 1941, Mike took up a special posting to the newly formed
2 Reconnaissance Regiment, Reconnaissance Corps, a part of the
Royal Armoured Corps; his number was 189576. The regiment
was for elite officers only. On arrival at Driffield, Yorkshire, he was
posted to C Squadron and took over a troop. As an armoured unit,
they had armoured cars which Mike described as 'an assembly of
old crocks'. They were waiting for the Humber armoured car. It
was here that Mike met Teddy Lane, the senior lieutenant in the
squadron, and a lawyer in peacetime. They became firmest friends
and were to meet again.

After about nine months of training, which included a course
for leaders in Lincoln (August-September 1941) the whole division
moved to Berkshire prior to an overseas posting. Mike went back
to Stanmore on two weeks' embarkation leave,[17] to find his mother
on her own – with June presumably at a boarding school. Mike's
sister Marion was no longer at home, having married a naval officer,
Percival John 'Jack' Young. 'Then an awful thing happened. His ship

(*SS Empire Light*) was sunk in the Indian Ocean (near Madagascar) and he was made a prisoner on a German cruiser which in turn was sunk by the Royal Navy ... with all the prisoners down below. The navy, being the navy, gave Marion a job at the Admiralty and somewhere to live.' Marion married Robert Huart, a Belgian, in 1947 and they emigrated to Melbourne, Australia, having two daughters, Anne Marie and Danielle. Marion died on 2 August 1962.[18]

On 11 April 1942, the recce unit boarded ship in Glasgow. They were issued with tropical kit, prompting them to think they were going to the Middle East; Mike recalled they even had the same topees (pith helmets) as were issued to the British forces in the Sudan 50 years previously.

Their route took them across the Atlantic Ocean to South America to avoid the German U-boats and back across to Cape Town, South Africa. Mike's first taste of Africa was to be life-changing though he did not know it at the time. 'We had had lectures for life on the ship, and now I was seeing what Badcock had conjured up in my imagination. We spent a week or ten days there with sunshine and magnificent girls; even regular blokes seemed to be driving Cadillacs. This is too much, I thought. It was terrific! I was very taken with the place.

'I remember visiting the main post office one day and was surprised to see a sentry outside. It turned out that the previous week an Australian unit had cheekily lifted an Austin 7 motorcar onto a counter, and the authorities were concerned that we British might try to better their effort. No one was homesick when we left Britain, but we were all sorry to leave Africa.'

The ship anchored off Durban, and seeing the golden beachfront from the ship, Mike said to himself, 'Wow, this is for me.'

By now, the British had decided to capture Madagascar, a French island that had been overrun, so the ship stood off the island for a period, but it was then directed toward Egypt. Then there was a change of plan: possibly in the wake of the fall of Singapore, the ship was diverted to Bombay. They made their way to nearby Poona by train, where life was pretty comfortable – nothing like the war in Europe, in fact. Mike recalled that he and the other officers all employed Indian bearers who would come and shave them in bed in the morning, under their mosquito nets.

In due course, however, General Archibald Wavell, Commander-in-Chief, India, paid a visit and his first order was: 'We are a British division and no Indians will be employed whatsoever.' On another occasion, Earl Louis Mountbatten, Supreme Allied Commander South East Asia Command, came to meet the officers, but Mike said when it came time to be introduced, 'our colonel was so dim he could hardly remember his own name, let alone ours; so as Mountbatten and the colonel came down the line, the colonel blithely called out arbitrary names. I was introduced as Rogers.'

It was here too that Mike had a stroke of luck. 'One day I was approached by the quartermaster and the squadron leader, with whom I was friendly. They explained that they were going to the horse races in Poona and needed another 2000 rupees or whatever it was, which they would gamble on my behalf. I was naive; I gave it to them. They won an unbelievable amount – I had never had so much money in my life. Naturally, I joined the Poona turf club, which was very select and expensive, but I had the money.'

Mike later said that he had hired a car and had uniforms made by a British tailor in Poona. He also said the money had come easily, so he had had no trouble in spending it. He would, however, have nothing to do with any of the many groups that played bridge in spare moments, regarding it as a 'terrible waste of time'. Rather, he adopted a habit that he later called the 'secret of life': a rest after lunch.

Meanwhile, Mike was still training men in the use of armoured cars and carriers. In August of that year (1942), Mahatma Gandhi, the famous political and spiritual leader, was arrested and taken to Aga Khan Palace in Poona. Other leaders were also arrested, and rioting crowds formed in protest. Mike, still a second lieutenant, was called out with a Humber armoured car, probably the Mk IV, to face the immense mobs. 'They had a good system in India. You took an Indian magistrate with you, which relieved you entirely of responsibility. He was trained to understand the political situation, and you were – as you ought to be in the army – an extension of the political will. The rule was you couldn't open fire without a special pink form being signed by the magistrate. It seemed ridiculous in theory, but it worked well. You anticipated the time might come soon when you would have to open fire, and he would say "OK, I am signing the pink form" and then he would say "Control the crowd by shooting that man there" and we would take him out with a rifle – machine guns were not permitted for this purpose. All it needed was one shot, such was the crowd psychology in India.'

Now, in December 1942, it was time for jungle training at Belgaum, near Goa. As a signals officer, part of Mike's duties was the command and training of a signals troop. There were 23 motorcycles in that unit and the men were all from Lancashire where trials-riding was the sport. The Lancashire lads taught Mike how to ride a 500cc BSA 'bone shaker' properly, he said.

But, on 22 February 1943, having to report to divisional HQ with all the secret codes, he rode off through the jungle on a motorbike. Unfortunately, he did not notice an exposed and slippery root. 'Next thing, I am lying unconscious on the track, with the motorcycle on top of me. I am bleeding from my right knee and ankle. A truck came along and took me to hospital. The Indian surgeon said the knee-cap was cracked and the knee very badly damaged. They did not operate, they just put my leg on a board for six weeks.'

Mike was left with a large round scar on his knee, but he would always make light of it when we, as small children, questioned him as to its origin, by saying things like: 'All I can say is that there were eight of them (Japanese soldiers).'

'From the hospital, I was sent to Ootacamund hill station in the Nilgiri Hills where I had to learn to walk again. Then to a reinforcement camp at Deolali, near Bombay, an awful place. The colonel heard I had been an articled clerk and gave me an office job. I loathed it; I was furious; then an influential friend managed to get me back to my unit.'

In July 1943 Mike rejoined his regiment but was unable to do long marches. By the September, his injury had caught up with him and he had to spend three weeks in Ahmednagar Hospital. But the trend was upward, the knee was strengthening. After the war, Mike was awarded a £75 gratuity for the fracture.

The unit was now based at Combined Ops (offensive amphibious operations) HQ on Madh Island, near Bombay, and the commanding officer, Colonel Bradford, started giving Mike his own command. Mike led all the experimental work on an American amphibian carrier, the LVT 1 (Landing Vehicle Tracked), with the aim of being able to supply a training unit. The LVT was a 16-ton monster that could carry 24 men or two tonnes of equipment; it was powered by an aeroplane engine, and steered with two levers.

'This was good fun and part of preparations for the impending invasion of Malaya. I made a good job of commanding that unit; Bradford was very impressed and I was promoted to full lieutenant (1 October 1943).'[19]

Now, in March/April 1944, 'Suddenly, we got a signal from Poona to take the unit and report to Calcutta. It was going very bad for us, the Japs were taking everything. They had knocked hell out of the brigade there (to the north, near Dimapur), so it was a case of "2 Div to the rescue". This was the role for which we had been prepared, a division in reserve for just this sort of thing. However, we had not been trained for the jungle, we were combined ops.

'I took my unit and joined Col Bradford's 2 Recce Regiment in Calcutta. From there, the whole regiment got on a train and we travelled for three days up the Brahmaputra River valley to Assam. As we got close to Dimapur railhead, we started hearing rumours: the Japs are in Dimapur. But it was not so. Just as well, because if they had taken Dimapur, nothing was going to stop them coming into India.

'A few hours before Dimapur, the colonel called an O Group. I remember it so well. We had done it in training 200 times. There is a certain structure: information enemy, information own troops, intention, method and so on. When Bradford said "information enemy" it was a real thrill for me; "information own troops" and he gave our details; "intention" is to defeat the Japanese – I found that so exciting.

'We arrived in Dimapur, but had to get to Kohima as quickly

as we could. As a reconnaissance group, we were supposed to be working ahead of our troops, touching the enemy here and there, and reporting back. I was sent on three patrols in three days. The squadron leader said, "Sorry, we haven't got anyone else". He apologised profusely as the chances of getting killed were good. Now we were 19 miles from Kohima, and coming towards us were ambulances and trucks; then they started moving the wounded at night so as not to demoralise the (incoming) troops.

'We were a mobile armoured reconnaissance unit (2 Recce, 2 Div, 33 Corps) playing an infantry role! We were placed on the right flank of 6 Brigade, 2 Div. My troop were in trenches in the most forward position facing the enemy. They (the Japanese) are dug in to bunkers about 400 yards in front of us. Now we can see the bastards, they are digging. We came to realise that they had new tactics, much better than ours. Better to dig behind the hill and tunnel through.

'Some time later, after a very heavy preliminary bombardment by our artillery on the Jap positions, we advanced. We can see Kohima on that hill there. It is World War 1 stuff, bayonets, whistle, over the top, after 200 yards, down there. A lieutenant got a bullet through his head, but no one stopped. We held the line and went on till we got to the Jap trenches. They had gone. This went on for quite a few days.

'After that action, 2 Recce were sent on an encircling movement around the Aradura Spur which overlooked the town of Kohima. The unit reached the Kohima-Imphal road behind Kohima several days later.

'Kohima was the worst battle of the war for the British Army. We under-estimated the ferocity of the Japanese. Another thing: in three months of fighting on that front, we took nine prisoners. If you got them cornered, they did not put their hands up, they took out a grenade and put it up against their stomach. To be taken prisoner, you were a rubbish and not prepared to die for the Emperor, they thought. This spilled over into another area: they also regarded our prisoners of war as rubbish.' He later wrote, 'I don't think any of us who fought the Japanese can ever forgive them their unbelievable cruelty to our men taken prisoner at Singapore in January 1942.'

The battle of Kohima-Imphal was later voted Britain's 'greatest ever battle' by the National Army Museum in London, and it marked the first time the Japanese had been defeated in a major WW2 battle up to this point. In effect 1000 British combat troops who were being besieged at Kohima, ultimately held off multiple attacks by 15 000 Japanese troops until reinforcements, including 2 Div, arrived in time to deny the Japanese the big prize: a massive supply depot at Dimapur, which was also the gateway to the Indian sub-continent.

Writing about the 'horrendous battle in such a remote place' after a 'pilgrimage' to Kohima in 2009, the respected military historian, Dr Robert Lyman, wrote, 'Kohima was where the Japanese turned back. The men who I have met may all be nearly in their nineties, but in their hearts and minds they know they are still the men who beat the Japanese. I cannot tell you how much I owe them.'[20]

'Then Bradford said, "We have an order to send you to Combined Ops HQ in Bombay." I said I preferred to stay, and he said, "No. We want you to join the director, Brigadier Fergusson".'[21]

The aristocratic Bernard Fergusson became Mike's role model and, more than anyone, taught Mike how to lead. 'Fergusson was an incredible man. I really admired him and I modelled myself on him. It is hard to define what it was about him, but for example, the very first night in the mess, he came in and said he didn't want a lot of rules, but one thing he did want was no smutty jokes to be told; nor should a woman's name be mentioned, ever. Another thing, he took a great interest in the welfare of his men, getting to know them, and seeing them right. He was a brilliant leader of men, he understood soldiering, he understood propaganda, and he understood the mind of the ordinary soldier. He could be charming too; one of his tricks was to switch from his normal posh Etonian to a low-class Scottish accent; the men loved that.'

In 1942, as part of the Joint Planning Staff in Delhi, Fergusson had met 'a broad-shouldered, uncouth, almost simian officer who used to drift gloomily into the office, audibly dream dreams, and drift out again. Soon we had fallen under the spell of his almost hypnotic talk; and by and by some of us had lost the power of distinguishing between the feasible and the fantastic. This was Orde Wingate.'[22]

The aggressive and controversial Brigadier Wingate invited Fergusson, then a major, to lead one of the columns of his 1943 expedition behind Japanese lines beyond the Chindwin River in north-west Burma. He was to use Wingate's newly developed guerrilla warfare tactic of long-range penetration. And in 1944 Fergusson led the 16th Infantry Brigade into the same area again, using the same tactics. Wingate's 'special forces' came to be called Chindits. Fergusson was a Chindit. Mike was sometimes referred to in the media as a Chindit, but was not. No doubt, however, he inherited a bit of Chindit from Wingate via Fergusson.

Most likely it was later in 1944 that Mike, now a captain[23], served in Burma with Fergusson and visited the Arakan front with him as his staff officer. 'It was deadly dull warfare really. In a country like Burma, the battle is for the road and its milestones. So you have a frontal assault by a brigade coming up the road, and simultaneously you have a left and a right hook which involves marching through the jungle. A mile a day was a good rate, and you were losing men all the time through exhaustion and dysentery. We would encounter small groups of Japs, sometimes they had roped themselves into trees (and would snipe) – a dirty type of war, with no staged battles.'

By now, Mike had met Elizabeth (Betty) Margaret Stott and wanted to be stationed closer to her. Fergusson helped Mike get a post at GHQ (I) Delhi, Section MT2, on the staff of General Claude Auchinleck, Commander-in-Chief, India. 'It was great training for me, learning how armies work, and of course very useful later on in the Congo. I thoroughly enjoyed this time. The approach to everything was different; one had to learn to understand the HQ mentality. The key thing I remember was the importance of commanders keeping HQ informed; if you forgot, you might not get any food, for example, sent up for your unit.'

Mike had met Betty at a dance while he was on leave in Simla. The story in the family goes that Betty had been invited to lots of dances, and that the night they met was her 32nd dance. Betty was bright, quiet and attractive, with blonde hair and blue eyes; Mike described her as 'a fabulous dancer'. Betty shared a common background with Mike: born and raised in India initially, then schooled in England.

Doubtless, Mike would have called her 'a looker'. This was something very important in his life and he would always notice what lookers might be around, and he would pronounce if he felt a woman was a looker (or had been a looker); and indeed he would always come alive in the presence of a looker and invariably would flirt with her.

Betty's father, Raymond Stott, was in the civil service, working in intelligence and forensics, later becoming a specialist in handwriting analysis. He was always spoken of as having a 'brilliant' mind. Her mother was Mary Ethel Stott, née Smith, a gracious woman and a product of the times. Ray was born and brought up initially in Seattle, USA, of Yorkshire folk, and Ethel's people came from Triangle, Yorkshire, England.

As Ray was a senior civil servant, the family could afford to live in a certain style. They had a big home in New Delhi, but during the hot summers, they moved, as did the whole New Delhi government, to the hill station of Simla, the summer capital of India. As an only child in India, Betty had a charmed childhood – the household boasted five dogs and 10 domestic servants. Oh, and horses, so many and for so long that Betty became something of an equestrian.

By this time, married life must have looked attractive to both Mike, then 25, and Betty, 20, what with the war dragging on and the possibility of Mike being killed in action. The wedding took place on 10 February 1945 in New Delhi. Ben, who was in the Royal Air Force, was there; Teddy Lane, Mike's friend from Driffield days, was the best man – he had travelled over 1000 miles from Assam to be there. Mike wore ceremonial dress, with sword.

But Mike was soon on the move again. 'One day, incredibly, an officer came to see me. He said, "You did the initial training on the LVT 1. We now have the LVT 3 and we need you, we want you to go back to Madh Island. Three hundred LVTs, combined ops, highly secret".' In June 1945, now 26 years old, Mike accepted the new challenge and started to train units for an amphibian assault on Malaya. He was promoted acting major.[24]

'The set-up was so big that I was not in command. An Australian called Colonel Herder was in charge, while I had my training team and focused on certain areas. Scads of men were arriving from England (as the war in Europe was now over) and we were busy training them.

'Around this time, some of the other officers asked me if I would like to drop on Sumatra and gather intelligence. I liked the idea, but I knew it would be a bit awkward because I had just got married. Betty did her nut at the idea.

'Then came 9 August 1945. We were about to go and attack Penang in Malaya. The whole fleet was ready. We had 40 amphibians in each LST (landing ship tank). Herder and I went for a last drink at the yacht club, followed by dinner, and a visit to the pictures. Halfway through the film, a runner came in with a torch; he had a telegram for the colonel. Herder passed it to me, saying, "War's over". The telegram said: "Atom bomb falls on Nagasaki." Herder knew the Japs would now surrender, but I often thought afterwards that if there had been no atom bomb we would still now be fighting the bastards.'

After the war, Mike adopted a policy never to buy Japanese goods, and he stuck to it for more than 40 years.

His tour of duty abroad had been three years and eight months – a long time. He had not seen much real action – only five weeks at Kohima and a spell in Burma – but he had gained experience in training, small unit tactics, combat leadership skills and HQ practices – good preparation for the Congo.

'My work in Delhi taught me a lot about how a big HQ works; years later, it was essential for me to know all this when dealing with the Belgians in Leopoldville. And of course ordinary soldiering helped me to learn to organise a group as big as a battalion.'

What did Mike learn? 'About the futility of war. It is not something I liked to face at the time, because, compared to being an articled clerk it was a great adventure. But warfare can in no way be described as adventure. My remembrance of warfare on a national level is only of its utter futility.

'The poet Thomas Hardy expressed my feelings exactly when he wrote:

"I have beheld the agony of war
Through many a weary season,
Seen enough to make me hold
That scarcely any goal is worth
The reaching by so red a road".'

Mike was repatriated, travelling first class with Betty on the troopship *Cameronian*, via Suez and Gibraltar, disembarking in Glasgow on 15 December 1945. After reporting to the Royal Armoured Corps depot at Catterick, he went on leave, and on 28 January 1946 was posted to a Polish Army repatriation camp at Macmerry airfield near Edinburgh. Ultimately, he escorted 5000 Polish soldiers back to Gdynia, Poland, in the troopship *Princess Sobieska*. On 4 May 1946, back in England, Mike went on 100 days' leave as the war was finally over for him.

Mike had enjoyed army life, been influenced by it, and had thrived on it. And had not his fellow soldiers been a substitute for the family he had never had? 'You are divorced entirely from ordinary life, paying rent, buying food, etc. All that is taken care of, there are no problems of that nature. I liked that. Also, the raw material was men. I might have stayed on (in the army) as I had enjoyed the war. It suited me in every way, but there was at that time an upsurge in all forms of learning and culture. I got caught up in it.' Another time, Mike said that Betty had been against him remaining in the army as she did not want to be an army wife.

So, in what later probably seemed like the wrong decision, he left the army, as a major, being released on 12 August 1946. The army did not leave him, however, as the die had been cast. Although his blood and his spirit were Irish, Mike had become the archetypal British officer and gentleman: correct in dress, formal in language, proper, punctual, well-spoken and well-mannered. And right wing.

Like his mentor, Fergusson, Mike had become a brilliant leader of men. His compass was set for life.

3. The Walker

'I was never able to run a great distance, but I could out-walk anyone.' – Mike Hoare

After the war, Mike and Betty went to live at 58 Hallmead Road, Sutton, Surrey, near London. Life for the young major was dull in the extreme. Mike had gone back to work for John M Winter & Sons in the West End, and was studying accountancy at the same time. Then he discovered he could earn more on a government-sponsored study scheme, and left the company. Now, being best early in the day, he used to rise at 5 am to study; but there was still food rationing – not to mention one of the severest winters on record (early 1947). When he had passed his board exams in November 1947, he joined Moore, Stephens & Co, a prestigious firm of chartered accountants in the City of London. Later he would always describe the effect of this lifestyle using the same words: 'Going down to the City in striped trousers started driving me barmy.'

It was time for a move, time for action. The obvious place was the Union of South Africa, a British dominion, which by now Mike saw as a country of opportunity; he would be able to explore the fabled Anglo-Boer War battlefields for himself, and enjoy the 'sunshine, magnificent girls and Cadillacs'. Also, Betty's parents had retired to Durban from India after World War 2, and had Mike's father not told him many times that Durban was one the two most wonderful port cities in the world?

Mike took his little family on a BOAC Solent flying-boat

to South Africa. What a trip it must have been! They flew low over the land and spent each night in the luxury of a hotel, also visiting some of the local sights. No doubt Mike made mental notes about some of the places he would like to see again. The journey began on Southampton Water (England), with overnight stops at Augusta in Sicily (Italy), Alexandria (Egypt), Port Bell on Lake Victoria (Uganda), and Livingstone on the Zambezi River (Northern Rhodesia). The journey ended at Vaal Dam, just south of Johannesburg (South Africa).

Mike, now aged 29, wife Betty and three-month-old Christopher Sean (the author) in a basket, flew the last leg in a DC-3, landing at Stamford Hill aerodrome, Durban, in the province of Natal, on 19 November 1948. They had arrived at what was later to be dubbed 'The Last Outpost of the British Empire'. The right-wing National Party had just come to power in South Africa on an apartheid ticket, and it was a time of uncertainty. But Mike loved the lifestyle, describing South Africa then as 'Europe in Africa'.

Mike passed his driving test the next day and very soon toured South Africa, climbing Majuba hill for the first of an eventual seven times, and visiting some of the other Anglo-Boer War battlefields. He loved to tell how, finding himself in the Karoo town of Beaufort West overnight, he went to 'the pictures'. After the film, *God Save the King* was played, and the whole audience, being Afrikaners, immediately walked out. Laughed Mike, 'I thought to myself, being an Irishman, "I'm going to like this country".'

Ray Stott had bought a house at 10 Grace Avenue in Westville, a developing suburb just inland of Durban. Ray was shrewd, had money, actively played the Johannesburg Stock Exchange, and dabbled in arbitrage and foreign currency deals. He and Mike really got on – they shared an entrepreneurial spirit.

Mike took offices at 6 Old Well Court in downtown Durban in 1949, and opened for business as a chartered accountant. But, he said, it was hard to get going because the old Durban families had everything sewn up under the 'old boys act'. He went around to introduce himself to the established chartered accountants, and they all said his practice would never make it even if he was London-qualified. Why? Because he had not been educated at Hilton College or Michaelhouse, the two most prestigious high schools in the province – if not in the entire country. Mike said he decided there and then that his sons would go to one of those schools.

Mike continued to offer a chartered accountancy service, but his heart was not in it. So now, seeing potential in used cars, the London-qualified chartered accountant went rogue. He borrowed from Ray and dived into what he called the 'motor business'. Quality Motors was born, but it was a rough game, way too rough for a gentleman like Mike, London-qualified or not, and in 1950 he went under.

But Mike was a dreamer and a schemer and, wiser now, he bought Hilton Motors at 37 Ordnance Road; soon he opened a branch in nearby Alice Street, and one in Pietermaritzburg. Another business was called U-Drive Car Hire. He also had the Vespa scooter agency. And a car repair workshop. Mike soon had about seven different businesses going at the same time, and told me he had made 'a lot of money' from these businesses.

One of his business cohorts in these early days was his brother Ben who had worked as an actor at the Abbey Theatre, the national theatre of Ireland, in Dublin after the war. Mike said that at that time he had 'always looked after Ben' and had encouraged him to emigrate to South Africa, which he did, probably in 1950. Ben had met Imelda O'Meara on stage at the Abbey and in due course she came out, some say eloped, from Nenagh, County Tipperary. They married in 1953.

Ben was altogether bigger than Mike – and altogether larger than life, with a sense of humour to match. He was charming, quick-witted and compassionate. He had come out of the war ill-equipped to earn a living, but he had been wonderfully blessed with the gift of the gab. He was an ideas man, a weaver of stories and a schemer of schemes who was never happier than when closing a deal. To his small children and their friends, he purported to be the 'King of Ireland' and even had a 'throne' (a huge chair) to prove it. He found a successful niche, with Imelda, in business in Durban as Ben Hoare Advertising. Of course!

Another who joined in the fun at Hilton Motors was John

MacPherson. John was born in India, schooled in Edinburgh and in 1941 was seconded to the Scinde Horse; however, he was captured by the Japanese in Malaya, and shot in the leg while escaping. He remained with the Scinde Horse until 1948 when he was demobbed as an officer, coming to Durban via Southern Rhodesia. A man's man, he was just the type that Mike enjoyed; they became life-long friends, later sharing sailing adventures.

In 2007, John's widow, Meg, sent me an amusing titbit from Canada: John and Mike 'were both interested in cars and, as cultured as your father is, motor dealers were a rough bunch of con men! Mike used to buy stock – used cars of all values – and I remember an incident which caused a lot of mirth. A man pushed his car on to the lot and was paid after he had mentioned that its only fault was that the engine was missing a bit. John had to park the car later on and, when he couldn't get it to start, he lifted the bonnet and then went to the office and said to Mike, "You know that man said the engine was missing? Well, it is – there is no engine there at all!"'

The family expanded with the arrival of Timothy Patrick in May 1951 and Geraldine in January 1953; soon it made more sense for the family to be nearer to his in-laws in Westville, and so Mike bought a piece of vacant land next to them at 12 Grace Avenue, and had a large and stylish house built. It was the perfect party house for Betty and Mike and their expanding group of friends who of course included Imelda and Ben, Meg and John, and other close friends such as Barbara and Richard de Gale.

Meg MacPherson later wrote in a letter to me: 'I always thought of Mike as intelligent, witty, adventurous, a good raconteur and hard. He loved company of all types and had many parties with very mixed guests. He was a born leader and an attractive personality. Never still for long, he was always trying something new. Your poor mother adored him.' Mike later remembered a party at the MacPhersons and an interaction with one of their friends, Joyce Wrinch-Schulz. According to Mike, Joyce admired the bowtie that he had put on 'for a bit of fun', and proclaimed him 'the best-dressed man at the party ... and the best looking'. Barbara de Gale later described Mike as 'an attractive man, amusing'. Ian Gordon, a Durban accountant and fellow right-winger, bought a Packard from Mike in the early 1950s; it was the start of a long friendship. He described Mike as a 'fresh young man, very enterprising; my God, but he could enjoy a night out'. Certainly Mike was impossibly charming ...

Around 1956, Mike sold his businesses and took over a corner site that Ray had bought at 289 South Coast Road, Rossburgh, for a new venture: buying crashed or second-hand vehicles, breaking them up and selling the parts. This new business thrived and, known as Autoscrap, continued under his ownership until the late 1960s, but almost always under a manager as Mike had other things to do.

Meanwhile, in the early 1950s, adventurous living was a much-talked-about subject, especially for relatively young men who had had a taste of it during the war. 'Mountain climbing and other dangerous pursuits had a vogue at that time, and this resonated strongly with me. The philosophy was that you get the most out of life by living dangerously. It was largely as a result of Freddie Spencer Chapman and his adventures; he was certainly an influence in my life.' Spencer Chapman was headmaster at St Andrew's College, Grahamstown, from 1956 to 1962.[25]

Spencer Chapman was, like Mike, a great reader and was able to express his thoughts on adventure clearly.[26] He said the happiest people were those whose occupations brought them into close touch with the elements, like farmers and fishermen. This satisfaction derived from four sources: a simplification of the objects of life, a degree of companionship, beautiful surroundings and the element of danger. The key was the essential background of danger; one had to live dangerously, but as carefully as possible, so to speak.

And so it was that Mike was caught up in this wave of adventure, post-war style. He loved nothing more than walking, and would on occasion say that in his day he could out-walk anyone. So, naturally, his adventures began with walking. And where better than the nearby Drakensberg Mountains, a 200-km 'barrier of spears' on Natal's western side? With peaks of over 3000 metres, the second-highest waterfall in the world, and more than 30 000 San-art images (known then as Bushman paintings), these mountains were to prove ideal for Mike to cut his teeth on. In time, probably 1955, he graduated

Orange
Free State

Natal

Leribe

Matsoku River

Nkau

MALUTI
MOUNTAINS

Tlokoeng

Mokhotlong

THABANA-
NTLENYANA
△
3 482m

MASERU

Basutoland
(now Lesotho)

Sani Top

SANI PASS

Himeville

Semonkong

Maletsunyane
Falls

Underberg

Orange River

Seforong

Qachas Nek

DRAKENSBERG MOUNTAINS

Quthing

Natal

Eastern Cape

ORANGE
FREE
STATE

NATAL

BASUTOLAND

EASTERN
CAPE

to the mountains of the then Basutoland, a British crown colony totally surrounded by South Africa. This was a different situation to the rock-art hikes in the Drakensberg; here, he walked for the love of walking in challenging country. Along the eastern side of Basutoland is the Maluti range of mountains, a summit plateau of around 3000 metres, complementing the Drakensberg on the western side of Natal. Typically, weather conditions could change suddenly and dramatically, bringing severe thunderstorms or even snow, and temperatures down to −15°C. With rainfall of about 1300 mm a year in the Malutis, most of it falling in the summer (October to April), rivers could become treacherous very quickly.

Summarising from *Mike Hoare's Adventures in Africa*[27], Mike began modestly enough with a trip of several days, everything on his back. He hiked up Sani Pass (altitude: 2895 metres), then little more than a rough and dangerous bridle path, crossed into Basutoland and tramped on around Thabana-Ntlenyana, the highest point in southern Africa at 3482 metres, to the village of Mokhotlong, about 55 km from Sani Top.

Next, probably in the winter of 1956, came a long trek from Qachas Nek to the spectacular Maletsunyane Falls with a guide, Sipho Sipho, who had brought along two ponies and two mules. But Mike and horses were never a good combination, and Mike walked pretty much the whole way.

'We covered about 10-15 miles each day, enjoying the magnificent vistas and pellucid atmosphere. It was sunny by day even though the temperature hovered around zero centigrade. I always made camp about three in the afternoon in the lee of a hill, but Sipho Sipho looked askance at this peculiar behaviour; he didn't care for camping in the open one little bit. Excusing himself, after making certain the mules were properly tethered and my pony hobbled for the night, he would make off for some distant village, usually going like the clappers of hell. Why didn't he want to stay with me? He couldn't look me in the face when giving his answer but it was clear he was mightily scared of something. Ultimately, when I got to know him better, he told me. In a phrase, ritual murder!'

Some Basotho witch doctors believed that traditional medicine (known as *muti*) which contained human flesh was superior to *muti* which did not – and all the more so if obtained from a living victim, hence the ritual murders. Sipho Sipho told Mike that bands of young men would attack at night, removing eyes, ears, lips, tongue, sex organs, heart, etc. Mike grew to take Sipho Sipho's point, and they then spent the nights in village huts along the way, rather than in the open.

At Seforong, Mike entered a crowded trading store. Brisk business was being done in blankets, saddlery, food, and even mohair and skins. Mike asked the man behind the counter if he and Sipho Sipho could camp within the compound that night. Before he could answer, a strong east European accent was heard to shout from another room: 'No, tonight you sleep wiz me.'

Mike was about to meet the hospitable store manager, a high-born Pole named Jan Glogowski whom Mike came to admire. We can tell from his description of Jan, what characteristics Mike appreciated in a man. 'Jan had been a cavalry cadet before World War 2. He took part in the last cavalry charge by the Polish Army: line abreast, they charged the German tanks and were mown down by the hundred. Jan was a man of breeding, superbly good manners and consummate charm. He was highly intelligent, spoke fluent Sesotho and was an avid reader. Each evening Jan took his bath in a galvanised tin tub, after which he would dress for dinner. Then he would mix and serve Martini cocktails in glasses that had been chilled in the refrigerator. Dinner was a formal occasion, served by the housekeeper. He had his standards and he observed them.'

In fact, the core elements of this description of Jan fit Mike himself perfectly: brave soldier, good manners, charming, intelligent, a reader, formal and traditional. No wonder they became lifelong friends.

'Two days later, Sipho Sipho and I saddled up and made our way down to the Orange River which was flowing quite strongly and about 70 yards wide at our crossing point. We dismounted, turned the packs on the mules upside down so they wouldn't fill with water and began the crossing. My guide showed me how to conduct myself. All I had to do was to ride my pony into the water and get him to swim. Easier said than done. Then I had to slide off his back and hang on to the bridle without tugging at his bit in any way, gripping his mane with the other hand. We were carried quite a long way downstream, but emerged wet and cold, and made camp at once in a nearby village. That night we suffered a shattering storm with thunder and lightning, some of it striking the ground not far from our hut, leaving the air steaming and smelling of sulphur. We were lucky to get away with it.'

A few days later, they arrived at Semonkong. They followed the river for a few kilometres until they got to the Maletsunyane Falls, probably the second highest in southern Africa, with a spectacular single drop of 192 metres.

In 1955, David Alexander started operating a transport service between Himeville and Mokhotlong via the treacherous Sani Pass, using four-wheel-drive vehicles. As he tells it in his book *Sani Pass – Riding the Dragon*[28], at that time, there were 37 tight corners where the vehicles had to reverse to get around. Soon, ready to extend his business, he wanted to pioneer a route from Mokhotlong to Nkau where there were diamond diggings. The distance was a mere 50 km; for 16 km there was a bridle track to a trading store at Tlokoeng, leaving 34 km, including a shallow valley and what appeared on the map to be a fair-sized river, the Matsoku.

Mike signed on for Alexander's expedition. The other adventurers were Arthur Bowland, a photographer and mountain enthusiast; Jim Alterskye, a black-marketeer who could cook; John Webb, a former coal miner; and, at the last minute, Paddy and Phil Peel-Pearce joined up to help Paddy recover from a bout of tick-bite fever!

Their vehicle was an open Land Rover. The equipment included sledgehammers, crowbars, picks and shovels, winches and steel stakes, stout planks, snow/mud chains, and so on, plus two tents and a tarpaulin to camp under, as well as food and liquor for three days. They were totally unprepared for the extreme cold and unforgiving terrain they were to encounter …

The seven left Alexander's home on the farm Dieu Donné near Himeville, on 28 October 1956. They negotiated the zig-zags of Sani Pass and overnighted at the rest hut at Mokhotlong. Even the next 16 km to Tlokoeng passed without incident, although they had to cross the wide Orange River – with all members of the party pushing the vehicle through the icy water. If the river came up any, there would be no returning this way.

The next day they followed a path toward Nkau – certainly no vehicle had ever ventured here before. The third night they camped at a school, and the next day they made 10 km. The following day dawned extremely cold, with relentless rain penetrating clothes and equipment. Two kilometres were covered.

The next night, one of utter misery, was spent under a primitive overhang. A mere 150 metres were covered the next day, with the party sheltering in an abandoned shepherd's hut. The next day they achieved a ridge marked on the map as 3050 metres high. They were now on the 'Roof of Africa'. The cold was perishing – and then it started to snow; they could not escape the cold as the doors of the Land Rover were now off in case the driver had to jump out quickly; they were also totally out of food and hunger was gnawing their stomachs. Yet they continued.

Now a large rock barred their way. Alexander describes what happened next: 'Arthur jumped off (the vehicle) with a sledgehammer and took a swing at it (the rock). Another blow with the hammer and a rock chip flew up and struck Mike in the left eye. Immediately blood welled up. The eye became a bloody mess. Mike was in intense pain and blinded in the one eye. There was little we could do for him. I had some aspirin which he declined; a wetted handkerchief gave some relief. Mike must have been severely shocked; his stoicism was an inspiration. It was weeks before Mike was to recover the sight of his left eye.'

The situation was now dire: two casualties (for Paddy was in a bad way with exposure), no food, not yet half way and trapped between two rivers – they could not turn back as the heavy rain and snow would have brought the Orange River down in flood by now. They limped on, soon to see the Matsoku River at the bottom of a deep valley; it was raging. As darkness closed in, they descended to a hut near the river. An old man fed them with *mielie* bread and sorghum beer.

The next day, something had to be done. Mountain-man Bowland managed to swim the icy torrent, ending up way down-river, and hired a horse in a bid to reach Nkau, some 19 km away. A blizzard soon stopped him and he overnighted at a nearby kraal. The next day, he traversed the snowfields to Nkau and got food sent on mules to the stranded group.

On this side of the river, a Basotho shepherd arrived with a few sheep. A deal was struck in double-quick time, and Jim did the knife work. Soon they feasted – Jim could really cook.

But Mike was still in pain – and he had to get back to work. A scrawny horse was produced. Mike mounted for the return journey but the horse refused to move. Mike was last seen leading the horse over a ridge. Most likely he walked back to Mokhotlong and got a lift back down the pass, arriving at Dieu Donné days later. Eventually Alexander and Webb limped into Nkau – it had taken them 11 days.

Mike wrote up his version of this madcap venture into the 'Alps in Africa', and it is reproduced below. He gave the escapade a witty slant to disguise the agony and the fact that it was a near disaster for Mike. It is called *Sojourn in Basutoland*:

Friend, should life have turned a bit sour on you, even if the bank manager, creditors and girlfriend are no longer giving you the green light, these are but small discomforts in comparison to a trip across Basutoland.

Sani Pass – Mokhotlong – Tlokoeng – Nkau – Leribe, names that conjure up the vast mountain fastness that is Basutoland, and the route that Alexander wanted to attempt to see if any sort of track across country was feasible.

In our path were a couple of mountain ranges and some formidable rivers such as the Orange, but we went out nothing daunted, seven strong, in a long-wheel-base Land Rover, loaded to the gunwales and looking something like the Italian Army before Alex.

The Orange was running fairly shallow and peaceable when we struck it in the evening of the first day, but we bellied out on a pebble the size of a 45-gallon drum. We dug whilst the river swirled pleasantly through the cab. This was only a foretaste of things to come. From then on, it was tote that pick, lift that shale, as a path was cut into the steep mountainside.

The next day we covered 12 miles crossing a number of streams, backing and filling up traverses, lifting impedimenta and generally indulging in light road engineering. Progress was being made and the mountains seemed smaller. Came the dawn – and the rain. Such rain, so wet, and so much of it. Soused herrings were bone dry by comparison.

That day we manhandled the truck three miles. By nightfall, the damp had entered our souls and we sought shelter in a cave – no mod cons and certainly no hot and cold chambermaids running through it. For sheer unmitigated misery that night stands alone. Amazing how pleasant it is to look back on torture of this kind.

Days followed when we inched the truck a few more miles up Mount Everest. I think it was Mount Everest – if now, it was only a few feet shorter. Liquor ran out, grub ran out and spirits began to flag. When life was at its lowest ebb, snow began to fall in all its silent beauty. There was nothing left to do but to cry softly in our beards – handsome things which had crep' up on us unawares.

Finally, of course, the journey received its quietus at Matsoku. Here the river ran turbulent at 25 mph (miles per hour), chest high, trundling along boulders the size of small oxen. Maybe they <u>were</u> oxen. It was the end of the track for the time being and the next day I walked back to Tlokoeng carrying my pack, my rations and my horse. The rest of the party struggled through the snow to Nkau and Leribe by horse and Jeep, and lived, bowlegged, to tell the tale. The leader and his lieutenant returned with incredible fortitude to pacify the Matsoku, fit a new clutch under appalling conditions and to complete the trek in a few more days. Stout lads.

Dramatis Personae
Leader, a man of inflexible determination: David Alexander
Lieutenant, a getter of things done: John Webb
Cook, conjurer and keeper-up of spirits: Jim Alterskye
Rhubarb: Arthur Bowland, Mr and Mrs Peel-Pearce from Johannesburg, and your humble servant.

An article in the *Sunday Times* of 18 November 1956 said in part that the expedition had made 'the first crossing of Basutoland by motor from Natal to the Free State', and Alexander said the expedition 'proved that a road capable of carrying 1,5-ton trucks equipped with four-wheel drive, could be built along practically a direct route from Mokhotlong to Leribe at little cost'.

A visit in 2013 to the dining room of Sani Lodge, at the foot of Sani Pass, revealed a display of magnificent photographs taken by Bowland, preserving the story of the pioneering expedition in the area.

4. The Motorcyclist

'Life on board a passenger liner contrasted badly with the weeks
I had spent alone on my motorcycle. Here I felt cribbed, cabined
and confined; there I roamed free as a bird, nearly every new day
bringing me some unexpected joy or problem, and fulfilling my
spirit of adventure.' – Mike Hoare

In the early 1950s, Betty and Mike were leading their lives in the
normal way for the times: Mike went out to work while Betty ran
the house and brought up the children. The trouble was, by 1953
Betty had her hands full with three children under the age of five –
and Mike could no longer resist the 'magnificent girls'.

Meg MacPherson put it to me this way in an email in 2012:
'Betty and I used to meet every week for lunch for quite a long
while. She was a very intelligent and well-informed person. She
was good natured and fun, but rather shy. Betty was an only child,
unsophisticated, and secure in the total love of her parents. Don't
forget that she had very little competition in India at that time, and
she adored your father. When Mike started going around with Nora,
I think her name was, your mother had no guile or tricks to use, and
Nora was a sexy mongrel. Men with personality and a background
like Mike's always attract the attention of women like Nora and, to
my sorrow, I know that most men will take what is offered. Nora
was a red head and one day, since Mike seemed to like red hair, we
gave Betty's hair a henna rinse. It didn't work and we just giggled
about it.'

In August 1953, Africa was 'British red' almost all the way from South Africa to Egypt. Mike decided to seize the opportunity while it was still possible, he said, and ride a motorbike from Cape Town to Cairo via Southern and Northern Rhodesia, Tanganyika, Kenya, Uganda and Sudan. It was to be a case of 'Two legs good, but two wheels better' and below I draw on his later writings on the subject.[29]

'A motorcycle has always been for me the most romantic form of travel. Crank it up, rev gently and away you go. The world is open to you at minimal cost. You are free, fast and independent. The wind in your face, that feeling of freedom and the sheer exhilaration of speed race through your veins and make you tingle with excitement. In one day you can travel several hundred miles, bringing distant places within easy reach. Come the evening you unfold a small tent, pitch it almost anywhere and live like a king.'

Mike believed in careful planning, and furthermore he relished this aspect of his adventures. First he read books on the countries he would be traversing, and books by 19th century explorers such as Burton, Speke, Baker, Stanley and Livingstone. Next, he bought a second-hand, 1951 model, AJS 350cc single-cylinder motorbike with workshop manual, fitted two panniers, and got a mechanic to show him what could go wrong and what to do about it, and how to service the bike. For headgear, Mike wore a tweed trout-fishing hat, complete with flies, for the whole journey. Boots, black leather jacket, goggles, shorts, kidney belt and pigskin gloves completed the picture. He was to regret the shorts when, in the Sudan, a wasp flew in through a convenient gap, causing considerable pain but no lasting damage to his 'wedding tackle'.

Mike booked into the Mount Nelson Hotel in Cape Town for a night of absurd luxury before heading off across the Karoo, a semi-desert region, and making his way north on what would be an increasingly rough journey.

'I passed through the border post at Beit Bridge into Southern Rhodesia and made for Bulawayo, intent on visiting their Central African Centenary Exhibition, billed as an international affair, which had just begun in that small city. But more particularly I wanted to hear Sir John Barbirolli and the Hallé Orchestra, that had been

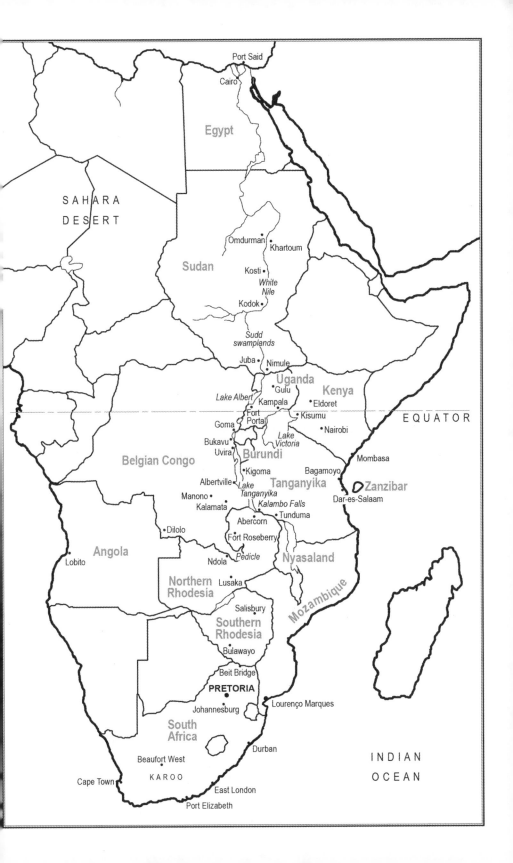

flown out from England especially for the occasion. I arrived at a hotel with half-an-hour to spare, changed rapidly and flew down to the concert hall just in time to hear the opening bars of the overture to *The Marriage of Figaro*. The excess of sun and fatigue which had threatened to depress me vanished in a flash as I sat transported by Mozart's heavenly music into that other world which soothes our troubled spirits. Contrast is the name of the game.'

In Salisbury, Mike was miffed to be treated shabbily at the five-star Meikles Hotel simply because he appeared to be a biker. In Lusaka, he met an English architect who was about to return to England after completing a contract, and who had decided to travel by public transport via the Sahara Desert rather than endure the 'gin and sin' routine of a passenger ship from Cape Town to Southampton. The architect later sent Mike a postcard saying the worst part of the trip had been the train journey from Liverpool Street to Chelmsford! Mike loved that bit.

Just before Ndola, Mike had trouble with a shock absorber but was able to nurse the bike into town. He booked into the Rutland Hotel, the best in town, and, referring to the workshop manual, fixed the bike in his room – incurring the wrath of the hotel manager. Now he crossed the Katanga pedicle, and, having been delayed when crossing the Luapula River by ferry, was riding in the dark for Fort Roseberry when an owl crashed into his chest, almost throwing him off the bike. Thence to Abercorn to see the Kalambo Falls, the second-highest uninterrupted waterfall in Africa at 235 metres.

He crossed into Tanganyika at Tunduma, and before long came across a broken-down pantechnicon that had been there for 27 days.

From Dar es Salaam, where Mike spent a lot of time at the David Livingstone museum, he made his way down the coast to the dhow port. He found a dhow that was bound for Zanzibar and negotiated a ride with the captain. They left in the late afternoon, the sailors raising the huge lateen sail to an Arab chant. A warm beam wind filled the sail. At sunset, the prayer mats came out and Mike joined them. The captain navigated by the stars and they reached Zanzibar around noon the next day – having sailed the whole way on one tack. Mike was fascinated to be visiting the hub of the east African slave trade of the previous century, and the spot where the great explorers recruited some of their porters. Back on the mainland, a stop at Bagamoyo, further north, was essential as it was the starting point for some of the 19th century expeditions into the interior.

After a few days' rest in Mombasa, Mike rode to Nairobi and on through Eldoret to Gulu in Uganda. 'The roads were fair to damnable and even so no preparation for the mild hell which greeted the naive motorcyclist when he entered southern Sudan. Just beyond the border at Nimule, the Albert Nile joins the White Nile. Here it was at long last, the mighty river. This was the very core of adventure, the translation of ambitious intention into fact.'

At Juba on the Upper Nile, he was told the road to the north was impassable, but a boat was expected 'soon' that could take him to Kosti, part of the way to Khartoum. When it arrived, Mike negotiated a passage for his bike, and they chugged north, taking four days to cross the difficult Sudd swamplands. Eventually, they arrived at Kodok, formerly known as Fashoda, where in 1898 the British and French were brought to the verge of war. Thence to Kosti, and from there by truck to Khartoum and across the river to Omdurman; Mike loved his history, and was now happy to be literally following in the footsteps of his boyhood hero, General Charles Gordon, and Lord Kitchener.

North of Khartoum there was no track as such; rather, the way through the soft desert sands was marked at random by low piles of stones. This was no place for a 1951 single-cylinder 350cc AJS, and Mike reluctantly changed his plan, taking another boat down the Nile to a point from which he could ride to Cairo.

From Port Said he took a passenger ship to Venice and rewarded himself with two nights of luxurious contrast at the Hotel Danieli. Thence across Italy and France to Barcelona, Spain, where, now low on funds, he had to travel steerage on a Spanish boat to the Canary Islands, transhipping there to a Union Castle liner bound for Cape Town and Durban.

Three months and many thousands of miles later, Mike had come to regard the AJS as a 'thing of beauty' and 'a reliable little gem' and had nothing but admiration for the Wolverhampton craftsmen who had made it. He cleaned it up and sold it back to the same dealer for £300 – which was only £25 less than he had paid for it.

'The trip was a great achievement and a true adventure; it gave me great pleasure. The lesson I learned was: go out and get hold of life and you will reap a rich reward. True, the first step is the most difficult, but take that and you are on your way.'

It was later rumoured in the family that Mike did not do this trip alone, that she had red hair, and so on. Decades later my pre-teen daughter asked him outright if he had done the trip alone, and he replied smartly, 'Officially, yes!' I asked Mike about this in 2015, and he remembered Nora, saying things like, 'She was a very fast mover', and 'When I told her I was married with three children, she said "So what?"' So yes, Nora did do part of the trip with him.

The Cape-to-Cairo trip had further stimulated Mike's interest in the Victorian explorers, and the following year, 1954, he decided to do another motorbike trip – partly in their footsteps. This time he bought a brand new bike, a 500cc twin-cylinder AJS, as he knew he would be travelling in remote areas where a breakdown would probably mean abandoning the bike completely and walking.

He travelled first by ship to Mombasa via Lourenço Marques and Zanzibar. Mike rode to Nairobi again, and from there to Kisumu on Lake Victoria, and Jinja in Uganda to admire one of the headwaters of the Nile River. At Kampala, the capital, he naturally stayed at the Speke Hotel.

He now visited Lake Albert and the places which corresponded with the three kingdoms of the 19th century, before riding to Fort Portal to see the Ruwenzori mountains, also known as the Mountains of the Moon, in particular Mount Stanley which is more than 5000 metres high. But, as they were covered in cloud and predicted to remain so, Mike moved on. Now, just south of Kampala, no doubt for a bit of fun, Mike stopped at the side of the road and got some ciné footage of himself standing astride a concrete plinth which marked the equator.

In Rwanda, he passed Ruhengeri, still black with lava from a volcanic eruption 16 years previously, and entered the Belgian Congo at Goma, 'a delightful holiday place' on Lake Kivu. Having booked into a guesthouse, he decided to do a recce of the area on his bike. Mike's upbeat description of what happened next is worth quoting in full.

'Put-putting gently down a narrow sandy lane I was confronted by a Great Dane who denied me peaceful passage. Dogs and motorbikes are sworn enemies; they live on different sides of the fence, so to speak; leastways they should do if they are law abiding in the Congo. This one had all the brashness of a dog who didn't give a fig for bylaws; probably couldn't read them either. I noticed with trepidation that he was *sans* leash. He held his ground, daring me to come on while salivating at the mouth in anticipation of I knew not what, nor did I care to imagine. I decided to rush past the brute and accelerated hard. That was my undoing; the sand was loose and I skidded right into the wretch, who, taking fright at this unwarranted attack on his person, went for my leg. Seizing my boot he bit hard causing me to fall to the ground with a cry of anguish, uttered in equal proportions of alarm and despondency. Whereupon the monster, sensing he had betrayed his master's trust in some manner, streaked off home and disappeared in a cloud of dust as if to say, "Don't blame me, I had nothing to do with it".

'I picked myself up, dusted myself off and limped back to the guesthouse, my one foot (as we say in South Africa) bleeding profusely. The guesthouse was owned and run, from time to time, by a remarkable lady who went by the name of Baroness Goldberg.

'This attractive personality, who was also a trained nurse, was half-American, half-Belgian. To complete the sketch she was extremely handsome, outrageously wealthy, and the owner of coffee plantations situated on islands in the lake, which she visited in her speedboat, hair streaming in the wind, glamour personified, you get the picture.

'But when she clapped eyes on the bedraggled creature wheeling his motorcycle along in a crestfallen manner, blood pouring from his boot, she lost no time in small talk but went into action at once. A bowl of water, a powerful disinfectant, cotton wool, an anti-tetanus injection and the gentlest of nursing followed. The bleeding stopped, my pulse returned to normal despite the proximity of Madame la

Baronne, and a couple of drinks later I was my revolting self again. The boot was still serviceable albeit with additional ventilation.'

In due course, Mike took the 'corniche' road along the western side of Lake Kivu to Bukavu. Soon, the road became nothing more than a 'downright villainous' track – and then it began to rain. By now the track was red laterite and Mike was skidding – and falling. On his thirteenth fall, he was pinned under the bike, the exhaust manifold searing his naked thigh. He limped into scenic Bukavu and sought out a doctor. Then the burn turned septic. Mike had no choice but to remain in bed at his hotel on one of the five promontories that make up the town, resting and reading.

A sign on the road to Uvira, on Lake Tanganyika, said that road works were in progress 50 km ahead, and that the road was closed. Mike ignored the sign. However, when he got to the road works, he could see that an old bridge had been completely removed. The gap was more than 5 metres wide, and the chasm some 50 metres deep. To the left was a sheer drop, to the right a sheer mountain.

Mike asked the Belgian engineer to bolt two long planks together and place them across the gap, but he refused. However, being lunchtime, the engineer offered Mike something to eat, and Mike contributed a bottle of wine to the occasion. Now, after lunch, things were looking a little different, and the engineer arranged for the planks to be worked into position ... but still against his better judgement. 'I took it slowly, trying to kid myself that I was riding down a solid white line with a tarmac road on either side. I made it across, the Congolese builders raised a cheer, and with a wave of my hand I raced down the remainder of the track to Uvira.'

At nearby Usumbura, the capital of Urundi, he found a 1200-ton lake steamer, the Baron Dhanis, ready to sail the next day. She had been built in Belgium, then disassembled and brought to the lake in boxes! At Kigoma in Tanganyika, Mike walked to Ujiji, 7 miles south, to examine the place where Stanley had found Livingstone in 1871. At Albertville, back in the Belgian Congo, the AJS was lowered from the ship to the wharf in a net, and Mike was off again.

His way lay south, but there were problems. After a tropical downpour, the red laterite was building up between the tyre and the mudguard and, in the end, stopped the bike. Worse, the local tribe, the Baluba, were reputed to be unfriendly. Mike removed the mudguard, and of course was soon covered in laterite; perhaps it was his extraordinary appearance that kept the Baluba at bay, for he reached Kalamata without incident. Seven years later, he was to serve in this area in a military capacity, and in fact he was to return to Kalamata in tragic circumstances.

Crossing the Luvua River by ferry, he encountered a new problem, loose sand all the way through elephant country to the tin-mining town of Manono. Now, his thoughts turned homeward. He made the unusual decision to travel by steam train on the Benguela railway from Dilolo, on the Congo-Angola border, to Lobito, some three days away on the west side of Angola. It was 'luxury indeed', with its saloons, restaurant cars and oak-panelled compartments. He described the journey which completed his traverse of Africa, as a 'continuous joy' after 'bumping along the tortuous roads of the Belgian Congo'. At Lobito, he was lucky and quickly found a liner bound for Durban.

Later he wrote, 'Life on board a passenger liner contrasted badly with the weeks I had spent alone on my motorcycle. Here I felt cribbed, cabined and confined; there I roamed free as a bird, nearly every new day bringing me some unexpected joy or problem, and fulfilling my spirit of adventure.'

5. The Explorer

'We did 71 miles in 11 hours. The tracks were described by the Leader in his initial reports as usually outrageous and frequently downright villainous. This of course is pure British understatement.' – Niels Lindhard, expedition scribe.

Mike struggled with the role of family man. Firstly, he had no personal experience of family life after the age of 8 to draw on, and secondly, he was not a man who could give voice to his feelings. I do, however, remember a lot of good hugs throughout my life and understood what they meant. But he gave little fatherly advice when I was a schoolboy. 'It's all in the struggle', 'Do your best' and 'Grin and bear it' was about it.

He taught us children how to use a pellet gun and .22 rifle, and we often had target practice on the lawn. He also had a 12-bore shotgun and when his friends came around, they would shoot clay pigeons from our large verandah.

Interestingly, Mike had his own way of disciplining me. I remember how once when I was small, my mother reached the end of her tether with me; furious, she phoned Mike at work, and she told me he was going to come home and 'thrash me into the middle of next week'. When he came home he took me into his study where he always conducted serious stuff, and gently explained that I had upset my mother which was not a nice thing to do, was it, and did I understand that? Best go and say sorry to your mother, give her a hug, and best don't do it again, there's a good lad ...

Though he was big on discipline in his military life, it played no part in his parenting style. I remember later as a young teen I was thumbing a lift into town when Mike drove by. He had expressly forbidden me to hitchhike, so I thought I was in for it. After a minute of mostly mock indignation, he moved on and took me to lunch at the Royal Natal Yacht Club where he was a member.

We children later used to laugh at what we thought was a strange custom our parents had. Whereas other parents would speak to each other in Afrikaans if they did not want their small children to understand, Mike and Betty, both having grown up in India, would speak Hindustani to each other at such times. And many of those words came into permanent use in our family, including for example, *garam* (hot), *chai* (tea), *wallah* (-man), *jaldi* (quickly) and *chokra* (child).

By the mid-1950s, the original motivating factors for Mike and Betty's marriage had been overtaken, and their relationship was in trouble. Mike was not only having affairs but also going off on adventures, sometimes extended adventures, most years; but notably, Betty's father, Ray Stott, was not particularly sympathetic to Betty. Yet, in his old age Mike wrote to Betty apologising for his 'abominable behaviour', and certainly Betty had seriously resented Mike's misconduct for decades.

And then in 1956, Ray died. Betty sued for divorce and it was made final in 1960. In terms of the order, she was awarded custody of the three children and Mike had to pay maintenance.

Mike went to live in Assagay Road, Hillcrest, outside Durban, and Ethel, my grandmother, came to live with Betty and us children. The alimony Mike paid was minimal under the circumstances, even though Mike also paid medical bills, school fees, etc, and Betty leaned heavily on Ethel for financial support. Betty often said Mike was extremely generous to his friends, giving away his possessions left and right, but did not look after his own family's needs properly. Indeed, he was often difficult about money, but spitefully so toward Betty after the divorce, delaying reimbursements, etc. From this time on, my mother always referred to Mike as 'your bloody father'.

Clearly, as a father in the 1950s, Mike was somewhat absent.

After the divorce, he was more absent of course, but we children enjoyed regular weekend visits and holidays with him. Mike often spent Christmas with us, arriving on Christmas Eve and sleeping on a couch in the lounge. And every time, at lunch the next day, he would pull the same trick on us children: my mother would carefully serve the 'tickey pudding', making doubly sure that each child got a tickey coin; naturally we were all quite pleased with ourselves when we found our tickies, and did not notice Mike putting a far more valuable two-and-six coin in his mouth, and then taking it out noisily and pretending he had found it in his helping of pudding!

More than once, Mike explained to me that his responsibility as a father now would amount to providing the best education money could buy. The Anglo-centric Mike started talking about sending me to boarding school in England. Given that he himself had missed out on a sense of family while at boarding school in England, I found it absurd that he would want to inflict the same thing on me.

However, it is true that in those days the 'problem' of the children of divorcing couples was often 'solved' by packing them off to boarding school, and no doubt this helped inform his line of thinking in some strange way. Then Mike suggested a private South African boarding school for me, namely Cordwalles in Pietermaritzburg, to be followed by Michaelhouse, also a private boarding school, in the Natal Midlands. This combination was generally regarded as the best schooling available in South Africa at that time – and the cost would have been ruinous.

Now, in the late 1950s or early 1960s, Mike decided to tackle a new project: the building of a wooden sailing dinghy from scratch, 'assisted' by Tim and me. It was to be a Dabchick, a flat craft of some 4 metres, and in truth the hull was little more than a large hollow surfboard.

Our basement was swiftly transformed from Mike's home-gym to workshop: out went his punching-ball and boxing gloves, and the simple rowing machine, etc, and in came an electric table saw, work bench and woodworking tools. Though Tim and I were later to criticise his somewhat elementary woodworking and handyman skills – in fact, we playfully nicknamed him the 'artful bodger' in this regard – my memory is that he did a good job on Dabchick 1037.

In due course Mike took us children and *Ding Hao* (Chinese, Mike said, for 'It goes well') on holiday to Peattie's Lake, near Pietermaritzburg, where we camped rough in the waterside gum trees with the consent of the farmer whose land it was. In the afternoons the wind would come up, and the Dabchick lived up to her name – and hao!

Indeed, Mike took us children on a lot of camping and other holidays during those years, including Cathkin Peak, Royal Natal National Park, St Lucia, Sani Pass, the then wild Richards Bay estuary, and of course many stays at Peattie's Lake. Sometimes, a friend of Mike's, Donald C Rickard, the American 'vice-consul' in Durban, and his wife Elaine and their many young children would join us at Peattie's Lake, bringing with them the latest in fancy American outdoor equipment, for example pop-up tents and massive walk-on-water plastic footwear. As a youngster, I thought of Rickard as a typical American: tall with black-rimmed glasses, crew-cut hair, informal, friendly and big-hearted.

Meanwhile, Mike's love affair with Africa was waxing, and Africana books, Anglo-Boer War books, and books on the bush and desert started to fill his study shelves.

In the 1950s, there was a surge in exploration of the Kalahari Desert in the then Bechuanaland Protectorate. An American family, the Marshalls, for example, made many expeditions into the Kalahari in the 1950s, filming the Bushmen and no doubt raising interest around the subject.

In 1955, Laurens van der Post mounted an expedition to the Kalahari, finding in the heart of the desert a 30-strong pure Bushman group living a stone-age life. His party also visited the Tsodilo Hills where, having upset the spirits of the hills, Laurens wrote a letter of apology and buried it in an empty lime-juice bottle. During the expedition, Van der Post's cameramen shot footage for a series of television documentaries for the BBC, and in 1958 his book, *The Lost World of the Kalahari*, was published.[30]

Even Alan Paton, the distinguished South African novelist (*Cry, the Beloved Country*), joined a group of six adventurers on the 'Natal Kalahari Expedition' in the winter of 1956 – in the role of scribe and bottle-washer. The aim of the expedition was to search for the ruins of a lost city that was rumoured to exist in the desert sands, and that was gripping the public imagination at that time. They did not find the lost city.

Mike would have been aware of all these developments, and in this context met Reg Ibbetson, a smooth talker who had been the motivating force on the 'Natal Kalahari Expedition'. Indeed Reg was a fanatic when it came to the lost city of the Kalahari. Mike later wrote, 'Reg was a man in whom the spirit of adventure burned brightly – he was a carrier of the virus. Ten minutes in his company and you were making plans to do things you didn't know you were capable of.' Reg and Mike agreed to search for the lost city in the winter of 1958, and Mike started reading everything on the subject.

An American who called himself Gilarmi A Farini claimed to have discovered the ruins of a lost city while trekking through the Kalahari in 1885. He wrote about it in a book, *Through the Kalahari Desert*, published in 1886, but from the beginning, there were sceptics. Then, after World War 2, interest in the subject revived and a steady stream of expeditions ventured into the Kalahari which, it is worth noting, covers almost all of Bechuanaland and more. Bechuanaland itself is slightly bigger than France.

Meanwhile, Mike bought a used but low mileage four-wheel-drive Willys station wagon, pale green, and at Autoscrap he custom-built a trailer with two 44-gallon drums for petrol.

At the last moment, however, Ibbetson cried off and Mike decided to go on his own – with the intention of searching in the Aha Hills area, west of the Okavango Delta in Bechuanaland. The expedition marked the beginning of a new phase in Mike's life – that of explorer and safari leader. He was to learn his new *métier* by trial and error ...

Mike documented two different versions of the first half of the two-month expedition: the story as told in the first chapter of his book, *Mokoro – A cry for help!*, and that described in a diary that he wrote at the time. Obviously, the diary would be the true record of events, and the *Mokoro* version would probably be a composite of later journeys.

The diary is in the form of filed carbon copies of Mike's typewritten letters, mainly to his 'fiancée', Phyllis Barbara Sims. Mike wrote in 2010 he had met Phyllis on 7 December at a bus stop outside the Blue Waters Hotel on Durban's Snell Parade. She was 19, he said, and had a flat nearby. It would thus have been 1956.

Phyllis had grown up in Turffontein, Johannesburg, in a horse-racing family. Her father, Robert 'Bob' Sims, had been a jockey and was a well-known racehorse trainer. Her mother, also a jockey in her day, was born Gladys Hodgson, but at this time she was known as 'Tickey' – a nod to the coins of the day: the shilling (Bob) and threepenny piece (Tickey).

Phyllis had a brother, also 'Bob', also a jockey and an accomplished polo player, who was destined to feature in Mike's life as well. When Phyllis was a teenager the family moved 'home and horses', she said, to Newmarket, also in Johannesburg. Then, having been a beauty queen, she became a professional skater and toured with an ice show to Brazil.

So in May 1958, Mike drove to Mafeking, the then capital of Bechuanaland which, curiously, was in South Africa. There, he had to obtain permission to do the expedition as this type of exploration was not encouraged – Mike was decidedly ahead of his time.

At Palapye, he sent Phyllis a cable asking that she fly to Bulawayo, Southern Rhodesia, where he would meet her. They arrived at Wankie Game Reserve, north-west of Bulawayo, on 1 June and stayed for four nights, doing the usual game-viewing drives. Phyllis flew back to Johannesburg from Livingstone.

Now for the bush. Mike filled the drums on the trailer, two jerry cans and the vehicle's tank: he had 110 gallons of petrol in all. He also had 25 gallons of water. He took a sandy track toward Kasane in Bechuanaland, and soon the game was on. 'I was shaken rigid when, on coming round a tight bend, I had to stand on everything – not 15 yards away, an enormous elephant was facing me. I looked back to consider how I could reverse in the event of necessity. Nausea overtook me. For one thing, a trailer makes it almost impossible to reverse, and secondly another monster was on the track aft about 30 yards away. The chap in front came closer to examine me and my blood froze. After two-and-a-half years he backed a few steps, waved large ears and disappeared into the jungle.'

At Kasane, Mike learned that his intended route to Maun was under water, and he was advised to take a bush road and join the Nata-Maun road some 250 km to the south as the crow flies. It is possible he turned off at the wrong place, for 'exactly 7/10ths of a mile and eight minutes later the birds stopped singing. The track was unbelievable. The middle grass was over seven feet high. Another 100 yards and I was in four-wheel-drive, low ratio, and another 50 yards and I was stuck. Livingstone where art thou? Michael hath need of thee. The great expedition had come to a full stop.'

This was the bush proper, a vast wilderness of flat sandy terrain. The sand was covered in tall grass, with bush and trees in many places. The rich habitat overflowed with a diverse profusion of life: birds, reptiles, insects, aquatic life, and animals of all sorts, especially antelope, baboon, warthog, elephant, giraffe, buffalo and lion. And no humans, for the most part.

Mike managed to free the vehicle and slogged on, but the sand was deep and the *middelmannetjie* high. 'It was absolute agony. The first hour yielded 8 miles and cost I imagine two gallons of fuel. Unworthy thoughts crept into my mind – what happens, chummy, if you should blow a cylinder-head gasket?' Today (2018), I have no doubt a solo expedition of about 300 km along such a track in a second-hand vehicle would be regarded as lunacy – especially as this was lion country and Mike was unarmed except for a Bowie knife.

Now, at twilight, and lucky as ever, he came upon a river with a rickety wooden bridge – and fish jumping. It was a delightful spot and he called it Angels Pool. In a typed letter to his friend Robin Alexander, the well-known radio broadcaster, he said, 'I came across this spot by accident. It is not of this world. Man in all his vileness has seen it little. I have been today in places where the hand of man hath not trod, as the Irishman said. And I like it. So much so that I have been here two days, writing under my canvas awning ...

Kasane
Livingstone
Victoria Falls

• Mohembo
Shakawe • *PANHANDLE*
△ Sepopa
Tsodilo Hills • Seronga
Mababe
Depression
Pandamatenka
Wankie
Game Reserve

Guma
Lagoon Chief's Island
Okavango Delta

Nokaneng •
N G A M I L A N D

△
Aha Hills
Tsau •
Maun •
Bulawayo •

△
Drotsky's Caves Sehithwa •
Lake Ngami
Nata •

Francistown •

K A L A H A R I   D E S E R T

Ghanzi •

Palapye •

Lone Tree •
Mahalape •

Bechuanaland
(now Botswana)

Letlakeng •
Sekoma •
• Molepolele
GABORONE ●

Kanye •
Lobatse •

● MAFEKING

Elephant there are here by the dozen. We have decided to leave one another alone – we are fighting in different weights.'

His diary for 8 June was typed at 'Camp 2: Despond' after a day that he sarcastically refers to as 'a pearl in the jewel box of my years'. First, it rained, and then the Willys would not start due to a dry carburettor. Mike waded the 50-metre river and thought it a better bet than the unsound bridge. In the middle of the crossing 'the xxxxxxxxxxx trailer slid off a boulder and was firmly wedged in the bed at an angle of 45 degrees ... and the floor of the cab was awash'. He got out his block and tackle and 'an hour and one half later a perspiring, bedraggled, foul-mouthed lascar was violating the rules and drinking the day's ration of scotch direct from the bottle and breathing fire and defiance at anybody within range of his doleful eye. It was now ten o'clock and I had progressed the fantastic distance of 80 yards.'

Up ahead, an elephant had pushed a tree down, blocking the track. Mike had to chop it in two, and tow the halves out of his path. Meanwhile, the going was 'villainous – at one stage, the path was so overgrown that it was impossible to see anything but one feeble track and wham! straight into an elephant hole.' Then, 'a spider, large and hairy with a body the size of a florin was exploring my calf. With a yell that could have been heard in Lusaka I whipped it off my precious body and flung it out the window, at the same time inadvertently accelerating and bringing the entire caravan to grief in the bush. More scotch. Rules or no rules, the day required extra-curricular stimulant.'

The truth is that Mike was a near-beginner when it came to the raw African bush, and he was making mistakes – a baptism of fire, you might say. Except in this case it literally was, for now, in particularly heavy sand, 'suddenly whoosh, a sheet of flame shot up through the opening where the two levers for the transfer box go through, and dense smoke filled the cab. I don't make any pretence about it, panic gripped my innocent frame and shook it.'

Grass and leaves had accumulated around the gearbox and the friction generated by the rotating driveshaft had caused it all to catch fire. Mike hastily smothered the flames with sand. After more rain, and discovering a puncture in a trailer tyre, Mike figured it was time to call it a day.

The next day, he had to fit a new inner tube, and removed from the casing 'a thorn the size of a carrot'. He pressed on, at one point driving for two hours in first or second gear; he covered 71 miles. That night, not finding a suitable camp, he had to sleep in the Willys and 'lions roared just before dawn and scared the life out of me'. The next day, near the Nata-Maun road, he came to a cattle ranch and, over tea with the manager, found out that he had just passed through an area with 'a hell of a lot of lions'.

Mike stopped in Maun for a day or two, and he remembered making some friends in the bar at Riley's Hotel where there was a sign outside saying, 'Please don't bring your rifles into the bar'.

North of Sehithwa, the *disselboom* of the trailer snapped. Then the stub-axle welding sheared. Mike stopped for the night, calling the place Richmond Park as it was 'so like the original'.

Back in Maun, Mike sold the trailer, now in pieces, to Aidan Riley for £15. Riley suggested Mike should visit a crocodile hunter at Sepopa named John Seaman. Around this point, Mike's diary peters out.

The route described above comes from the diary. The route described in *Mokoro – A cry for help!* was: Mafeking – Gaborone – Molepolole – Ghanzi – Lake Ngami – Nokaneng. Why did he claim to have travelled this route? Mike himself would have said, and here I string together some of his remarks in later years, that a writer need not be shy of embellishing the facts as the reader has to get his money's worth, that an author has a certain amount of licence and that there is nothing wrong with a bit of embroidery to make a story more interesting.

Following *Mokoro – A cry for help!*[31] now, it appears that Mike tramped the Aha Hills, finding nothing except perhaps himself. 'Over the years to come, I returned again and again to the Kalahari Desert, making it in some strange way my spiritual home, seeking that stillness.'

Mike was now ready to explore the nearby Tsodilo Hills. It seems the hills had until then been visited by only a few Westerners, for example, Dr Sigmund Passarge (1893), Andrew Wright (1935), François Balsan (1951) and Laurens van der Post (1955).

Turning off the main road near Sepopa, Mike bashed his way through the scrub and heavy sand toward the hills as there was no track of any sort in those days. Male Hill, Female Hill and Child Hill rise individually above the semi-desert plane and have 'an aura of mysticism about them and are reputed to be sacred to the Bushmen. I began at once to explore the caves for rock paintings which I found by the score, some of outstanding beauty'.

Toward the end of June, Mike got to Sepopa, a camp on a waterway known as the 'panhandle' that accommodates the Okavango River and its roughly 10 billion cubic metres of water (on average) a year that meander through the papyrus and reeds. Eighty kilometres later, as the water gets to the Okavango Delta, it fans out across 16 000 square kilometres, forming a brilliant water wonderland that is also one of the most pristine wetlands in the world.

Here, in this complex ecosystem, the wildlife is abundant. The species include lion, leopard, buffalo, elephant, cheetah, wild dog, hippo and crocodile, hyena, giraffe, and a wide variety of antelope including the shy and rare sitatunga and the widespread red lechwe, not to mention the more than 400 species of bird and the more than 70 species of fish.

And, incredibly, the water that supports all this life then disappears: most of it evaporates into the air and a tiny fraction flows out into the great thirstland of the Kalahari that surrounds the delta. None of the water reaches the sea.

Here, at Sepopa, Mike met Seaman who, his son Shane later told me, was the first commercial crocodile hunter in the northern part of the delta. Mike said Seaman 'had a concession to shoot 2000 croc that season' for 'a Port Elizabeth firm of leather and skin merchants; they supplied their clients in Paris, France, with the skins'. Seaman knew the bush and its creatures intimately, was an expert hunter and marksman, was good-looking and attractive to women, spoke fluent Setswana and was as fearless and gung-ho as Mike; he was also a prankster of note. They were a good match and became friends for life.

They went into the delta together to hunt crocodile, travelling in a large aluminium dinghy powered by a 25 hp outboard motor; a barge, no doubt for transporting Seaman's assistants and the crocodile skins, followed. At night, Mike and Seaman would camp on one of the thousands of treed islands that dot the delta, or at one of Seaman's satellite camps.

'I spent a few weeks with John in the interior marvelling at the ways of nature and learning of the smallness of man in the grander scheme of things. I loved this place with a passion, the pure air, the pure water and the utter quiet broken only by the cry of the African Fish-Eagle, the grunt of a hippo or the plop of a jumping fish. Even to talk loudly seemed an intrusion on nature.'

Then Mike headed for home, possibly via Ghanzi as an ancillary objective of the expedition was to consider ranching in the Ghanzi area.

After the lost-city expedition, Mike could see the tourism potential of the Kalahari Desert and the Okavango Delta – and no doubt a way out of the motor business that didn't suit him. He obtained permission from the Bechuanaland government to run two three-week expeditions the next year (1959): the first one was to cross the Kalahari, go north to the delta and have as its ultimate destination the Tsodilo Hills.

Mike advertised what he called his Ngamiland Expedition and got an enormous response. One of the group was John Yelland, at that time a young architect in Salisbury, Rhodesia, who was passionate about rock paintings. Listening to the radio one Sunday, he heard about the expedition Mike was going to lead: its aim was to find and record the rock paintings at the Tsodilo Hills, and to try to find a Bushman who could still paint. Thus, John said, for the first time, the two would be connected irrevocably.

Another on the expedition was Don Rickard, whom we met earlier. Rickard was born in the Burmese capital, Rangoon, where his father was both the Principal of Judson College and a Baptist missionary. In December 1941, Rickard, then aged 14, had to flee from the invading Japanese with his parents and three brothers. There was only one way to go – north to Assam, India, about 500 miles away as the crow flies – and much of the distance was on foot. Their walk-out ended seven months later at Imphal in India. Rickard finished his schooling in America and graduated from Bucknell University with a degree in political science.

No doubt this common link to Burma and India sparked a friendship between Mike and the widely travelled Rickard. They played golf and had African adventures together, and ciné footage shot by Mike shows Rickard having fun on the beach at Salisbury Island in Durban harbour. The friendship bloomed, in time bringing far-reaching consequences for both men …

Having paid the £100 fee, the 15 expedition members assembled at the Victoria Hotel in Johannesburg at 5.00 am on 1 July 1959. Transport consisted of a new Land Rover 109 (Series 2) and two Land Rovers 107 (Series 1); each vehicle carried five expedition members plus a Sechuana cook; they travelled three in the cab and three on the open back. The vehicles were named Male, Female and Picannin, after the three main hills at Tsodilo.

The route was to be: Johannesburg – Mafeking – Lobatse – Kanye – Sekoma – Ghanzi – Tsau – Sepopa – Tsodilo Hills – Mohembo – Sepopa – Maun – Kasane – Victoria Falls – Kazangula – Pandamatenka – Nata – Francistown – Johannesburg.

Yelland later wrote a detailed account of the expedition called *Kalahari and I*. It is distilled as follows:

Each vehicle was a self-contained unit and towed a trailer carrying two 44-gallon drums – one for water and one for petrol. The first stop was at Crewe's Hotel, Mafeking. Mike insisted we turn out in formal evening wear, and there was one helluva party with the whole of the white population of the town. The next day, Mike arranged weapon licences and a permit to shoot for the pot, and we headed west into the Kalahari Desert after picking up three cooks and a guide; our destination for now was Ghanzi, on the western side of the desert.

It was uncomfortable going, and sometimes equipment broke. By the end of the day we were exhausted. Mike said only by strict personal discipline and order could general morale be maintained. And so each person was allocated set duties.

Mike's duties involved determining our position on the map and working out the day's run. They must have been exceptionally strenuous because they always seemed to last until the rest of us had set up camp, and would only cease when the sundowner drinks were broken out. The evening meal was quite a posh affair with all the best crockery and cutlery set out. Then coffee and fireside tales followed until late.

The nights and early mornings were extremely cold. Keeping clean was a challenge as water was rationed. Dust was a constant annoyance. We continued to struggle with trailers that overturned, and even had to replace a broken half-shaft using a spare Mike had brought along. I remember him as very well organised. He must have known about the dust problem, because he always wore a black beret.

Eventually, we arrived in Ghanzi. That night we played touch rugby in the vehicle headlights, and drank the pub dry.

We headed north again, covering 72 miles in 12 hours, and collapsed near Lake Ngami to the sound of roaring lions. Now we were in tsetse-fly country and passed through several control sheds as we headed north. The way became a living nightmare. In many places there were no roads at all. ..... there were sections where road and swamp were indistinguishable. And as for the bridges ...... they comprised flattened bundles of sticks and tree trunks which semi-floated on the swamp.

We eventually arrived at 'Crocodile Camp', Sepopa, having covered 1000 miles from Johannesburg in a little under 10 days. We camped on the banks of the Okavango River among trees. It was better than heaven. The water was crystal clear and cool; we splashed about in the river, only later to find out a crocodile had taken a goat a little downstream that very afternoon.

John Seaman was adviser to the expedition. That night, we went on a crocodile hunt in the delta. Using a powerful torch, Seaman would pick up the crocodile's eyes which shone like rubies in the night. With the croc mesmerised, the hunter approached and shot it between the eyes.

It took four hours to cover the 31 miles to the Tsodilo Hills.

We pitched camp between Male and Female and set out to find and record as many rock paintings as possible. None of us, even in our wildest dreams, was prepared for the hundreds, maybe even thousands, of rock paintings that were discovered by the expedition. On the first afternoon at the Hills we discovered 11 new sites with up to a dozen paintings in each.

From there, we made our way to Maun and up through the Mababe Depression where we virtually had to make our own roads through one of the richest game areas in Africa. We went on to Kasane, Victoria Falls, Francistown and Johannesburg to complete a journey of 2400 miles on some of the worst roads in Africa. End of summary.

(On a long visit to the Tsodilo Hills in 1961, Yelland found a lone Bushman who could paint, not perhaps in the magnificent style of his forefathers, but at least in his own way.)

Mike posted out a long report on the expedition. It included such information as the 'discovery of a considerable number of hitherto unrecorded rock paintings on Mt Male and on Mt Picannin'. Petrol consumption in the Kalahari was between 6 and 7 miles per gallon; and speed in the Kalahari was 10 miles per hour.

Mike also mailed out a detailed and up-beat 'log book' written by the expedition's official 'scribe', Niels Lindhard, a Dane. Lindhard describes Day 4 as follows: 'Letlakeng – Barotse Pan. We did 71 miles in 11 hours. The tracks were described by the Leader in his initial reports as usually outrageous and frequently downright villainous. This of course is pure British understatement.' The next day, they covered 127 miles in 12.5 hours. 'The road was 80 feet wide and 2 feet deep. Day 6: The highlight of the day was the meeting with Magon Bushmen at Lone Tree Pan. All the 25 cameras belonging to the 15 members of the expedition came into action.'

At Tsodilo, he says, 'No Sunday was ever like this. Begins with a leopard hunt and ends with a crocodile hunt. As Lindhard and Yelland drifted leisurely towards Balsan's painting before breakfast, suddenly comes out of a large cave a leopard and two grown cubs right in front of them ....' Day 12: A great party was held overnight. All enjoyed themselves and we are most happy about the excellent results of the Tsodilo investigation. Day 18: (At Victoria Falls) 'Don (Rickard) said he saw a girl today.'

Concluded the scribe, 'It was a truly great achievement of the Leader to finish his programme on time. All the know-alls, everybody with years of experience in Bechuanaland, told him that it could not be done. At one stage, most of the expedition's members told him at a kgotla (meeting) that the pace was too hard. But Mike did it, and for the sweat and tears he imposed on us, for the new worlds he showed us, for the adventures he brought to us, we are all very thankful. From us all, and for us all, I the duly authorised Scribe, say THANKS MIKE!'

Almost certainly the expedition found hundreds of Bushman paintings that had not been recorded by Westerners before, but the modest Mike did not brag about their discovery. A Johannesburg newspaper said simply: 'The Bushman paintings discovered in the Tsodilo Hills by a Natal expedition last week may prove to be about the most important collection so far found at one time. Mr Hoare said, "When we set out, only a few rock paintings were known in these hills. I like to feel that the results of my expedition have added something to the knowledge of Bushman primitive life".'[32]

It is believed that there are about 4000 paintings in all at Tsodilo, most of which were probably done by the San, and that the red paintings were done mainly in the first millennium AD. In 2002, Tsodilo was declared a Unesco world heritage site.

One of the expedition members, Woden Odendaal, wrote a long article about the expedition, and it was published in a Durban newspaper with a photograph of Rickard and Odendaal holding three-year-old crocodiles.

Rickard later reminded Mike how at Tsodilo they had found Van der Post's message in a buried bottle, saying it had begun: 'Dear Gods ....', and how they had replied: 'Dear Laurence, don't feel too bad, we all make mistakes. Signed "The Gods".'[33]

In 2006, Yelland told me, 'Mike was the kind of guy I would have followed to the gates of hell and back. He was very well organised and had tremendous leadership skills – he usually got his way without sacrificing too much.'

Later that year (1959), 'in blistering heat', Mike took the second Ngamiland Expedition to Drotsky's Caves which are near the Aha Hills. The apparently spectacular caves are devoid of light and a visit is 'an exhilarating experience – one that makes the adrenaline rush the minute you descend into the unknown darkness. Not recommended for the faint of heart!'[34]

Mike simply said, 'The element of danger in exploring and drawing maps of the caves which were very little known at the time, gave the expedition a further zest.'

The 'immensely wealthy' Delphine 'Fifi' Renaud, who, Mike said, had visited every game park in Africa, was one of the members of this expedition.

John Vigor, a young press photographer at the time, later said of the expedition, 'There were about seven of us on that trip in three vehicles and there were some hard drinkers among us; a black retainer did the grunt work of setting up and striking camp. There were two women, one fairly young and beautiful, with long legs and short shorts, and I can tell you there was some intense competition for her company among the older men in our group, with the exception of Mike, who was the proper gentleman.

'And it struck me right from the beginning that Mike was firmly in charge of them all, despite his quiet manner and his lack of theatrics.'

Early in 1960, Mike and his now great friend Don Rickard read in the newspapers about an unidentified ape-like creature that was on the loose in northern Nyasaland (now Malawi). Called 'Ufiti', it was described as a sort of African 'Abominable Snowman'. In due course Mike and Rickard were invited by the Nyasaland government to get some close-up photographs of the mysterious animal and thereby identify it. Perhaps they hoped it was a previously unidentified species.

They left Durban for Johannesburg in Mike's Land Rover on 21 March 1960. It was the day of the Sharpeville killings. Rickard had thus to report to the American embassy in Pretoria, and initially Mike was concerned that Rickard might have to pull out of the trip. The thing was, 'Don was not what he appeared to be. He was

Belgian Congo

Tanganyika

Nyasaland
(now Malawi)

Lake Nyasa

Nkata Bay

Northern Rhodesia

LUSAKA

Blantyre

Tete

SALISBURY

Mozambique

Southern Rhodesia

Bechuanaland

INDIAN OCEAN

PRETORIA
Johannesburg

Sharpeville

Swaziland

S o u t h A f r i c a

Majuba Hill

Basutoland

NATAL MIDLANDS

St Lucia

Richards Bay

Pietermaritzburg
Hillcrest

Durban

Scottburgh

not the American vice-consul in Durban. He was a CIA (Central Intelligence Agency) agent.'

The next stop was Salisbury where Phyllis, who loved flying, was now working as an air hostess with Central African Airways. Driving into Salisbury, Mike and Rickard encountered an old friend from the previous year's first Ngamiland Expedition, John Yelland, who joined the party. The following is a summary of Yelland's *Abominable Ufiti*, a detailed description of the adventure.

They left for Blantyre, travelling on a typical Southern Rhodesian strip road, a sort of tarmac version of a railway line. The countryside was what Mike was known to describe as 'miles of nothing, and goats eating it'.

At Nkata Bay they heard Ufiti, apparently a female, was nearby. They jumped in the Land Rover to do a recce and get the lie of the land. Incredibly, they soon spotted Ufiti up a tree. By the time they had loaded film into their cameras, Ufiti had disappeared into the dense forest. They returned to the rest house to get properly organised, and to cook up what was Mike's traditional expedition fare: coarse-cut onions, plenty of potatoes, and bully beef – all fried up with copious curry powder.

As if they had not already been exposed as amateurs, the next sortie only confirmed it. They left before dawn. At sunrise they stopped in the road, waiting and listening. After a time, they became aware that Ufiti was sitting quietly in the middle of the road behind them. Once again, Ufiti had made monkeys of them! Pandemonium broke out again, and Ufiti scaled a large tree with the sun behind her. As our three intrepid lensmen were making plans to trick Ufiti into coming down, a noisy tractor appeared and Ufiti disappeared into the undergrowth. Despite searching extensively in the days that followed, Mike and Rickard were not to see her again.

As the area was wet, stinking hot and mosquito-ridden, it was no surprise when Rickard went down with malaria, and he flew out in a chartered plane. Then Mike got malaria and had to lie low.

Now it was time for the final act. Spotting a type of nest high in a tree, Yelland managed to climb up with the aid of six-inch nails and a hammer, and verify that the nest was Ufiti's. Then, suddenly, he saw her ... on the road ... standing on her hind legs ... next to the Land Rover ... examining his camera. Yelland had missed the photograph of a lifetime, but was able to gauge the still unidentified animal's height at about five feet.

Mike conceded the trip had been a failure, what with the incessant rain, shocking roads and malaria – not to mention the absence of decent photographs. Later he heard Ufiti was a chimpanzee that had escaped from a circus in Tanganyika and that she had died in a zoo in England in 1964.

In 2006, Yelland said of the trip: 'My main impression was that Mike had a wonderful spirit of adventure and a wicked sense of humour. He was an excellent organiser and able to improvise when things didn't turn out as planned.' Mike simply said the trip had ended in 'disaster'.

Probably around this time Rickard introduced Mike to the 'brilliant' George Calpin, who had written a book called *There Are No South Africans* and who had been a heavyweight political writer and editor of *The Natal Witness* newspaper in Pietermaritzburg. Mike and Calpin used to meet for a drink at the Royal Hotel on a Friday evening, and probably during one of these meetings, Mike asked Calpin for advice on how to write.

Calpin counselled him to get a good fountain pen and some expensive foolscap paper; he was to 'feel the paper' and to start writing by hand. But try as he might, Mike found he could not work like this; his weapon of choice became the typewriter. Then he attended a course run by Calpin for people interested in learning to write.

Meanwhile the British prime minister, Harold Macmillan, was visiting Britain's colonies in Africa and indicating that Britain would be prepared to grant them independence. The tour ended with his famous 'Wind of Change' speech to the South African parliament in Cape Town on 3 February 1960.

Then, very suddenly in mid-1960, war drums started beating in the Belgian Congo. It was a call to arms that Mike could not ignore.

6. The Mercenary Officer

'We were really in the heart of darkness. It evoked memories of what Vachel Lindsay, the poet, had written: "Then I heard the boom of the blood-lust song/And a thigh-bone beating on a tin-pan gong".'– Mike Hoare

Mercenary soldiering is an old profession, as old as warfare and no doubt almost as old as the oldest profession. It is also a modern profession – look no further than the popular French Foreign Legion and the esteemed Gurkhas. And recently we have seen mercenary soldiers become more acceptable as 'private military contractors' in Sierra Leone, Afghanistan, Iraq and Nigeria.

Mercenary soldiering reached its apogee in Africa in the 1960s, against a backdrop of cold war and the ending of the colonial era. During that time Mike Hoare became 'the most famous mercenary leader in the world', according to Anthony Mockler in *The New Mercenaries. Soldier of Fortune* magazine said he was 'THE mercenary of our time'.

It must be said, however, that Mike's debut as a mercenary leader in 1961 was brief and not covered in glory – two of his men were caught and eaten by the enemy.

It all started for Mike in the Congo, a country which straddles the equator and is usually described as being almost as large as Western Europe; some say the distance across the Congo is equal to that between London and Moscow.

It is also blessed – some say cursed – with scandalous quantities of minerals such as copper, gold, diamonds, tin, coltan, uranium and critically, cobalt.

In 1875 the area became the personal fiefdom of King Leopold II of Belgium. In 1908 the area became a colony: the Belgian Congo. The Belgians ran the country for their own ends; their rule was 'severe' but their administration was 'excellent – they were brilliant town planners', Mike said.

Standards were high but 'fewer than 20 Congolese had graduated from university by 1960. None were educated in the disciplines required of high political office. The Belgians controlled the populace through the Force Publique (FP), or colonial army, but as independence approached, the officers and senior NCOs were mostly Belgian. About 20 Congolese candidate officers were at military school in Belgium. The approximately 125 000 Europeans, particularly Belgians, in the Congo .... occupied the skilled positions on every level and had intended mostly to remain after independence.' However, during the run-up to the May 1960 elections, the Congolese politicians created 'the perception ... that the source of all the iniquities, challenges and hardships visited upon them in the past was to be ascribed to the Belgian government, the missionaries and the European settlers'.[35]

On 30 June 1960, the Belgian Congo hurriedly became independent from Belgium, becoming the Republic of the Congo. The soldiers in the FP mutinied when instant improvements were not forthcoming. Virtually all European officers and NCOs in the FP were fired. Inexperienced Congolese replaced them. At a stroke, the army was rendered ineffective and anarchy gripped large parts of the country. The FP now became the Congolese National Army. A sergeant named Joseph Mobutu was made colonel and appointed chief of staff of the army. Tens of thousands of Belgians left the country.[36]

Katanga, a province practically the same size as Spain and with copper and other deposits which generated half of the Congo's foreign exchange earnings, seceded from the Congo on 11 July 1960; its pro-West president, Moise Tshombe, a member of the Lunda tribe, famously described the move as 'seceding from chaos'.

But the secession was never going to be sustainable and in addition it made the Congo more vulnerable to the Soviets.

In an attempt to restore law and order and to keep the cold war out, in the second half of July 1960 the United Nations sent a peacekeeping force, known as ONUC (*Organisation des Nations Unies au Congo*), to the Congo. Leif Hellström, a Swede who in 2007 completed an immaculately researched paper on mercenaries in the Congo, says that ONUC's strength varied between 15 000 and 20 000 men over the next few years, almost bankrupting the organisation.[37]

Then, in August 1960, according to Mike, 'Tshombe and the Belgians decided to bring in gendarmes to protect the mines. Who could blame them? They knew if they were ousted the mines would go out of production in less than a year. Union Minière was the paymaster, everything was Union Minière, not the Americans; their role in Katanga was simply background. Don't forget the uranium for the first (American) atom bomb came from Shinkolobwe in Katanga.

'Tshombe wanted to keep the enormous wealth of Katanga in Belgian hands; he was a wide boy and a charming rogue – he had been bankrupt about six times. Meanwhile Russian planes were flooding Leopoldville (the capital). Patrice Lumumba (the Soviet-aligned first elected Prime Minister of the Congo) responded to Tshombe by sending troops from Leopoldville to invade Katanga. Meanwhile, the Baluba tribe in the north of Katanga, generally regarded as the "Kings of the Congo", did not want to fall under the Lunda and rebelled against Tshombe.'

The attempted invasion of Katanga stalled when the Congolese Army got bogged down in Kasai province en route to Katanga, before withdrawing. For the next year, the 'Baluba problem' in the north became the main focus of Katanga's military operations.

The Americans, for their part, regarded the Congo as the key domino in central Africa; they feared that if the Congo fell to the Soviet Union, its many neighbours would also become vulnerable.

As the CIA's station chief in Leopoldville, Larry Devlin, later wrote, this would give the Soviets an 'extraordinary power base in

Africa. Control of the Congo would also give the Soviet Union a
near monopoly on the production of cobalt, a critical mineral used
in missiles and many other weapons systems, since the Congo and
the USSR were the world's main suppliers of the mineral. Such
a scenario would put the United States' own weapons and space
programs at a severe disadvantage.' Clearly, the stakes were too
high for the Americans and so, in August 1960, Devlin was tasked
with the removal of Prime Minister Lumumba. He was authorised to
spend up to $100 000 to achieve this objective, but Devlin later said
he could not justify such a step.[38]

In the end Lumumba, who had insisted ONUC use force to end
the secession in Katanga, was assassinated on 17 January 1961 in
the Katangan bush 'by a firing squad in the presence of President
Tshombe and the leaders of the Katangese government, and in the
presence of four Belgians: Police Inspector Verscheure, Captain
Gat, Lieutenant Michels and Brigadier Son'.[39] Over the years, moral
responsibility has been laid at the feet of ONUC, the Americans and
certain Congolese including Mobutu. Lumumba became a cold war
martyr.

Naturally, the turmoil in the Congo was very big news in South
Africa at the time, and, coupled with the Sharpeville massacre and
action campaigns by the African National Congress (ANC) and the
Pan Africanist Congress (PAC), dread began to grip many white
people; they began to talk about emigrating, and indeed my mother
started talking about us moving to nearby Swaziland.

'Then it became necessary to bring in a better type of soldier (than
the abovementioned gendarmes). There must have been collusion
between South Africa and Katanga, because South Africa gave the
OK for local recruitment,' Mike said.

Enter Carlos Huyghé, the chief mercenary recruiting officer in
South Africa (and elsewhere described as *Chef Cabinet, Defense
Nationale,* Katanga) and Captain Roderick Russell-Cargill.
According to a 'Top Secret and Confidential' letter signed by Huyghé
from Johannesburg and addressed to Colonel JM Crèvecoeur (the
Commander-in-Chief of the *Force Terrestriale Katangaise* or, in
English, the Katanga Army), recruitment of what were to be called

'volunteers' got under way in Johannesburg in February 1961; the pair said they would be visiting Durban, East London, Port Elizabeth and Cape Town during March.[40] There was also a recruitment office in Bulawayo, Southern Rhodesia, around that time.

The letter makes it clear that the South African government was aware of the recruiting; the signatories explain how they had a meeting with the 'South African Government Security Department' who said 'they would not interfere whatsoever as long as we were guarded (and) did not involve the South African Government'. The recruiters, however, 'could not ask for reports on the volunteers as this would show, if it ever came to light, that the South African government were co-operating'.

Captain Richard Browne, a Briton who had fought the communists as a Company Commander in Malaya, signed up on 27 February 1961 and flew to Elisabethville, the secessionist state's capital, on 3 March. He was joined by about 38 men from Johannesburg on 5 March; the first of a number of intakes, they were the cream of the 1100 applications that had been received by that time.[41]

These men were usually referred to as the *Compagnie Internationale*. One of their number was Sergeant Nigel Osborn, then 23, who had served in the British Army for three years. Osborn said the unit initially trained at the Shinkolobwe army base. 'Our first action was for the 44 of us to drive 6000 Balubas out of Manono! (30 March)'

Then, on 7 April, as Osborn later told a newspaper, 'We (30 men) landed on an airfield (at Kabalo) and saw UN troops. There was no shooting. There had always been co-operation between UN troops and the Katanga Army. We were promptly arrested after the UN colonel tore up our written permission to take half the town.'[42 43]

After several weeks in custody, Browne and his men were deported by ONUC to South Africa. However, Osborn and Lieutenant Ian Gordon, now without passports, were determined to go back to Katanga and swam the river at Beit Bridge from South Africa into Southern Rhodesia and from there hitch-hiked back to Elisabethville. But they were eventually deported by the UN again.[44]

The thing was, on 21 February 1961 the UN Security Council

had passed a resolution urging 'that measures be taken for the immediate withdrawal ... of all Belgian and other foreign military personnel .... and mercenaries'.[45]

At this time, Mike had become thoroughly bored with the car business and was considering running safaris again – more his style, he said. So, during the second week of March 1961, when Russell-Cargill arrived in Durban, Mike wanted to find out more – despite the UN resolution. In his own book on the subject, Mike did not reveal how it all started for him ... but by 2006 he was ready to talk about it.

'I met Russell-Cargill and we had a drink. He was recruiting a gendarmerie; now, a gendarme is not a soldier but a policeman. He gave out that he was recruiting a force to protect Elisabethville, which he was not of course. He was also looking for people with actual combat experience – I thought he was being naive. He also explained to me there might be a problem regarding my rank as they were offering one rank above whatever one retired at. I had retired as major.

'At school, I had always wanted to go into the army. I was training to do the Sandhurst exam when my father died. You could not become an officer in the British Army without some sort of support, it was impossible, so I was forced into another line – articles to a chartered accountant. It didn't suit me at all. I was a soldier at heart, soldiering was what I wanted to do, and now here was an opportunity to be a soldier again. And it would bring in monetary reward and immense adventure. The main attraction was the adventure.'

There was also, of course, the political attraction, and in this regard Mike had been influenced by Don Rickard, the CIA agent. Were they not both adventurous, bright, literate and right-wing types? Had they not, just the previous year, spent a month together on an expedition to Nyasaland?

'At that time (early 1961), America was rabidly anti-communist; we seem to have forgotten those days. I must have inherited a bit of anti-communism from Don, what was likely to happen if the communists were successful in Africa, and so on. The threat was considerable. Knowing Don altered my life completely. I was interested in the political situation – more so than most people – and I was in alignment with the political purpose I could serve (in Katanga). So, I signed on for the gendarmerie. I hoped it was going to be minor warfare.'

Mike admitted to being politically naive in those days, and did not give much consideration to the morality or otherwise of taking up arms for the cause of a rebel state that no one, not even the Belgian government, officially recognised.

Nor was he concerned that Tshombe now had three enemies: ONUC's so-called peacekeeping force, the Baluba, and the Congolese Army who might invade Katanga.

All he knew was, the overall situation in Africa south of the equator was worrying. But he was not among those whites in South Africa who were running scared; no fear, he chose rather to use his military skill and *do* something to counter the looming danger. He was taking action, albeit maverick action, to help block the Red tide that was threatening the Congo, and that he believed would eventually swamp his adopted country if not checked.

Nearly 25 years later, Mike worked up a memoir on his role in Katanga entitled *The Road to Kalamata*. It is a slim volume that is light on dates, historical, military and other detail. I have referred to the book in writing the rest of this chapter.

Mike left Autoscrap in the hands of Bob Sims, Phyllis's brother, and flew to Katanga, arriving most likely in the first part of April 1961, finding himself with about 120 men, mainly English-speakers, at the first-class Shinkolobwe army base. The HQ of the Katanga Army, with its efficient Belgian staff and known as Etat Major, was in Elisabethville.

Mike wrote that, although a major, he was given the lesser rank of captain and command of a 'half company'. Captain Alistair Wicks was to lead the other half company; he was an Oxford University graduate who had trained in law, and had served in the Royal Gloucestershire Hussars during World War 2.

The bigger plan was that the English-speakers would be divided into five sections: one group at Etat Major under Major Jeff Lardant and Capt Russell-Cargill, and a platoon each under Captains

Browne, Wicks, Hoare, and a Captain Lombard. But Osborn says this four platoons idea did not 'take off'.[46]

Mike said the Belgian officers at Etat Major referred to the English-speaking unit as *Compagnie S.A.* but he did not like 'silly little names like that', and called his command '4 Commando'. This was because it was his fourth command, and he knew the South Africans would like the name Commando as the Boers in the Anglo-Boer War had named their units commandos. And indeed, carbon copies of communiqués handwritten and signed by Mike show that he used the name 4 Commando in official correspondence with Etat Major.[47]

In fact, 4 Commando was the name Mike applied to what was from 4 May 1961 officially the 4th Company (consisting of the 'remains of *Compagnie S.A.*, reorganised and reduced') of the 1st Motorised Infantry Battalion (*1e Bataillon d'Infanterie Portée*).[48]

The uniform of 4 Commando was that of the Katanga Army and included an Australian-type bush hat which Mike found 'less than practical in the field'.

There were many nationalities in the unit, but the majority were South African or British. They were not to be confused with the Belgian and later French mercenaries who, in what was the birth of the modern mercenary, had surfaced in September 1960, and whom Mike described as 'tough yeggs' who were also 'ill-disciplined louts' and 'unsoldierly', and who were soon dubbed internationally as *Les Affreux*.

'I wanted no "frightful ones" with me; every man would wash and shave every day without fail regardless of the difficulties or the circumstances, in action or out of it; a proper soldierly appearance and soldierly behaviour were essentials if we were to succeed in behaving like a professional unit.' This attitude was later to earn Mike the sobriquet of 'Boy Scout Soldier' (most likely from the Americans in Leopoldville), but it shows that he wanted his men to be regarded as 'professional soldiers' rather than 'mercenaries'.

Mike wrote that volunteers were paid $150 a month, with $5 a day danger pay. This $300 was about double an artisan's wage in South Africa at that time. Mike's wages as a captain were double the volunteer's wage. A UN report, written after interviews with the Kabalo 30, says the base pay ranged from £100 to £180 a month, plus danger allowance, family allowance, etc. The mercenaries signed on for a six-month contract.[49]

Unquestionably, Mike was a superb leader of men. Osborn said, 'His leadership was excellent, not a big man but very fit, and he made sure the men were too.' In Mike's book, he spells out his leadership style: 'I inspected the men and had them call out their names as I came to them, a trick I had learned years before as a second lieutenant. This little dodge had always helped me fix a man's name and face in my mind. The second part of the trick is more difficult – to go round the ranks again, but this time (as you get to each man) you call out the men's names yourself from memory. This comes with practice. When you get it right, it never fails to impress your men. Better than that, it gives them to understand, very rightly, that you intend to know them as individuals. Getting to know your men is ... the very first rule in man management and leadership. The second follows logically from that: get close to your men and care for them; a remote leader is an abomination.

'I have always believed that one of the most important things a leader must do is to talk to his men. I cannot think of anything as important as this for establishing that vital link which must exist between him as their leader and those he leads. By talking to his men, formally and informally, he lets them get to know what makes him tick. This is every bit as important as his getting to know them. There has to be a meeting of minds. Soldiers must be made to feel that they are a vital part of their organisation. To build on their natural enthusiasm a good leader has to capture their minds. He can do this only by talking to his men and impressing his personality on them ... if possible with a touch of humour.' (See Appendix C.)

Mike said initially it was given out that 4 Commando was 'not intended ... to be part of the Katanga Army proper but to serve as a form of gendarmerie whose duties would be of a paramilitary nature, in support of both the army and the police'. But, by the time the unit was ready to move, their role had changed – they were to be more like a small army than a gendarmerie. Their main purpose was now to 'subdue the groups of lawless Baluba rebels that were still roaming the country perpetrating atrocities, mostly against defenceless Belgian missionaries, and to defend the country against the possibility of attack by the Congolese National Army'.

In this regard, Osborn said many of the volunteers felt they had been lied to by Cargill. 'We were to hold towns after the Katanga Army captured them and moved on to the next town. Then we were embedded with them to provide backbone. This proved too dangerous to us as they shot wildly in all directions. Then Browne said it would be safer to be well in front and so we became the main fighting force. So in a few weeks we went from police to frontline! These lies caused quite a few to desert especially after all the fighting to take Manono.[50] Our purpose was to push the Congolese, Balubas, etc back ... where they came from, and liberate the Katangan towns and villages they had occupied on the orders of Lumumba. We were very successful at this which is probably why the UN were worried as they thought we would take over all of the Congo. Not true as Tshombe just wanted Katanga back.'[51]

No expense had been spared in equipping the unit with Jeeps, trucks, FN rifles, and a number of Uzi and Vigneron submachine guns. They were to be a mobile unit and their tactics were to be simple: maximum speed, coupled with 'reconnaissance by fire'.

All the men had been recruited on the basis that they had actually been in action, so the training was limited to getting fit and mastering the weapons, including time on the firing range. However, Mike found it necessary to give the officers some formal leadership training himself. In addition, he had to drum into both officers and men the importance of taking malaria prophylactics, and the dangers of both gangrene and the local strain of venereal disease – the Baluba were not the only enemy. In addition, he briefed the unit on the ways of their adversaries, including their use of poisoned arrows, pit traps, spells, marijuana, jungle drums and cannibalism ... all of which 4 Commando was soon to encounter.

The first assignment given to Mike's unit was to escort a column of 51 laden five-ton trucks, using a back route, to Nyunzu, some 1350 km to the north. Most likely, they set off on 18 April; the journey was expected to take four days. Mike led the way in a Jeep; his driver was Company Sergeant Major (CSM) Stan Dowsey, who had also served with the British Army in India and Burma during World War 2. On the first day, the column covered 160 km and stopped early as per Mike's custom. That night, Mike examined the column and engaged with the Katangese drivers ... to find that most of them had only just learned to drive.

After several days the column crossed the Luvua River on a two-vehicle ferry ... and moved into Baluba country. Then it started to rain and the road turned to mud; the trucks slid into the ditches alongside the road and most often could only be extricated by building a new track under the vehicles. Faced with continual rain, appalling equatorial heat and mosquitoes in profusion, morale sank. Then, men started going down with malaria.

One of the volunteers, now mentally unstable, stepped off the back of a moving vehicle and ran into the forest. They searched for him, but withdrew when he fired on them. They waited and then they searched again. Mike had to make the difficult decision to abandon the man and asked Etat Major to send a search party. Some of the men were horrified, no doubt at the thought of him being caught by the Baluba and hideously tortured.

According to Mike, 'the usual method was to tie the prisoner to a stake and begin by cutting off his arms above the elbow and legs below the knee. A sharpened bamboo stake would be forced up his anus while the witch doctor took out his heart while he was still alive. The object was to keep the man alive while the heart was still beating in the witch doctor's hands. Once dead he would be dismembered slowly and his flesh shared out to be eaten.'

Near Baudoinville, during the night they heard jungle drums start beating, and then the sounds of several hundred enemy preparing themselves for an attack. This involved drinking *mai* (water) which had had a spell cast on it, turning it, they believed, into a *muti* (medicine) which would render them immune to enemy bullets; and smoking marijuana.

At two in the morning the Baluba approached noisily but withdrew in response to heavy fire from Mike's unit.

A day or so later, one of the volunteers went into the bush, against orders, to relieve himself. They found him on his knees, a poisoned arrow having pierced his torso. He died within the hour.

Clearly, the journey to Niemba had been a 'total disaster'. Wicks had already arrived there, having come via a different route, with orders to patrol the area to the north of Niemba. Mike's column rolled westward to its ultimate destination, the village of Nyunzu, which had by now been deserted by the Baluba.

Lieutenant Jerry (aka Josh) Puren, a South African in another platoon, was already there and later described Mike's mobile group as 'easily comparable in discipline and turnout to the UN's best troops. His column arrived early one morning in a cloud of dust and gunning Jeep engines. It was the first time I had met the energetic Irishman.'[52] Puren later recommended Mike to Tshombe – with far-reaching consequences.

The village was the base of a well-equipped 1000-strong ONUC force, mainly Malayans. They were in a quandary, however, largely due to the poorly worded Security Council resolution that urged 'that measures be taken' against the mercenaries. Each ONUC commander, it seemed, was interpreting the 'measures' in his own way. In the field, ONUC seemed content for the moment to hold a watching brief. However, at Nyunzu, things were yet more relaxed – the mercenaries even attended a variety concert presented by the Malayans.[53]

Malaria was taking its toll and some of Mike's unit had to be evacuated. Mike and the CSM were among the few untouched – some said it was because they took several doses of a golden Scottish 'medicine' every evening at sunset.

The unit began patrolling the nearby railway line. Then, a young soldier arrived by light plane. Literally tall, dark and handsome, Simon Donaldson spoke Swahili (an important language in Katanga) fluently, had some military training, and was a 'natural leader of men' and a 'born adventurer'. Mike was impressed and appointed him Second Lieutenant. Soon, Donaldson struck up a friendship with Mike's batman, now mess major-domo, the diminutive Volunteer Ted MacKay who just then had malaria.

Now, Mike received a warning from HQ that his unit, possibly 20 to 30 men, was about to be arrested by the UN, and he commanded each man to prepare for an escape. Early on 6 May, however, two ONUC Ferret armoured vehicles drove into the unit's camp at speed. Mike was taken to the colonel, Prince Nazirmuddhin, who said his instructions were to capture Mike's unit. Mike said some of his men might want to surrender, and persuaded the colonel to give him time to talk to his men. It was that kind of war.

After Mike had explained the situation, most of the men opted to march with him through the bush to Niemba, some 50 km to the east. In *The Road to Kalamata* Mike writes that Donaldson, who was recovering from an accident and still walking with a limp, said he had hidden a Jeep in the bush and asked permission to make his way there with the sick MacKay, and join up with Mike later; Mike refused them permission.

However a typed report among Mike's papers states that the request was 'at first refused but later allowed'.[54]

Seven men chose to surrender, and were instructed to create a diversion as they marched to the ONUC compound. Mike and the balance of the group raced for the bush in all directions. At their rendezvous point, Mike decided his unit would initially do two legs through the thick bush to avoid capture, and then join the road to Niemba.

The fittest man, the 'superb' Volunteer Des Willans, hacked a way through the tangled vegetation on a compass bearing. Mike counted the steps. In the staggering heat, and with many of the men in poor shape, the going was slow. Mike wanted to hit the Niemba road before nightfall, where they would be better off than in the bush if the *jeunesse* (12-to-20-year-old rebel fighters) attacked.

Leaving the men to rest, he and Willans scouted ahead. They spotted the road – and three ONUC Ferrets who were looking for them, halted about 100 metres away. The crews were standing around casually.

Willans took aim at one of the six crewmen, but Mike stopped him. 'The armoured cars were empty, the men would scatter, maybe we would have to kill or wound one or two of them, but we would end up with three vehicles. It was the logical military action. Perhaps I was wrong but I have never regretted my decision. Apart from other considerations, there is something repulsive about firing at an unarmed man.'

When the Ferrets left, Willans went back for the rest of the group while Mike made his way to a stream at a point where it went under a road bridge. Totally naked, he was washing himself in the stream when three more ONUC Ferrets stopped on the bridge for a pee break. Mike lay doggo in the water. After they left, the rest of Mike's unit arrived and feasted on some bananas growing wild there. That night they marched 10 km toward Niemba, before collapsing near a deserted village for the night. Two days later, they made Niemba, only to find that Donaldson and MacKay were missing.

According to the typed report, on 8 May a 4 Commando patrol learned that a 'single Jeep with two Europeans in it' had passed through Kiambi on the evening of 6 May, heading for the road to Kalamata, the HQ of the Baluba who were 'hostile in the extreme'. On 10 May, patrols led by Wicks and Mike went out to different sectors, but could not reach Kalamata.

When the UN announced that all mercenaries were to be arrested, Mike's unit was ordered back to Shinkolobwe. But there had been some changes: Tshombe had been placed under house arrest in Coquilhatville, 'an event ... fraught with latent danger', and on 7 May it was announced that Tshombe was to be tried for high treason.

Now, as French officers were replacing some of the Belgians in the Katanga Army, Mike had to report to a French major, Roger Faulques, a 'bold commander' and 'a professional soldier through and through'. As there was still no sign of the missing pair, Faulques arranged for Mike to meet Colonel Crèvecoeur, who was unsympathetic and said nothing more could be done. Mike then visited Colonel Bjorn Egge who was in charge of UN intelligence in Katanga, and who, extraordinarily under the circumstances, congratulated Mike on his march. But, he could do no more than offer to put all ONUC units on the alert.

In mid-June, after a period of inactivity, Mike hand-picked 16 men for a four-Jeep five-day patrol, which Faulques regarded as 'highly dangerous'. They left Shinkolobwe on 18 June. Outside Kalamata, ominously, they found straw effigies of two soldiers, one tall and one short. The village was deserted. Despite searching the whole area, they found nothing more than some Jeep tracks, and Mike returned to Elisabethville on 22 June. The typed report concludes that Donaldson and MacKay were 'captured and in all probability done to death', and recommends a punitive expedition of 100 men be despatched to the Kalamata area.

Enter 'Speedy' Donaldson, the father of the missing lieutenant and a millionaire mining magnate in South Africa. He cannot accept his son is dead. Mike arranges meetings for him with Crèvecoeur and Egge, who offer no hope. With his visa about to expire, Donaldson senior, a man of influence, has to leave but he makes it clear he cannot just stand by while his son in unaccounted for. Mike offers to help in any way he can.

Meanwhile, Tshombe agreed to (but did not) reunite Katanga with the Congo, and was freed on 22 June.

The last members of 4 Commando, including Mike, were expelled from Katanga by the UN on 26 June.[55] Back in Durban, Mike decided that he would propose marriage to Phyllis, now 23. She was everything a man's man could have wanted: with her blonde hair and blue eyes, she was the looker of lookers – and she was playful, sexy, caring and game ... yet conservative ... yet a risk taker. And she loved fishing. And, according to Ralph Labuschagne, an employee of Mike's, Phyllis 'worshipped' Mike.

So Mike took Phyllis out to Durban's best, the Edward Hotel, for a romantic dinner and to propose. However, before he got to the point, Phyllis proposed to him, almost ultimatum-style; he produced a ring (to her chagrin, by some accounts), and they were married in a civil ceremony on 30 June 1961.

Mike had literally zero skill in dealing with matters of emotion, and for example, never sat us children down to explain what had gone wrong with his marriage to our mother, that he had decided to leave, or that he had married again. In matters of this sort, his style was always the same: total silence.

I learned about his marriage to Phyllis when I came across an envelope in his car addressed to 'Mr and Mrs Mike and Phyllis Hoare'. My brother Tim found out when he saw a ring on Phyllis's finger, and in answer to his question, Phyllis explained it was a wedding ring.

Of course, we children knew Phyllis well by this time as she had moved into Grace Avenue while our mother was away on an extended visit to Europe a few years earlier – and naturally this gave people in Durban something to talk about at that time …

The honeymoon was to be in Mombasa, Kenya, and Phyllis was busy making the arrangements at a travel agency when Donaldson senior phoned Mike. Within minutes, he had enrolled Mike into helping him do an aerial search for his son and MacKay, leaving early the next day. He was not called Speedy for nothing, it seemed. Now Mike had a predicament on his hands: how to say to Phyllis, er, darling, don't you think that Elisabethville would actually make a much better honeymoon destination? But Mike was nothing if not persuasive ….

Mike joined Donaldson senior in Johannesburg and they flew in a four-seater Cessna 310 to Abercorn. First they searched the Nyunzu-to-Kiambi road from the air; then they methodically covered the area between Kiambi and Kapona. The next day (14 July) they focused on the Kalamata area, but without success. Now Donaldson senior was ready to cause a stink about his missing son and they flew to Elisabethville where Mike asked John Latz, a journalist friend, to arrange a press conference for Donaldson senior. Phyllis arrived from Durban.

Meanwhile, Mike and Donaldson senior went to see Crèvecoeur again. Something had prompted a change of heart; the C-in-C authorised Mike to lead a fighting patrol to establish the fate of the missing men and/or find the Jeep. He also permitted Donaldson senior, a former captain in the South African army, to accompany the patrol. Donaldson senior had to agree to finance the whole operation and to call off the press conference.

The substantial patrol, supported by two light planes, assembled at its forward base, Kiambi, and started searching the area. On the fifth day, they found the Jeep about 4 km north of Kalamata. As it had been more than two months since the two had disappeared, they had to conclude that Donaldson and MacKay were unlikely to be alive, and Donaldson senior returned to Elisabethville by plane and bus.

Mike, however, wanted witnesses or at least some intelligence, and at dawn the next day surrounded the nearby village of Kasongo; it was all but deserted. Meanwhile, his mobile force was speeding toward Mwenge when the leading Jeep fell into an elephant trap, the sharp stakes fatally wounding the driver. Now the jungle drums began to beat. The element of surprise had been lost, but the mobile force returned later with 80 Baluba prisoners.

The next day, Mike witnessed what he called a 'callous and brutal' incident. All the prisoners were lined up some distance from the trucks and had to run, one at a time, between two lines of Katangese soldiers. The prisoners all received a severe beating with rifle butts and boots. Then, a youngster made a dash for the bush but was taken down in a burst of automatic fire. Mike became furious, but was unable to stop it immediately and many of the prisoners were unconscious when they were thrown onto the trucks.

He later wrote, 'It came as a profound shock to me that human beings could behave in this barbaric way, but I had to remind myself that this was a matter of tribal custom and tradition.' Later, the Katangese shot two of the prisoners dead. Mike wrote, 'We were really in the heart of darkness. It evoked memories of what Vachel Lindsay, the poet, had written: "Then I heard the boom of the blood-lust song/And a thigh-bone beating on a tin-pan gong".'

Slowly, a picture emerged from the prisoners. Donaldson and MacKay had arrived by Jeep at Kalamata. The headman, one M'Buyu Kepo, had ordered the *jeunesse* to kill them that afternoon. Mike laid the blame on the village of Kalamata and, in ruthless retribution, ordered its 500 huts to be burned.

'I hurried back to Elisabethville to resume my extraordinary honeymoon and to bring Speedy Donaldson up to date with my news. The marble floors and crystal chandeliers of the Leo Deux (hotel) brought me back with a jolt to the so-called civilised world we live in.'

A letter signed by Mike at the Leo Deux Hotel on 7 August 1961 shows that he had spent some time attending, inter alia, to the 'pay affairs' of his men, and that he intended to leave Katanga that day.

But Mike, always a schemer and a go-getter, devised a plan to get some more action. On 28 August 1961, he wrote from 289 South Coast Road, Durban (ie, Autoscrap), to Osborn, saying in part: 'Over the weekend I was getting very worked up over a scheme to offer (Godefroid) Munongo (Minister of the Interior, Katanga) a small unit of hand-picked men to give UNO (in Elisabethville) a go, but just as I went to send the wire to him this morning I got the news that UNO had taken over the post office and were scrutinising all telegrams. Rather put a damper on the idea but I am still working on it. I am afraid UNO have won the day there; I bet Munongo wishes he had held on to us in June.'

Later, Mike said that post-Katanga he had liaised with Rickard who 'wanted me to go back after it was all over to report on the UN and one thing and another, but I didn't see myself in that sort of role at all'.

Four years later, Mike received documented eye-witness reports that Donaldson and MacKay had been shot dead near Kalamata. Mike told me that the bodies of the two had been eaten – standard practice for the Baluba.[56] Osborn corroborated this, saying the pair had been 'tragically caught and eaten by the Balubas'.[57]

In his very old age, for what it is worth, Mike told me casually one day that he had later returned to Katanga by road with Phyllis, and on his way there they had stayed at the Rutland Hotel in Ndola, Northern Rhodesia. He could not remember why he was going back, but he could remember the date, 17 September 1961, for it was on that date that Dag Hammarskjöld, the UN Secretary-General, was flying to Ndola to arrange a truce with Tshombe when his DC-6B aeroplane crashed nearby, killing all 16 people on board.

Mike, who was by nature suspicious and took nothing at face value, felt that the real cause of the crash had been covered up – and would never come out. He made it clear he personally knew nothing about the crash and had had nothing to do with the crash.

7. The Safari Leader

'Tears ran down my face unashamedly as I said my own private prayer for help. I believed in that minute with every fibre of my being that ... God would answer my prayer. I had done everything I could and I was beaten. Deep in the African bush, I came face to face with my Maker in my desperate hour of need.' – Mike Hoare

By 1962, I was at Michaelhouse, an Anglican boys-only high school in the Natal Midlands; Mike had kept the vow he made in 1949. The school was regarded as the best education money could buy and Mike knew its name would open doors for his sons. And he was right – I got every job I ever interviewed for.

One day at school, I received a letter from Mike inviting me on a safari to the Okavango Delta in the July, along with several other teenagers including the De Gales' son, Tom.

Part of the marketing effort was a printed pamphlet which proclaimed: Okavango Canoe Safari – new exciting wilderness trail, 14 days. The blurb ended: 'Naturally, there is an element of danger but I am sure you will agree with me that this only adds spice to the adventure. One thing I can promise you – you will never forget your days in Ngamiland on your Okavango Canoe Safari.'

One who responded to Mike's marketing was Maud Jefferay (later Frean), a teacher in her twenties. She wrote to Mike after seeing the 'wonderful descriptions' of the Okavango Delta in an advertisement. Mike said he would be available to meet people who wanted to know more about the safaris at the Langham Hotel in

Johannesburg on a certain day. However, before the appointed day, Maud said she 'chickened out' and changed her mind about going on the safari.

She went to the meeting, however, describing it thus: 'Mike walked in, short, bearded, with piercing blue eyes. I soon realised he was the sort of man I would follow to the end of the world ... the way he looked at me with those blue eyes that went right into my head. I could not say no. He had charisma. I know it is hackneyed, but he did. He was also a wonderful raconteur, speaking in that clipped officer-class English. I asked if any other women would be on the trip. He said, "Yes, we observe the proprieties, you know." Not that they did!'

With the safari due to start from Johannesburg the next day, we left Durban well before dawn in one of the three Land Rovers (station-wagon type) that were to be used for the safari; the other two Land Rovers were already in Johannesburg along with a Bedford five-ton truck which would carry what was termed the 'heavy luggage' – mainly a small mountain of beer, as I recall – and also the camp equipment and cooks. It was to be an old-style African safari.

A few miles before Colenso, less than halfway to Johannesburg, we appreciated the wisdom of the early start when the vehicle ground to a jarring halt. Mike announced that the rear differential had seized. He got a ride into Colenso and arranged a tow-truck. Now, in the late morning, it was too late to have the vehicle repaired and still be in Johannesburg early the next day. Mike had no Plan B, but it did not take him long to find one. He phoned Phyllis in Durban and gave her the awkward task of asking 'Fifi' Renaud if Mike could borrow her almost new Land Rover for a few weeks. Later that day, Phyllis arrived at Colenso in the vehicle, and we rolled into Johannesburg late that night.

Fifteen of us assembled early the next morning. Maud was there, and her friend Paddy Withnell (later Holdcroft); both were to become lifelong friends of Mike and Phyllis.

Each of the three vehicles was equipped with a custom-made wooden box with a hinged lid. Inside were sets of plates, mugs, cutlery, plus a tin opener, etc. Every day the box was replenished with our 'rations' for the day: tins of sardines, dry biscuits, and oranges, as I recall.

That evening, we were met at Mahalape in Bechuanaland by John Seaman, whom Mike had retained to help run the safaris and provide local expertise. We set up camp in the bush outside town. As the cold started to bite, the party sought warmth from the fire and alcohol. After a braai, we went to the village hall to a dance that was being held for the white community; it was the first (and last) time I ever saw a tea-box double-bass in a band. Our group really started to get to know each other; quite likely it was as early as Mahalape that some of the guys tested the proprieties ...

Our route was thence to Nata, Maun, and Sepopa where, that night, Seaman took some of us on a crocodile hunt. The next day, those who wished to paddle downstream into the delta to our next destination, were given two-person canoes; Mike had imported four from America as knock-down kits, and assembled them in our garage in Westville with Don Rickard, 'assisted' by us children. The rest of the group travelled in small motor boats laden with the 'heavy luggage'.

In the panhandle, which is about 10 km wide, the Okavango River splits into a number of lesser rivers. Our route, initially, was down a broad channel lined with papyrus and reeds. Ultimately we turned into much smaller waterways that had been made through the papyrus by hippos – we could see their footprints on the sand some two or three metres below our canoes. These hippo-sized paths also helped the water to flow through the dense floating papyrus.

Guma Lagoon, known to the locals as 'the enchanted place', was a veritable paradise. We spent a few days camping under large trees next to the lagoon, enjoying the unlimited Tiger fishing, hunting for buck, bird-watching, photography and walking.

On our return to Sepopa, we set off on a rough track for the Tsodilo Hills to examine the rock paintings; we were fortunate to meet a group of Bushmen living there, and bought or traded some of their bows and arrows, and other artefacts. We spent a day or two exploring the hills and photographing the paintings. We must have been delayed on our return to Sepopa, for we camped in the middle of nowhere that night, falling asleep around the campfire to the roar of lions.

Back at Sepopa, some of the party caught baby crocodiles to take home. Realising that crossing the border might present a problem, they put them in a cardboard box which they marked: 'Crockery – handle with care'. We got through the border, but the crocs did not get through the journey ...

Many years later, Roswitha von Glehn of Johannesburg, who did one of the 1962 safaris with her husband Kay, said, 'A few weeks before the safari, Mike sent us letters telling us what to bring and not bring, etc. He was always very polite and a real gentleman. He kept the camps in, how shall I say, military order. Everything ran smoothly, which was not always easy as there were some strong characters on those safaris. When we got to Francistown, there were no tents for some reason, so we had to sleep out. We were not well equipped with sleeping bags and so on. John (Seaman) and Mike were still in their short-sleeved shirts and we were already freezing. It was the coldest night I can ever remember. In the morning the water in the dishes was frozen over. Nevertheless, the safari was an enormous experience.'

Another 1962 memory comes from a Durban professor of anaesthetics, Harry Grant-Whyte. He recounts in his autobiography how after a lunch of asparagus and beer at Guma, he and Mike had gone Tiger-fishing in a canoe. After a while Grant-Whyte needed to urinate and stood up, turning the canoe over in the process. 'There were Mike and I in a crocodile-infested river hanging on to the hull of an upturned canoe. Mike was imperturbable as usual – not so yours truly. I was petrified with fear. The effects of terror on the excretory functions are well known, and to this involuntary reaction I ascribed my deliverance, coupled with the crocodile's dislike of asparagus and its teetotal propensities.'[58]

Maud Frean remembered how, after the expedition, Mike sent out a circular letter, obviously using it as an opportunity to hone his budding writing skills. Tom de Gale also received a personal letter in which Mike thanked Tom for saving his life! The night we slept around the fire near Sepopa, a log had rolled off the fire about

4.30 am, and Mike's sleeping bag had caught alight. Somehow, Tom became aware of this, woke Mike and doused the flames. By this time, however, the whole camp was awake, and in no time at all someone remembered the heavy luggage was still way too heavy – and so it was that pre-dawn beers were served.

Geoffrey Jochelson, later resident in Australia, said of the same safari: 'The trip was one of my great experiences. At that time, there was a famous American weekly magazine called the *Saturday Evening Post*. There was a section at the back entitled "The Most Unforgettable Character I've Met." I was tempted to write to them about Mike.'

Mike himself wrote a long article about the Okavango Delta. It was published in the August 1962 issue of *AA Review*.

Mike later listed the 75 people who went on these safaris. The names include Mr & Mrs DC Rickard and Miss D Renaud.

Mike thought, after the two 1959 and five 1962 safaris, that he and Seaman 'could fairly be regarded as the fathers of today's tourist industry in Botswana'.

Later, in the context of Shaw's 'dregs very filthy, scum very superior', I asked Mike where he placed himself. He replied light-heartedly, 'Muggins! Too good for ordinary bourgeois life, hence safaris etc.'

Mike was in his element running safaris and intended to run seven in 1963. In a printed pamphlet, he says, 'Each safari is led by Michael Hoare who knows the territory intimately. You will find him an ideal companion and leader. This is his fifth year conducting similar expeditions and safaris, and all the knowledge and judgement required for their success is enthusiastically offered to you.' On offer were Tiger-fishing, bird-watching, canoeing, a side trip to Tsodilo, even dinghy sailing, and a visit to Seronga where 'we can find the rare river bushmen of the Mxonakwe tribe'.

It seems the 'Okavango expedition-holidays' were to be for 18 days, including ten days at Guma, and more luxurious. For example, the pamphlet says: 'Amongst the amenities at Guma, I am providing a 10 x 8 (feet) tent with floor for every two people and a servant to every two tents; six canoes, a small cabin cruiser, a sailing boat, and fishing boats with outboard motors on the scale of one to every three people.' The cost was R175 (£87/10/-).

On 3 March 1963, the *Sunday Tribune* published a feature article with photographs taken in Bechuanaland the previous year. Probably, the spread was intended to promote the upcoming 1963 safaris. We learn Mike 'is of a fast-disappearing breed, an adventurer, a gentleman adventurer – the kind you read about in boys' adventure magazines – the swashbuckling hero off to find his fortune – to see the world.' He is 'the type of man who, just for 'kicks' will explore dangerous uncharted country, go on expeditions to discover fabled cities, mountains, rivers and people. The type of man who will risk his life, and has, for the thrill of doing it.'

Mike and Phyllis arrived at Guma Lagoon in early April 1963 to prepare the camp for the safari season, but soon things went awfully wrong and lives were lost. Decades later, Mike wrote up an account of what happened – improving it as he went along – and I published it in good faith as the main story in a little book called *Mokoro – A cry for help!* in 2007. The story was also published in *Mike Hoare's Adventures in Africa*, in 2010.

The way Mike tells it in the *Mokoro* book, the story starts in Durban early in 1963 when he and Phyllis revive an old idea: they will take a year off and go and stay at 'the enchanted place' in the depths of the Okavango Delta. They will get back to nature and fend for themselves by hunting, fishing and growing vegetables.

Mike bought a six-metre cabin-cruiser called *Snow Goose* which would travel to Sepopa on the back of the Bedford, and which they would use to transport their equipment between Sepopa and Guma. He also bought a small dinghy in kit form, some outboard motors, a 30-06 rifle, and a wood-burning stove with an oven. Then came the maps, aerial survey photographs of the lagoon and surrounds, books, cameras, medical gear including malaria prophylactics, provisions, etc, and they were off.

At Shakawe, Cedric Boast, the local manager of Wenela (Witwatersrand Native Labour Association), told them that the Okavango River, which rises in Angola and feeds the delta, was running extremely high that year; the floodwaters were expected to start arriving locally in about ten days. Boast warned Mike to consider all the consequences of the flooding, including a greater incidence of malaria.

At Sepopa, Mike renewed his acquaintance with Kiboko who ran the local Wenela transit camp. Kiboko was a Christian with a heart for evangelism. He warned Mike that no man could live in those parts 'without seeking the protecting hand of God as the river was full of lurking enemies'. Mike was not a practising Christian and had to admit to Kiboko that he seldom prayed, to which Kiboko responded prophetically, 'You will, Morena, you will.'

With Kiboko's assistance, Mike employed four men. One was a cook named Fury, and two were general helps – Mike named them Munye and Mbili (One and Two, in Zulu). As *induna* (headman), he took on a man named Simon Nari who could speak English, knew the interior of the delta intimately and was immensely strong despite having been seriously gored by a buffalo as a child. They loaded the equipment into *Snow Goose*, disconnected the battery in the Bedford, and set off for Guma, a seriously remote spot – the nearest hospital, for example, was several days' journey away. Turning into a papyrus-lined side-stream called the Kijelekatu, they found the slow-moving stream had become blocked with bits of dried papyrus and reeds. Working with bush-knives, the men cleared a way forward.

They set up their camp at Guma and settled into a routine. Fury made bread every second day, Mike did some fishing, the men went hunting for buck from time to time, and Phyllis planted a vegetable garden and started teaching the local children English. Mike said 'living was in a low key, but real and productive'.

After a few weeks, Munye went down with 'the fever'. Then Phyllis developed a temperature and flu-like symptoms. Two days later she had the symptoms of blackwater fever, including dark-red urine. 'The traditional treatment in the bush was to place a 44-gallon drum of water next to the patient's bed and find someone to see he drank it, all of it, and as quickly as he could. The crude first-aid sometimes saved the patient ... but generally not.' Susansho, the local chieftainess, arrived and confirmed that Phyllis had 'the fever' – adding that most people died when they got it.

Mike leaped into action. Soon Phyllis was lying on a bunk in *Snow Goose*, and they set off for Sepopa with Munye, Mbili and Simon. Fury was to guard the camp. Negotiating the Kijelekatu, they found the blocked section of stream was much, much longer, due to the heavy flood that year. Clearing the detritus by hand in the heat, they made painfully slow progress. Then Munye collapsed. It was about 38°C in the cabin and Phyllis was fading. They worked like men possessed. Then Mbili went down. Now Mike and Simon found they could not move the boat forward … or back. Phyllis was unconscious. They were trapped with only 20 metres to clear … and three people were dying.

It is now 6 pm. Mike takes stock of the situation. Examining the map, he discovers that their route has been circuitous and they are only 3 km from Guma. Three kilometres of floating papyrus, then some open water – and crocs most likely. But Mike can hardly swim. He decides to try and get to the camp somehow and bring some men back to help clear the blockage. Taking a pistol, torch, compass, map and panga, he cuts his way through the papyrus, counting the steps. Night falls. Fatigue. Then exhaustion. Mosquitoes. A hippo crashes through the reeds ahead. Mike swims across a hippo path. 11 pm. He sleeps briefly. Re-energised, he gets to the edge of the lagoon. He can see a campfire. He gives the local cry for help: '*Mokoro!*' No answer. He finds a way around the lagoon and eventually to the camp where eight men are sleeping around the fire. He shouts with excitement and two men run away. The rest are unwilling to go on the water at night.

'After pleading with them to come with me, I tried cajoling. None of them would do it. Finally, I drew my Beretta and ordered six of them down to the dinghy. One man broke and ran. I fired a shot over his head. The bullet hit a tree, the bark flying off and striking him in the face, drawing blood. He stopped and walked back sullenly. I didn't care. I was desperate.'

Towing two *mokoros*, the group got to *Snow Goose* at 2.30 am and cleared the blockage. Mike promised to reward the men, and soon they were speeding toward Seronga where they would borrow Bobby Wilmot's fast boat and be in Sepopa before noon, and then the last 60 km to Shakawe in the Bedford. There, the Wenela doctor would attend to Phyllis and the two men. But everything continued against them. Wilmot had left by boat the previous day. At Sepopa, they learned that the road to Shakawe was flooded in the Namasseri Valley, and that the water would be too high for the Bedford. They decided to go as far as they could in the Bedford, cross by mokoro, and hope that there would be a truck on the other side that would take them to Shakawe.

But no, the Bedford's battery is flat and no amount of trying alternatives makes any difference. They are trapped again. Then Munye dies. Mike realises Phyllis is going to die. He is not going to succeed. He is reduced to nothing. Then Simon says, '*Morena*, there is something you can still do: you can pray to Jesus.'

'With the sun beating fiercely on us, I knelt in the burning hot sand. The Bakuba formed a circle around me and dropped to their knees one by one. I began to say a prayer out loud. The only one I knew. "Our Father, which art in heaven ..." Kiboko took over, his rich and resonant voice boomed out across the water, followed by the deep harmonious voices of my African friends. They sang out with a fervour and supplication greater even than mine. They went on. I couldn't. Tears ran down my face unashamedly as I said my own private prayer for help. I believed in that minute with every fibre of my being that God would help me, God would answer my prayer. I had done everything I could and I was beaten. Now only His divine intervention could help me. If He would. It was a pure and holy moment, the only one I had ever known in my entire life. Deep in the African bush, I came face to face with my Maker in my desperate hour of need.'

An hour later, the villagers yell, 'A truck, a truck'. A ten-ton truck with extra-high clearance comes into view. The driver, Malcolm Wright, explains he was on the main road and had not intended to come to Sepopa but 'something had told him to do it'. It was the hand of God.

At Shakawe, Boast raises Eugene Szlamp, a Polish doctor in

Francistown who is a tropical diseases expert. He flies in by Dakota C 46 the next day to fetch Phyllis, now conscious, and Mbili, now in a coma. On the flight to Francistown, Mbili dies despite the doctor's attentions. At Francistown Hospital, the doctor diagnoses Phyllis with cerebral malaria. She is in a deep coma. Only a miracle can save her.

The doctor 'put his arm round my shoulder with genuine affection. "We must pray," he said. "When two or more are gathered together in His name ... you remember that, don't you ... have faith ... express it ... the Lord is greater than all the doctors and medicines in the world." We prayed. I found words I never knew I possessed.'

Then Mike goes down with malaria. For seven days Phyllis hardly stirs, while three nuns from the nearby convent of Our Lady of the Desert nurse and pray. Then she moves. She will live! The nurses send Mike to buy some ribbons for Phyllis's hair, so that she can look nice when she comes to. 'How many ribbons?' asks the Indian shopkeeper. 'I'll ... I'll take the lot,' says Mike.

The story in the *Mokoro* book ends with Phyllis surviving cerebral malaria (known as the four-day killer) and blackwater fever!

Of course, as Mike tells it, it is a riveting and emotive story, but some of it is not quite true. As we have seen, they did not decide to drop out in the delta – they went there to prepare a safari camp; perhaps we can overlook this, regarding the 'dropping out' simply as a cute literary device manufactured by the sentimental Mike, a bit of blarney of no great consequence.

More serious, however, is Mike's assertion that they were rescued as an answer to prayer. I have no doubt Mike, Kiboko and the Bakuba did pray, but it is also the case that in a letter that Mike wrote from Durban on 25 June 1963 to all those who had paid deposits for safaris that year, he says when he finally got Phyllis to Sepopa, that he 'got a message through to Cedric Boast at Shakawe … He came at once with his wife in his truck even though this meant crossing the Namasseri valley which was flooded and had destroyed the causeway ….'

Mike always saw things differently from other people, which, on the plus side, enabled him to play a leading role in the Congo when almost nobody in the world was up for it. Perhaps Mike's little fabrication about the rescue is an example of his unusual perspective: he saw nothing wrong with letting the overall story trump the literal truth; he would have said it was more important to be able to entertain people with a damned good story and more important to be able to stir the emotions and to inspire, than to worry too much about the actual facts. And surely, by the time the story was published, some 44 years after the events, it was true in his imagination.

In the letter Mike is real, describing Phyllis's healing as follows. 'For four days and four nights she hovered on the brink of death and it is my opinion that the miracle which saved her life was due to the volume of earnest prayer which was offered up by all who knew us.' He also explains how the blockages made it too risky to run the safaris in the coming season, saying, 'If any one of you had gone down (at Guma) with any illness requiring hospital treatment, it would have taken me at least two-and-a-half days to get you to Maun.' He refunded the deposits with apologies.

In due course, Mike hitched a ride with Wenela from Francistown to Shakawe to fetch the Bedford, and left Francistown on 15 June for Durban. The emaciated Phyllis remained in hospital 'making plans to join the Gandhi club!' Her mother travelled to Francistown in a station-wagon vehicle, made up a bed in the back, and brought Phyllis home, almost wasted away and with dreadful bedsores.

The saga was covered in a number of newspapers in South Africa and Rhodesia. *The Natal Mercury's* story of 3 May is headlined: Stricken Durban Woman In 100-mile Dash For Plane; the *Sunday Times* of 5 May went with: Husband's vigil as doctors fight to save wife.

They never went back to 'the enchanted place' but found accommodation on Durban's Bluff, not far from Autoscrap. Phyllis took up swimming to regain her strength and in due course made a complete recovery, but later she told me that staying at Guma had been a 'bloody stupid idea'.

Mike applied himself once again to Autoscrap. Ralph Labuschagne, the manager at that time (1962-66), later told me: 'I consider myself to be a self-appointed ambassador for "Mad Mike". I often wondered at that title as in my view he was about the sanest person I had ever met. Quite frankly I looked up at him in wonder as I have never come across such a thoroughly decent, moral and honest person in my life. I have used his character as a direction for my moral and ethical compass. Knowing him has made me a better person and I was honoured to have been under his guidance and in his employ. He was a strict boss, but damn it he was very fair to all.'

Later, I asked Mike why he had undertaken such adventures, some of which had turned out to be disasters. The answer was: 'It is difficult to describe an urge. I suppose I had a latent urge that could not fulfil itself in a (city) suburb. It was for no other reason than to fulfil my own spirit of adventure – and I had an extra helping of "spirit of adventure". I don't know where it comes from.'

8. The Loose Tongue

'We went round the circle, and when it came to Don Rickard's turn he said, "I can't really talk about this, but I was instrumental in having Nelson Mandela arrested." He had tipped off the police as to Mandela's whereabouts, who at that time was on the run ...' – Mike Hoare

A round this time Mike's now best friend, Don Rickard, the CIA agent, dropped a bombshell at a party at Mike's flat that would explode and play out in the media around the world only 50 years later.

In the early 1960s, much of the world was in the grip of a cold war between America and the Soviet Union. The fear in the West was that the communists would get a foothold in the Congo, and make their way south until they had captured South Africa. Why the preoccupation with South Africa? The superpowers knew it would give them command over the vital sea-trade route around the Cape, as well as access to the country's staggering mineral wealth.[59] It would make a spectacular prize.

Within South Africa the political situation was tense. After Sharpeville, a state of emergency was declared to neutralise political dissent, and the ANC and the PAC were banned. The ANC thus decided to abandon its policy of non-violence. The leader of the new armed wing of the ANC, Nelson Mandela, was operating underground against the apartheid state. The media dubbed him the Black Pimpernel. He was organising acts of sabotage and he later wrote that 'if sabotage did not produce the results we wanted, we were prepared to move on to the next stage: guerrilla warfare and terrorism'.[60]

So why was Mandela on the run? In 1956 he had been charged, along with 155 others, 'with high treason and a countrywide conspiracy to use violence to overthrow the present government and replace it with a communist state. The punishment was death.' All the accused were acquitted in March 1961. Fearing banning or arrest, Mandela went underground immediately. A warrant was issued for his arrest. Disguised, he travelled the country organising a non-violent stay-at-home, but in the end it was not the big success he wanted. Soon, the ANC launched Umkhonto we Sizwe (The Spear of the Nation) and the armed struggle was born. In early 1962, Mandela travelled to many African countries and underwent military training in Ethiopia. He learned how to use an automatic rifle and pistol, and was taught about demolition, and the making of small bombs and mines. After eight weeks' training he was called home. On his departure from Ethiopia, he was given an automatic pistol and ammunition.[61]

As a result, the United States regarded Mandela as a terrorist – and they continued to do so until 2008 when he was removed from their terrorism watch list. He was also a member of the South African Communist Party (SACP) and of the SACP's central committee.[62]

Then, on 5 August 1962, the police arrested Mandela as he was travelling by car, disguised as a chauffeur, between Durban and Johannesburg. How did the police know where Mandela would be? All sorts of rumours ricocheted around for decades.

Then, probably in July 1986, a Durban newspaper ran a story headlined: CIA man betrayed Mandela – claim. Written by journalist Luke Zeeman, it said in part: 'The United States government's alleged "double dealings" with the ANC have come under scrutiny in Washington. *The New York Times* this week claimed that US officials funnelled information, including political intelligence and specific warnings of planned attacks by the ANC, to South African officials from the early 1960s until the mid-1980s.

'According to *The New York Times*, the policy was established in the 1960s. US Secretary of State Mr George Shultz, testifying before the Senate Foreign Relations Committee, has denied the allegations, but sources in South Africa, including a former high-ranking police officer, back up the claims.

'An American diplomat who was stationed in Durban, Mr Don Rickard, has been accused of betraying Nelson Mandela. The ANC leader was arrested at a roadblock near Howick 25 years ago.

'This week, a senior police officer claimed that information that Mandela would be in the car came from Mr Rickard, who is suspected to have been a CIA agent. He is said to have tipped off the police in exchange for information wanted by America about the government's Bantustan policies.

'The retired police officer, who does not want to be identified, has told this story to a Paris journalist. He also said that the diplomat had boasted about his betrayal to a group of friends during a party at the flat of Colonel Mike Hoare in Durban. According to the retired police official, one of the guests reported the conversation almost immediately to the authorities.'[63]

Of his arrest, Mandela said in 1994, 'Someone had tipped the police off about my whereabouts. The most oft-cited story was that an American consular official with connections to the CIA had tipped off the authorities. This story has never been confirmed.'[64]

For more than 40 years Mike kept his mouth shut about all this, and there were too many unnamed players in the story for it to develop legs of its own. Then, out of the blue one day in 2004 as Mike and I were chatting in our kitchen, he casually related what happened at that party in 1963 ….

He and Phyllis were living in a block of flats called Hermanus in leafy Glenwood, Durban. Chubby Checker was all the rage and Phyllis had his latest album. Bill Haley's too. Mike preferred their *Satch Plays Fats* by Louis Armstrong. It was time for a party – Mike did not always relish the idea of a party, but once he was there, the opportunities for repartee and flirtation were endless, and he would be in his element …

Rickard and his wife Elaine were there. There were also some Congolese civilians, James Tomlins (a Reuters correspondent who had covered Katanga and who later moved to Paris), George Calpin and quite a few others.

'We had all had too much to drink and it was getting toward midnight. I then did something which was not abnormal in those days, given the types we were dealing with, but which I have regretted ever since. As the general intelligence level of our guests was pretty high, I suggested we should take turns to make a one-minute speech, and then go home.'

This would be typical Mike. He was not a late-night owl, and hated it when people stayed longer than he would have liked; 'Must you stay, can't you go?' was his usual barbed refrain to old friends, and even his first-batch children, who might have been lingering at the end of a visit. However, Mike held good manners paramount, so his idea of short speeches would have served the dual purpose of providing an amusing and stimulating interlude, while at the same time bringing the party to an end politely. In this case, however, the ploy backfired – big time.

'Calpin made a witty speech, and we went round the circle, and when it came to Don Rickard's turn he said, "I can't really talk about this, but I was instrumental in having Nelson Mandela arrested." He had tipped off the police as to Mandela's whereabouts, who at that time was on the run ... Well, the next day Don was summoned by Pretoria (the US Embassy) and fired; his case later went on review in Washington. When he got back (from Pretoria), I visited him and he said, "I must have said something bloody silly that night." He inferred in fact he had had Mandela arrested by putting the police onto him. Anyway, within a week he and his whole family were back in America. Don was demoted, retrained and sent to Burma.'

Mike later said Rickard thought Mike had leaked the information, and this had caused a temporary estrangement between them. But Mike told me clearly that it had not been him, and he and Rickard remained firm friends. Later, Rickard said Mike was his 'biggest hero' and usually referred to him as 'the good colonel'; and Mike dedicated his Katanga book as follows: 'To my great American hero, Donald C Rickard'.

Rickard took early retirement from the CIA in 1978 and went to live in a remote corner of Colorado. For decades, if anyone asked if he had tipped off the South African police, and journalists <u>did</u> ask, he would brush them off.

Then, about two weeks before he died aged 88 on 30 March 2016, Rickard apparently received a visit from the well-known English film director, John Irvin, who was making a docu-drama film called *Mandela's Gun*. Two months later the *Sunday Times* in London published a long article written by James Sanders, a writer and researcher working with Irvin. Sanders quotes Rickard as saying: 'Mandela was under the control of the Soviet Union. He could have incited a war in South Africa, the United States would have to get involved, grudgingly, and things could have gone to hell. We were teetering on the brink here and it had to be stopped, which meant Mandela had to be stopped. And I put a stop to it.'[65]

In due course, Mandela was sentenced to three years' imprisonment for inciting people to strike and two further years for leaving the country without a passport. Then, in 1963, while Mandela was serving this sentence in prison, the entire high command of the armed wing of the ANC were arrested in a police raid at Liliesleaf Farm in Rivonia, Johannesburg. Mandela was shown to have been a co-conspirator and was charged with incitement to sabotage, treason and violent conspiracy against the South African regime. He was sentenced to life imprisonment.[66] He was released from prison in 1990, and in 1994 became president of South Africa and famous throughout the world for his extraordinary willingness to reconcile.

In 1995, I visited Mike at his home in France. One day he presented me with a copy of *Long Walk to Freedom*, the autobiography of Nelson Mandela, which had recently been published.

I was surprised that Mike had such a book, but the note inside explained it all: 'Nothing for us to worry about here.' It was signed 'Don'.

9. The Legend

'There is a tide in the affairs of men,
Which, taken at the flood, leads on to fortune;
Omitted, all the voyage of their life
Is bound in shallows and in miseries.'
  Shakespeare, *Julius Caesar*, IV, iii, 217

(In prison, Mike kept a notebook in which he wrote out his favourite lines from Shakespeare; the above was on the first page of the notebook.)

Much had happened in the Congo since Mike left Katanga in mid-1961 – little of it good. By the end of 1961, conditions in Elisabethville were barbarous. As one scribe put it, 'Katangan gendarmes under the command of the drunken and drugged (General Norbert) Moke robbed, looted, tortured and terrified everyone and anyone they deemed to be Onusien – or a UN spy. UN troops (the Indians on a grand scale) looted all abandoned Belgian property and distributed shot and shell with equal abandon. The Congolese Army simply went on an uncontrolled rampage. The Balubas continued to sever and consume remaining supplies of human genitalia. Other tribes seized the moment to settle old scores. The mercenaries swaggered and shot at anything that moved.'[67]

In December 1962 the UN peacekeeping force began a final offensive against Katanga and brought the secession to an end in January 1963; remnants of Moise Tshombe's faithful gendarmerie and remaining mercenaries, some 2000 well-equipped men in all, took refuge just across the border in Texeira da Sousa in Angola, waiting for the call.[68]

Then, in early January 1963, Mike took us three children on a camping holiday to Peatties Lake. Somehow, he got hold of a newspaper which had huge, fearful photographs showing a male Belgian civilian begging for mercy. His wife and a friend had just been shot dead by Indian UN troops at a roadblock near Jadotville, Katanga. Mike was a low reactor, but I could see from his horrified expression that the images had shaken him to the core. Over and over that day and on subsequent days, he kept talking about the appalling situation in Katanga. I now realise it was those photographs, taken by the famous Ernie Christie on 3 January 1963, that provided the jolt for him to 'get off his backside' and stop the bloodshed.

In June 1963 the Europe-aligned Tshombe went into voluntary exile in Spain to escape a charge, Mike said, 'that he had been responsible for the murder of Lumumba', and to avoid any repercussions for seceding with Katanga. However, he soon started plotting his return to the Congo and in April 1964 he contacted Mike at his home in Durban.[69]

'I got a telegram from "Josh" Puren – Colonel Jerry Puren who is perhaps best described as "chief mercenary". The telegram said that Mr Tshombe had appointed me officer commanding his land forces with a view to taking back Katanga. No "are you interested?" or anything like that, just a straight directive. Now at that time Tshombe was not President or Prime Minister. He was just a man in exile in Madrid. There were seven battalions of the Congolese Army holding Katanga, and the idea was to go in from Dilolo with 300 men. I had a look at the map and then I said "No dice".'[70]

In early 1964, there had been a revolt in the west of the Congo in Kwilu where, Mike said, a 'Peking-trained agitator' and 'rabble rouser' named Pierre Mulele 'formed the hub of the rebellion'. A communist-inspired revolt had also ignited in the east of the Congo in May, and within months the rebels had taken hold in much of the country; among its leaders were Christophe Gbenye and Gaston Soumialot, who formed the Executive Council of the '*Republique du Congo'.* According to Ian Colvin, the *Daily Telegraph*'s well-regarded roving correspondent, 'China actively organised and financed the Congo rebellion of 1964'.[71]

Now the rebels, known as Simbas (Lions), were heading for Leopoldville with a minimum of fighting and a maximum of witchcraft. According to Mike, they were within 160 km of the capital; it was clear that the Congolese Army was incapable of stopping them – 'their fighting qualities were practically non-existent'. Worse, it was common knowledge that the Congolese Army used to reverse their vehicles into battle so that they could make a quick getaway when necessary.

So, who was going to halt the rebel advance? Certainly not the UN, for on 30 June 1964, believe it or not, they quit the Congo. The UN operation, which had lasted four years, 'cost £140 million and 236 men from 25 countries who had died under the UN flag to preserve the cohesion and order of the new Congolese state'.[72]

Mike was watching the Congo situation closely from Durban, and was ahead of the game. He told the CIA, 'Tshombe is going to be invited back from Madrid.'

'They had people all over the world and they didn't even know that. g (a CIA officer in Pretoria) had no understanding of where I stood in the knowledge. He thought I was one of the many going there to get a little job – and an advance of money. He wouldn't believe (Tshombe) had called me. He said, "Where did you get this information?" I said, "Never mind, I am telling you now, Tshombe is going to be invited back on the first of July 1964." And he was. They thought, "We had better take this bloke seriously".'

So, in an apparent reference to the CIA, Mike said, 'I went up there (Pretoria) and discussed everything with them. I was not on the payroll, I didn't ask to be on the payroll. But I said, "Whatever I do, I want your support, it can't be done without".'

Later, I asked Mike if he would not have liked to be on the payroll. 'Yes, but not so much a month; I like a large sum of money, boooom, and that is what they gave me from time to time. I never lost touch with them after Katanga.'

Clearly, inviting the apparently forgiven Tshombe back was a smart move as it precluded his army in Angola from invading Katanga – which of course would have created a second front for Leopoldville to deal with.

Mike said when Tshombe was installed as prime minister of the Congo on 10 July 1964, 'the first thing he did was send me a telegram'. Mike flew north from Johannesburg on a Brussels-bound airplane, most likely around 27 July, but the Congo was not a popular destination and he was the only person to disembark when the plane landed at Leopoldville airport.

Alastair Wicks, now probably in his late forties, was already there. Although Wicks had 'little military experience', Mike liked him and found him useful because 'he spoke fluent French and was officer material – he had been to Harrow, which lifted the whole tone of the operation'.

Puren, who had stayed on as an aide to Tshombe after Katanga, was also there. He later wrote of Mike that he had been 'tremendously impressed by the discipline and the effective force he had engineered from the disparate adventurers' in Katanga. He also later described Mike as 'correct but ruthless'.[73]

All three were essentially 'Tshombe men', but Tshombe would not see them – there was still some hope of a diplomatic solution with the rebels, and Tshombe had requested help from five African countries and was giving their leaders an opportunity to act … but no help came.

Then, on 5 August, the rebels captured the important eastern city of Stanleyville; it became their capital. All the white civilians – 1600 is the figure usually quoted – were taken hostage, among them 'the staff of the US Consulate, including three CIA personnel'.[74]

Meanwhile, the Belgian Foreign Minister, Paul-Henri Spaak, and the American Under Secretary of State for Political Affairs, W Averell Harriman, had had discussions and 'agreed that the only realistic course is to develop as rapidly as possible a gendarme force led by military technicians [mercenaries]. Belgians have agreed to supply arms, helmets and boots. US will provide vehicles, communications and air support as needed and not available locally. You are authorised immediately to inform Tshombe USG will support the development of a 3000-man force. As first order of business, the immediate objective is to have an effective force of up to 500 men in being, prepared for operation within seven days. Obviously a force which can accomplish this objective will require military technician leadership, must be amenable to American and Belgian military advice, and not subject to control or veto by Mobutu. ... planning must be done urgently toward eventual force of 3-4000.'[75]

On 15 August Tshombe summoned Mike. Could he bring a large force of 'foreign volunteers', as Tshombe was wont to describe the mercenaries, to the Congo and put down the rebellion? He could. The meeting lasted five minutes.

That night Mike met with the National Security Council that included Tshombe and Major-General Mobutu, Chief of Staff of the army. After some discussion, Mobutu drafted a directive. The scale of operations was to be much grander than in Katanga in 1961. One thousand mercenaries should arrive immediately and recapture first Albertville and then Stanleyville. Remuneration was to be based on the Katanga model. Mike, as major, was to be the commander, would have 'absolute autonomy' and 'no Belgians would be placed' above him. Nominally they would be assisting the Congolese Army. Tshombe walked Mike to the gate and took his leave saying, 'We count on you, major. You are our man of destiny.'

Mike wrote in the *Sunday Times* of 13 December 1964 that a name for the force now had to be found. 'With memories of my new home in South Africa I decided to call it a commando (as in Boer commando), and because this would be the fifth command I had held, I named the new force "5 Commando".' He said he did not call it '5th Commando' because British units did not use the 'th' convention, although the Belgians may have referred to the unit as the 5th Commando.[76] In 2010 Mike said that as 5 Commando was the successor to 4 Commando in Katanga, it was the natural name. It is, however, also true that there were already four commando battalions in the Congolese Army, so '5' was the next logical number.

Later, I asked Mike how he had got involved in 1964. 'I was very very close to Don (Rickard), though he was not there (South Africa) at the time. The whole idea of raising a mercenary force plainly was the Americans' idea, passed off by Mobutu as <u>his</u> idea. A thousand men, retake Stanleyville, ooohhhh, Mobutu didn't think that big. But he had the CIA behind him and he could get what he liked. Without doubt, the Americans funded the 1964 and 1965 mercenaries. Fortunately for Mobutu, he had been adopted by the CIA, who were there then in the form of Larry Devlin.'

Had Mike got involved for the same reasons as before – namely, the adventure, the love of soldiering, the political attraction (stopping the communists), and the money? 'It was the adventure. Money was not a factor for me.' Another time, he said, 'The greatest thrill I get is the command of men, real men. I love being in the company of hard men, men who can live hard and not grumble. I like that type.' Mike has often been described as an idealist, and he put his idealism like this in 2006: 'If the wealth of the Congo had been captured by the Russians and Chinese, Africa would be very different today. Everything south of the equator would now be under the domination of the communists.'

By this time, Mike is in his mid-forties and no longer has the light build we see in his wedding photographs. He is powerful for his size, but it is his sharp mind and aggression in the field that make him a force to be reckoned with. As it turned out, during the next 18 months he was going to be unstoppable.

Author David Reed says Mike at that time had an 'autocratic bearing' and was 'a no-nonsense British officer of the old school – used to giving orders, used to having them obeyed at once'.[77]

And Ian Colvin says in his biography on Tshombe, 'Mike Hoare struck me as a man with subtle powers of leadership .... well balanced and alert, endowed with unusual sensitivity and foresight in assessing a situation. Hoare's training as a chartered accountant had overlaid a flair for command in the field of action, which, bursting out at this time, made him a Ulysses to the thousand adventurers who were being formed into 5 Commando.'[78]

Commandant Wicks advertised in newspapers in Johannesburg and Salisbury for 'any fit young man looking for employment with a difference'. The volunteers were given six-month contracts and would earn £200 or more a month in regular and danger pay.

'By comparison, the Southern Rhodesia Army advertises for new recruits at £42 9s 6d.'[79]

However, when it became clear that white mercenaries from apartheid South Africa were going to fight and kill black rebels, a torrent of abuse from black Africa landed on Tshombe's head. But, as Wicks later told a military attaché at the British embassy in Leopoldville, both he and Mike were pro-Tshombe because he was 'now the only African leader brave enough to declare openly that a partnership of black and white is the best solution for Africa. He is the only African who has so far emerged to turn back the tide of African nationalism, to bridge the gap between black and white, and thus prevent Africa reverting to anarchy.'[80]

Tshombe, of course, had the considerable backing of Belgium who wanted to protect their considerable interests in the Congo, and America who wanted to keep the communists out. Although Mike says in *Congo Mercenary*, 'These two powers were not averse to the Congo's employment of mercenary troops, in the circumstances, providing they were neither Belgian nor American,' we have seen above how America and Belgium in fact engineered the use of mercenary troops. Later, extensive recruitment of Belgian mercenaries was permitted.

The *Concise Oxford Dictionary* defines a mercenary as a 'hired soldier in foreign service'. SJG Clarke, in his *The Congo Mercenary*, suggests a fuller definition: a mercenary is primarily 'a foreigner in the country in which he is fighting or serving; and he is paid by the government of that country, or some other body, to fight'.[81]

At that time, however, the international media took one look at the swashbuckling European thugs who had resurfaced in the Congo, and again dubbed them *Les Affreux*. Also 'hired killers', 'dogs of war', and so on. Mike's 5 Commando were tarred with the same brush. The world disapproved of mercenary soldiers.

Bernard Levin, a London *Daily Mail* columnist, is quoted as writing, 'Mercenary soldiering has not only gone out of fashion, it has gone out of taste too. Killing people for money is, as an occupation, generally felt these days to fall somewhere between pimping and being in the Home Office.'[82]

Mike said, however, that he had learned at school that thousands of 'noble' Irish mercenaries had fought in foreign armies in the 18th century, and they had called themselves 'Wild Geese'. Shrewdly, Mike bestowed this name on 5 Commando, at one stroke giving them an air of historical respectability and at the same time distinguishing them from *Les Affreux*. Thereafter, the Wild Geese flag flew in 5 Commando camps. (See Appendix A.)

Though later Mike would subtly seek to distance himself from his work as a mercenary officer, in *Congo Mercenary*, he says, 'I make no apologies for being a mercenary soldier. Quite the reverse. I am proud to have led 5 Commando. I am proud that they stood when all else failed.' Later, he would back this up by quoting AE Housman's poem, *Epitaph on an Army of Mercenaries*, in particular the punch line: 'What God abandoned, these defended'.

I now draw on my interviews with Mike, on a host of other sources, and occasionally on what Mike wrote later in his book *Congo Mercenary*. The Americans gave Mike a ride on one of their C-130 Hercules military transport aircraft to Kamina Base, just outside Kamina in Katanga, where the men were to be stationed initially. The base had been built by the Belgians at enormous cost as a pilot and paratrooper training base and as a 'safeguard against Belgium being invaded'[83] during the cold war. It was said to have the longest runway in Africa if not the world, could house 30 000 troops and was a 'military marvel set in the heart of Africa'. But it had been looted to ruin since independence. 'There wasn't even a cup and spoon,' Mike said.

Although Mike had expected that very few of the recruits were likely to have combat experience, and that he would train them on arrival, and despite the almost total lack of equipment, he was intent on a quick, morale-boosting victory for Tshombe. As no road transport was available, Mike and Mobutu devised a plan whereby his unit would creep up the lake by night and attack the airport at Albertville on 25 August. Simultaneously, separate Congolese units would attack from the west and south, along with air support.[84]

Mike did a personal recce of lakeside Moba (Baudoinville), his likely jumping-off point some 140 km south of Albertville, and surrounding areas. Here, he learned that Albertville was in the hands of a small number of rebels, mostly *jeunesse* who were happily committing acts of brutality and terror. One hundred and thirty Europeans had been taken hostage.

Mike had sent for 100 volunteers, but on 21 August only 38 men, of many nationalities and mostly untrained, flew into Kamina; nine withdrew when they heard they would be going into action within days. Nothing daunted, Mike chose some experienced men as platoon leaders, including Sergeant Donald Grant who had been with him in 1961; press reports at that time described Grant as Mike's 'bodyguard'.

Now the unit familiarised itself with the CETME and FN rifles, and on 23 August[85] Mike sent the men on ahead to Moba with four assault boats and outboard motors, but without radios – they had not arrived in time. When he got there himself, he found a mutiny on his hands. One of the men, a Belgian who had grown up in Katanga, had convinced the men they would drown on the lake, and they were refusing to go.

'I imagine there comes a moment like this in every commander's life when his authority is challenged. In a flash I whipped out my Browning 9 mm pistol and clouted him on the side of the head. He collapsed like a pricked balloon. It was all over in a second, but it was a watershed in my life. The leadership of mercenary troops by force of personality alone demands a hardness of character and a conviction in one's own invincibility which I did not possess. I was obliged to assume those qualities then and there. Without it I could never have done my duty or lived through the horrors which were to be my lot.

'I spoke to the men. "Now listen to me. We are going to raid Albertville from the lake in support of two Congolese Army columns and I am going to lead you. Anybody who refuses to go can take three paces forward." Nobody moved.'

By dawn after the second night, the outboards had all but packed up. They had to paddle and came ashore 24 km south of Albertville. They started to march. Mike soon found one of the men on the ground in tears. 'Please sir, let me go back. I should never have

come.' Mike ordered him to fall in, but the man worked himself into a state of hysteria. 'You're mad, major, you're mad. We're all going to be killed. I know we are,' he screamed terror-stricken, until Grant put a fist in his mouth.

Mike is quoted in the *Sunday Times* of 13 November 1966 as saying this man had later deserted and, in an attempt to cover his cowardice, had told the press in Johannesburg that the major was mad. This was Mike's version of how he came to get the *nom de guerre* 'Mad Major' – which soon became the shorter 'Mad Mike'.

However, Christopher Munnion, a former Africa correspondent for the *Daily Telegraph*, gives two other possible sources for the name. 'Mike Hoare was automatically dubbed "Mad Mike" by the journalists, more for the sake of appealing alliteration in copy than because of his behaviour.' He also says, 'Michael Brown of the *Daily Express* was the first to dub Hoare "Mad Mike" after accompanying him on one particularly hair-raising trip. The colonel resented the nickname but never held it against Brown.' Munnion himself did not find Mike mad – he describes him rather as 'the perfect gentleman, courteous, considerate and charming' and as 'friendly and accessible'.[86] And yes, Mike was always dismissive of the name 'Mad Mike'.

Further on, they repulsed an attack by a mob of doped-up Simbas (rebels) who advanced screaming '*Mai Mulele*', secure in the knowledge that the enemy's bullets would turn to water. Most of the 28 killed were *jeunesse*. From here, however, nothing went right for Mike's unit. Soon, their beach landing in impounded boats was repulsed, and a woman and her two children were mistaken for rebels in the dark, and shot dead. Several nights later, they found the airport deserted but surprised about 50 Simbas who were sleeping on the floor in a nearby building; in the ensuing action, two of the men were killed by enemy fire, and a Briton, Lieutenant Eric Bridge, sustained a bullet wound to the shoulder and a poison arrow to the face, and was losing blood. The unit withdrew, and after several days of paddling, they came ashore at Mpala, almost back where they started, on about 1 September. In the meantime, government forces had taken Albertville by 30 August.[87]

Over the years, I often wondered who this Lt Bridge was and why he had gone to the Congo. I found out in 2011 when Bridge, then aged 82, rode up my driveway on his BMW 1150 cc motorbike, having ridden from his home near Johannesburg, nearly 600 km away, to visit Mike. Before signing up for the Congo – 'for the adventure and the money, in that order' – he had served in the Royal Marines Commando in Malaya and Egypt. He was also in the Kenya police, the Kenya Regiment and a South African commando unit. After he recovered from his shoulder wound, he worked in the Johannesburg office of 5 Commando, handling the recruiting of the men. Later he worked in Biafra, and the Comores in the SA Defence Force's military intelligence unit. 'I have served in six armies,' he said proudly; 'I reckon that qualifies me as a professional soldier.'

The Albertville raid had evidently been a disaster, and Mike blamed himself for testing the men so severely without proper training. David Reed described the operation as 'something that might have been staged by the Marx Brothers'[88]. The *Sunday Times* of 13 September 1964 used such terms as 'comic-opera lake assault', the 'half-cocked army' and a 'tragic farce'.

In early September, about 500 men of 19 nationalities but mostly South African and Rhodesian, assembled at Kamina. 'I never saw such a disgraceful looking lot in my life,' Mike wrote. After he had weeded out the alcoholics, bums and no-hopers, he was down to 300 men, only a few of whom were found to be officer material after an initial scan. One was Jeremy Spencer, an ex-Coldstream Guardsman whom Mike later described as 'a magnificent leader, loved by his men whom he led with a grip of iron tempered with great understanding'.

Another was Second Lt George Schroeder, whom Mike would describe both as the all-round best soldier in the Congo and also in less complimentary terms. More of both men later.

Certainly Mike would have wanted more Celts. He once wrote, 'Can't have too many Celts. I love them. Sometimes a little hard to handle in barracks. The price one pays for fighting spirit I suppose, but worth it; always tremendous men in action.'[89]

Some of the men were ex-regular-army, some were there to find themselves, but most were simply adventurers. Almost all were there for the money – half of which was payable in sterling. The money was transferred directly from Leopoldville to the men's accounts, most of which were in Johannesburg and Salisbury. 'If there were more than five percent of us who had carefully considered the moral implications of fighting for money, I would have been surprised,' Mike said.

One of the new volunteers was Ivan Smith, a young giant who had been conscripted into national service in Southern Rhodesia, and who had then got a taste for danger, brawling and big bucks as a miner on the Copperbelt near the Congo border. Now, at a loose end in Salisbury after two wild years in Europe, he signed on as a volunteer; the pay was 'very high' and that was all that mattered. His first impression of Mike was 'bullshitter', followed at once by 'dangerous and strong'.[90]

Another volunteer was Flemming 'Pluto' Kerstein, a Dane. He had served with the UN forces in the Congo in 1962-63 and got 'hooked about being in Africa'. He then managed a coffee plantation in Équateur province, and signed on because he was 'an adventurous soul', and wanted to see if he 'could endure soldiering under fire'. (After the Congo, he spent about 40 years in the Danish Army, retiring as a major). Of Mike, Kerstein wrote: 'Mike Hoare was a most respected leader. He was a mixture of "management by fear" and "management by example!" He always tried to teach his officers new ways of doing things.'

The men were formed into commandos of 40 men (called 51 Commando, 52 Commando, etc), each with three sergeants and two officers. Mike was a great believer in talking to his men, and impressed on them the need for 'regular army standards'. 'Not for us the sloppy dress and three days growth of beard almost mandatory for a Belgian mercenary.'

Regarding dress, he said, 'I did not think the recently introduced camouflage jackets that were issued in the British Army in Europe would be suitable for us in the Congo. [I was quite right.] I refused to accept the bush hats we were issued with, and we bought our own green berets and khaki shirts on my orders.' Mike also designed a

hat's Mike with the cheeky face, and his siblings, from left,
8en, Marion and Alick, at their childhood home in Budge
3udge, Calcutta. ±1927. *Photograph: source unknown*

Mike and some of his school
family on their way for a swim at
Margate beach. 1934.
Photograph: source unknown

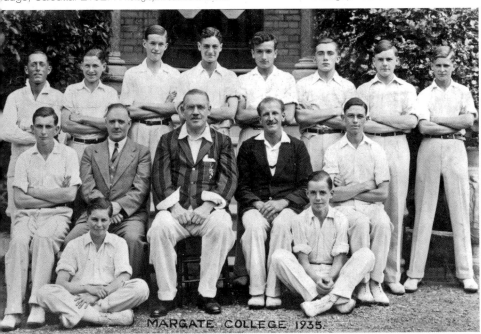

MARGATE COLLEGE 1935.

/like, far right, loved cricket, later playing for his club at
.ords. His brother Alick is seated at left. First XI, Margate
College, 1935. *Photograph: source unknown*

Mike's father was a master mariner. So
were Mike's grandfather and great-grandfather. Like Mike, they were all named
Thomas. *Photograph: source unknown*

Mike as a young British Army captain in 2 Reconnaissance Regiment, Royal Armoured Corps, in India. 1944.
Photograph: source unknown

Mike Hoare, in full dress with ceremonial sword, and 'Betty' Stott were married in New Delhi, India, on 10 February 1945; seen behind them, from left, are Betty's mother Ethel Stott, an unidentified woman, bridesmaid Liz Ogilvy, Mike's brother Ben Hoare (back), and best man Teddy Lane.
Photograph: source unknown

ike sports a traditional asuto hat in the mountains Basutoland. Mid-1950s. *otograph: source unknown*

Baby Chris with his father and mother, Mike and Betty. Grace Avenue, Westville. September 1949. *Photograph: source unknown*

Basutoland (see over) the ill-equipped pioneers had to take refuge in a hut at an altitude of bout 3000 metres, with snow roundabout; from left Paddy and Phil Peel-Pearce, John Webb, m Alterskye, Mike, and David Alexander. *Photograph by Arthur Bowland*

One day they managed only 150 metres.

Mike assisted in the first-ever expedition to blaze a vehicle track across the mountains of Basutoland. 1956.

Photographs by Arthur Bowland

One night they sheltered under a rocky overhang next to the zigzag bridle path used by donkey trains.

David Alexander, standing, keeps up the spirits of Jim Alterskye, John Webb and Mike.

Mike, left, and the others had to help the Land Rover across the Orange River.

ke straddles the
quator near Kampala
Uganda while
ossing Africa from
ist to west on a
)0cc twin-cylinder
JS motorbike. 1954.
otograph: source unknown

Mike hams it up for the movie
camera during his cross-Africa trip
in 1954. Having crossed a river on
a pont, he rides up to the camera,
removes his beret, unzips his
leather jacket and takes a swig out
of a bottle of scotch whisky, just
for fun. *Photograph: source unknown*

Mike with his 1951 model,
350cc single-cylinder, AJS
motorbike in Welkom, South
Africa, on his way to Cairo,
Egypt. August 1953.
Photograph: source unknown

Mike towed a trailer with 88 gallons of petrol in his search for the lost city of the Kalahari. 1958.
Photograph: Mike Hoare

Mike got totally bogged down while trying to rescue a cow from the mud of Lake Ngami, Bechuanaland. 1958. *Photograph: Mike Hoare*

There were some pranksters on the Ngamiland Expedition of July 1959, seen here, probably in Mafeking. Note the accessory on the Female vehicle. *Photograph: John Yelland*

Mike (third from right) supervises
puncture repair in the Kalahari
Desert. July 1959.
Photograph: John Yelland

Looking for an unidentified
ape-like creature known as
Ufiti, in Nyasaland. 1960.
Photograph: John Yelland

. . . an 'Ufiti's-eye view of 'Ufiti'

John Yelland's amusing illustration of his
sighting of Ufiti in Nyasaland. 1960.
Illustration: John Yelland

Mike borrowed Alastair Wicks's kilt to wear to a function – most likely at the Katanga Army base at Shinkolobwe. The women are the wives of local Belgians. 1961.
Photo courtesy Jean-Pierre Sonck

'Speedy' Donaldson (the father of the missing Simon Donaldson), left, and Mike at an airport in Johannesburg shortly before doing an aerial search in Katanga. July 1961. *Photograph: source unknown*

Mike, right, and members of the fighting patrol that found Simon Donaldson's jeep; next to Mike is Adjudant Edouard Lambrette, an officer in the Katanga Army. July 1961. *Photograph: source unknown*

Mike, left, and John
Seaman led five safaris to
the Tsodilo Hills in 1962.
Note the spectacular rock
images.
Photograph: source unknown

Blocked in the
Okavango Delta.
1963.
Photograph:
source unknown

A loaded *Snow Goose*
makes its way to 'the
enchanted place' in
the Okavango Delta,
Bechuanaland. 1963.
Photograph: source unknown

Joseph Mobutu congratulates Mike Hoare at Faradje in the Congo near the Sudan border. On the back of the photo, is written, "To my excellent friend, Lt Col Mike Hoare, senior officer of exceptional worth, both militarily and in the re-establishment of the regions that he liberated from the rebel regime. With all my gratitude for the exceptional service rendered. Joseph Desiré Mobutu, Maj Gen." May 1965. *Photograph: source unknown*

Mike Hoare, centre, leads the rescue of priests at the Kalima mission. 1964. *Photograph: source unknown*

Major Mike Hoare at Kamina base 1964. *Photograph: Norman Evans*

On the back of the photograph, presumably the missionary Mrs Holte has written: 'Mrs Greta Holte with brave South African soldiers at Bondo. 30 May 1965.' *Photograph: source unknown*

Wounded in action in the shoulder and the face, Lt Eric Bridge in a small boat on Lake Tanganyika during the withdrawal to Mpala. August 1964.
Photo: Siegfried Mueller and courtesy Eric Bridge

The fighting in the Congo was very big news in South Africa and in many parts of the world in 1964/5.
Photograph: source unknown

The well-known Major Siegfried 'Congo' Mueller was one of the characters in 5 Commando. Note the Iron Cross.
Photograph: source unknown and courtesy Eric Bridge

Mike supervises the evacuation of the wounded by helicopter after the landing at Baraka. Note the injured John Peters next to Mike. September 1965. A part of this photograph is used on the front cover. *Photograph: Bob Houcke*

Mike in discussion with CIA Air Operations Officer Larry Murphy at Baraka in late 1965. The CIA controlled both the air support and the medevac helicopters. *Photograph: Bob Houcke*

Mike sails his beloved *Colin Archer* in Durban harbour during the opening cruise of the yachting season; the author is crewing. On the left is (now Sir) Robin Knox-Johnston's *Suhaili*. 1966.

Photograph: source unknown
Courtesy Bob Fraser

elow, Mike's 36-foot
utter, *Colin Archer*, at
e yacht basin in Durban
1969. Seen preparing
r a television shoot
n board, are from left,
mon and Mikey, Gerry,
Gina' (back), one of the
V crew, Mike and Phyllis.
ote the Riviera Hotel in
e background at right –
ee chapter 13.

notograph: Chris Hoare

A studio portrait of Mike taken in about 1966. *Photograph: source unknown*

Phyllis with Mikey, 6, and Simon, 4, at Clementi Park, Singapore. November 1970. *Photograph: source unknown*

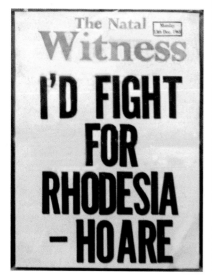

A *Natal Witness* poster dated 13 December 1965, just a month after Ian Smith's unilateral declaration of independence from Britain, shows Mike was already looking to the future. *Photograph: source unknown*

Sylvia sporting 'gunports' and topsails. Mediterranean 1972.
Photograph: Chris Hoare

Sylvia, a Baltic trader, under sail in the Mediterranean. 1971.
Photograph: Chris Hoare

ike on the set of *The Wild Geese* in South Africa in 1977 with the film director, Andrew V McLaglen.
otograph by courtesy of Euan Lloyd (©1978 Richmond Light Horse Productions Limited)

Mike's release from jail caused a sensation in the media. Here, he arrives for a press conference at the Hilton Hotel, Hilton. May 1985. *Photograph: Peter Duffy*

The media turned out in force for Mike's post-prison press conference at the Hilton Hotel, Hilton. Some of the Frothblowers can be seen at back left, namely Bob Sims, Barney Carey (obscured), Ken Dalgliesh and Aubrey Brooks. May 1985. *Photograph: Peter Duffy*

black cravat, which he wore, and a shoulder patch which initially said simply '5 Commando'; later it said '5 Commando' in red above a flying goose in blue, on a light khaki background. Mike also said he encouraged the men to wear the insignia of their previous unit.

Training commenced, with the men spending their time getting fit and on the range with some old FN rifles. The NCOs and officers were trained by Mike, mainly by means of sand-table and tactical exercises. However, almost no equipment was getting through. Then a Belgian, Colonel Frédéric Vandewalle, assumed overall command and began to sort out the immense supply problems, but, according to Colvin, Vandewalle found Mike 'difficult to harness to orthodox military obedience'.[91]

About 8 September,[92] 51 Commando was sent north to Gemena. According to Smith, they were not supplied with any food and had to literally forage every day; they had no Jeeps and had to liberate some from the Congolese Army at gunpoint; orders were not given – fear of death was the only commander. In a fire-fight, to avoid getting a bullet in the back from a fellow mercenary who may have felt aggrieved about something, the men formed mutual-protection cells. They were dubbed 'Mad Dog Killers', and yes, their advance on Lisala and then Bumba was a blazing saga of looting, booze, dagga, killing and more killing, some of it the wanton killing of innocents.

But, Smith says 51 Commando were mere beginners when it came to butchery, compared to the Congolese Army and the rebels. 'Each time control of a town changed hands the killing started again. The local black population tried to run for cover when the soldiers (Congolese Army) came to buildings in which they hid, seeking to rape, kill and loot. Anyone who ran was shot. All the males who put up their hands were taken captive; females were raped then and there in the street before being taken into captivity. Many male captives were first maliciously beaten to a pulp with rifle butts and then bayoneted at the mass grave instead of being shot. The women were pushed into the houses the soldiers commandeered, and abused day and night. All day and night gunfire rattled and screams of tortured men and women filled the air around (51) Commando.

When the rebels took control of a town, their law assumed that all were government agents and the same slaughter took place.'[93]

A long and extraordinary article in *The Daily News* of 10 September 1964, tells us Mike himself was in Albertville in early September.

The article – make of it what you will – is based on a report by Michael Brown of the *Daily Express*, who had had breakfast with Mike on the verandah of the Grand Hotel du Lac. We read that 'they ate frugally – tinned cheese, a bar of chocolate and a glass of whisky because the hotel was completely deserted, apart from the major's personal bodyguard, Donald Grant from Glasgow, who was roaming around … looking for water.'

Brown describes Mike as 'the sort of man who might invite you to play tennis or go sailing on Durban bay. It was difficult to imagine him killing 17 men single-handed only a few hours before while fighting his way out of an ambush. "I suppose we are all a bit touched really," Hoare grinned at Brown as they were finishing their breakfast. "But when you have been at this sort of business 15 years it's difficult to give it up. Do I enjoy killing? Certainly not. Actually, this business a few hours ago was pretty ghastly. They were a raw bunch and gave us no trouble. How did I get into this? It began after the war when I was an accountant, wearing striped pants, going up to the City every day. I got bored and pushed off to South Africa. I lost all my money, then made some more in the car business and virtually retired. I took my wife and children off to the Seychelles and relaxed. Nearly went barmy with boredom after a bit, so started safaris. Tshombe asked me to get the old team together again – and here I am".'

Meanwhile 55, 56 and 57 Commando had been training at Kamina to spearhead a column of Congolese infantry that was forming up to liberate Stanleyville. 51 Commando returned to Kamina and also joined the Stanleyville column. 52, 53 and 54 Commandos were working in the north to take the bigger towns around Stanleyville.

At the last moment, new FN rifles were issued, and the men flew to Kongolo to find probably several dozen vehicles waiting. Lt Col Albert Liegeois, a Belgian regular army officer, was given command of the column which consisted of about 130 mercenaries (mostly in 5 Commando), and about 370 Katangese and Kasaian soldiers.

5 Commando were to do most of the fighting under Mike's command and they led the column, known as Lima One, as it struck out to fight its way to Stanleyville, some 750 km to the north, on 1 November 1964.

They were to be supported by a small air arm, 'recruited by, paid for and run by the Americans' and consisting of some B-26 bombers and T-28 fighters. The pilots were anti-Castro Cuban exiles.

57 Commando was led by Captain Ian Gordon, the 'nearest thing to the perfect fighting man'. One of his sergeants was John Peters who had 'nerves of steel' and was 'tough and untameable'. 57 Commando considered themselves the elite.

Tactics were, as in Katanga, speed and a determined show of force coupled with reconnaissance by fire and a lot of noise. At night they would stop in a village and sleep next to their vehicles. Said Mike, 'You never sleep in a hut – too easy to be surrounded. And, interestingly, the men develop a strange mentality – they don't want to leave the hut.'

They ticked off the towns. Samba, Kasongo, Kibombo. Now for the last 100 km to Kindu, a major centre where rebel atrocities were taking place daily, and where 220 European and Asian hostages were being held. The town was heavily defended but 5 Commando went in hard and freed the hostages. The next day, by special request, they detoured to Kalima to free 48 Belgian priests and a similar number of civilians.

Meanwhile, Phyllis was about to give birth to their first child in Durban and was having problems with a breech presentation. Mike was called home for a few days and the baby was born on 15 November. Back in Leopoldville, Mike received the news that Jeremy Spencer had been killed defending the Elila bridge near Kindu. Mike later wrote, 'I am not a soft man, but this went hard with me. The death of Jeremy, sensitive, courageous and lovable man that he was, struck something deep down inside. I wept in the privacy of my room.' He sent a signal to Phyllis: 'Call the boy Jeremy'. And so it was that the infant was named Michael Jeremy.

After a battle at the Lowa river, Mike learned that elite Belgian paratroopers were standing by on Ascension Island. Mike wanted to push on for Stanleyville where the Simbas were holding 1600 white hostages to ransom, and where thousands of Congolese were being cruelly done to death. But Liegeois had orders to wait.

Then the paratroopers moved to Kamina. Mike was convinced that with surprise on their side 5 Commando could take Stanleyville, a mere ten hours away, and free the hostages. But all he got was a command to proceed to Lubutu where, that night, a rebel truck roared up to the hospital which was being held by 51 Commando who had joined the column at Kindu. Some rebels were killed. One of the mercenaries also shot dead a boy of 8 – in cold blood.

Of this, Mike wrote, 'When I saw the body of the child, I was furious. My anger knew no bounds when the brave murderer was paraded before me – it was the same bastard who had given me all that trouble on the beach at Moba! This time I fixed him for ever.' When I asked Mike in 2010 what he meant, he declined to comment.

Suddenly, Vandewalle arrived. The paratroopers were going to drop on Stanleyville at 6.00 the next morning and 5 Commando were to attack at the same time. At the last moment, 'the CIA dispatched a team of 17 Cuban exiles led by paramilitary officer "Rip" Robertson' (he of the Bay of Pigs) to join the Stanleyville column and rescue the American consular and other hostages.[94]

The column started for Wanie Rukulu in the late afternoon and pushed through enemy territory that night. But they were repeatedly ambushed and lost a sergeant and a journalist, both killed. Mike halted his men 'para drop or no para drop' and later wrote, 'I salute every man who took part in that column that night. It was the most terrifying and harrowing experience of my life.'

Just after dawn, 5 Commando passed through the sparsely defended Wanie Rukulu, 60 km from Stanleyville. At 6.35 am, a battalion of paratroopers dropped on the airport from C-130 aircraft and started making their way into the town; the Simba rebels, meanwhile, were lining up several hundred hostages in a street. Then they opened fire, massacring 27, including an American doctor, Paul Carlson, who had devoted his life to healing sick Congolese.

Mike later wrote, 'It was an act of unparalleled savagery. Stanleyville bore witness on 24 November 1964, to one of the most hideous and barbaric crimes of the century, a premeditated act of murder, for which the leaders of the rebel regime must one day be held accountable.'

The 1966 'shockumentary' film *Africa Addio* by Gualtiero Jacopetti declared that the Simbas had 'tortured and, in part, eaten 12 000 Africans' in Stanleyville during the 100 days preceding 24 November 1964.

Although the paras had beaten 5 Commando to Stanleyville by a couple of hours, *Argosy* magazine said in 1966, 'It was Stanleyville more than any other single event that made Col Hoare a world hero. Letters and telegrams of praise and congratulations poured in from all corners. The mercenaries' dramatic dash to liberate the Stanleyville hostages fired the imaginations of young and old.

'Captain Henry Kerby, MP, in a House of Commons motion, stated that a British decoration should be awarded to Colonel Hoare "who has saved more British and European lives and done more for humanity in the Congo than (UN secretary-general) U Thant and the entire population of the United Nations put together, and at a fraction of the cost".'

Mike simply said, 'We experienced a lot of delays on the road north, and every day we would hear of more senseless killings by the rebels. It was immensely frustrating – we were so keyed up we could not sleep. Taking Stanleyville was the greatest achievement of the Wild Geese. There is only so much a unit of 300 men can do, but here we were part of a very big push and clearing the rebels out of Stan was a major victory for our side.'

That day in Stanleyville, Mike was involved in some derring-do which he describes rather neatly in *Congo Mercenary*. I reproduce it in full, both for the range of emotions that it evokes, and because Mike refers to it again at an important moment later in his life. Quote: A runner arrived. 'Colonel Raudstein from the US Embassy and the American consul, Mr Clingerman, to see you, sir.'

I might have guessed that Knut Raudstein would have been in

to Stan on the first C-130 available. He was dedicated to his job as military attaché. There was nothing diffident or withdrawn about Raudstein, and he wasted no time in getting to the point.

'Mike,' he said, 'you've got to do something for me. There are two American families in the middle of rebel-held Stan about 8 km from here. I want them out. Clingerman will show us the way.' Mr Clingerman was a slight man with a studious, happy face. He was bubbling over with enthusiasm.

To know Raudstein is to obey Raudstein. 'OK, Colonel,' I said, 'but you better stay here. In your position as Mil ....' He stopped me short.

'Not likely,' he said, 'where you go I'm going. These are Americans, lad, Americans. Don't worry about me, I'm just going along for the ride. I'm under your orders, I'll do anything you say.'

The opportunity of having a full colonel, American Army, under command was not one to be resisted. I raised a patrol in 20 minutes and accompanied by Clingerman we set off.

I put the Colonel in an armoured car and took the consul with me in the tentacle (a three-quarter-tonne HQ and signals truck). He kept up a steady chatter the whole way, oblivious of the gunfire, as though we were out for a Sunday afternoon drive. We arrived at the two houses in a residential area.

Clingerman dashed in while I set the field. John Peters (now a lieutenant) sealed off one end of the avenue and engaged the enemy, whilst the other end was held by a group led by the Colonel. I just had time to see him kneeling behind an armoured car, blazing away with his M 14 before we got the two families out. A man, some women and two children. I think he was a professor at the university. I seated them in the back of the tentacle. One of the ladies was distraught.

'What about Aunt Millie's present?' she cried. 'I've left it in the kitchen.' The man said something crisp about Aunt Millie. The rest of the family shouted her down with protest. This was no time to be thinking about silly things like presents, they all said, let's get going for heaven's sake, they chorused.

In an effort to calm their nerves and show them there was nothing to worry about, I told the good lady to go back and get Aunt Millie's present and anything else she wanted. She would never see that house again. She wanted to go desperately, but she gave way to the others.

I blew my whistle and we were off. The sea of rebels which we had parted for a few brief moments closed in again, engulfing the house. Half-way back we stopped to engage some snipers and the Colonel opened fire on the Congolese Army by mistake.

'Hold it Colonel,' I screamed, 'that's our side! That's the Congolese Army – furthermore, dammit, you're doing what I've always wanted to do!'

Clingerman delivered the party to the aerodrome and four hours later they were in Leopoldville. Unquote.

Raudstein was interviewed by David Reed on 20 January 1965.[95] Quote:

Q. From a military point of view, what do you think of the mercenaries?

A. Ordinarily, they wouldn't be able to cut the mustard, but here, under these circumstances, they are more than adequate.

Q. There is not much discipline among them, is there? An officer can't do much if they rebel, can they?

A. Well, strangely enough, they can. This guy Michael Hoare has done a marvellous job. He has no legal backing of any kind. He has no court martial authority and he is just a little warlord.

Q. Do you think he's a good officer?

A. I think he's as fine a battalion commander as I have ever seen.

Q. What's Hoare's background?

A. He was in World War 2 with the British Army. He went through South Africa on a troop ship and was so impressed with the beauty of the women there that a few years later, he went back to take another look.

Q. He tells us he controls these troops by force of personality. Physically, he is a rather small man, isn't he? He's got quite a strong personality.

A. Extremely strong personality and also a very dominant character.

Q. Is it not true that 5 Commando has borne the brunt of the action here and that 6 Commando (mainly Belgian and French mercenaries) has not done very much, really? Is it true to say 5 Commando has seen a lot more (action)?

A. I would say yes. Unquote.

5 Commando, having been denied a showdown with the rebels, soon established themselves at strategic locations in Stanleyville and in due course took the left-bank area on the other side of the Congo river. But military action was not the only show in town. Take looting for example. The shops were full and, in spite of Mike's ban on looting, there is no doubt that members of 5 Commando took advantage. The Congolese Army were looting too, after all.

And sex. As Smith tells it, the members of 6 Commando were suffering with the heat and had found a sports club *avec* swimming pool. They 'had a taste for young black girls. Nearly all of them had two or more teenage girls hanging on. All around on the grass surrounding the pool, there was constant casual fornication taking place. No privacy was sought or required.'[96] A girl could be bought for sex for the same price as a hen's egg, Smith said.

Probably the day that Stanleyville fell, Mike did something that has usually raised adverse comment. A European mercenary, fit and strong, and a professional footballer at home, not one of 5 Commando, raped a young Congolese, marched her down to the river and shot her dead at the end of a small pier. Late that night, in a tropical downpour, three officers from 5 Commando roused Mike and asked him to try the man for murder. Mike demurred. The officers said Mike was the only authority in Stanleyville at that time, and if the man got away with it, every other man would think he had a licence to rape and kill. They brought the man in and set up a court. Three Congolese gave irrefutable evidence. The accused man did not deny it. It was spoils of war. She was a rebel.

Clearly he was guilty. Mike said, 'We shall now write down on a piece of paper the sentence we wish to pass on this man. If the sentence you give is confirmed, you will also be the executioner.' The officers chose a whipping, execution, and forced suicide. Mike's sentence read, 'The big toe of each foot will be removed.' Down on the pier, they held the man down and Mike shot off his big toes with his Colt 45. Within a week, the man was killed in a plane crash.

In 2011, I asked Mike if he felt his action was justified in the circumstances. He replied in writing:

'Let me begin by saying that anybody commanding a unit of mercenary soldiers and who is sensitive to adverse criticism of his actions by the press has very little chance of performing his duty successfully. It is quite impossible for the average person to imagine the horror and loathing a commander of soldiers will face from time to time when dealing with riff-raff, bums, uneducated layabouts and others who may emerge from time to time in his unit, most likely untrained, uninvited and totally friendless, and who commit this type of atrocity without the slightest regret or understanding of their actions. And how, as a unit commander, do you deal with these characters? In the cold light of after years, the bare facts of such events lead one to remember and regret them, sincerely. But memories are short and in many cases one deliberately obscures them from memory because of their intrinsic horror. What I still remember about this incident is that anybody in my unit who had in mind committing any such action himself in ensuing actions was in no doubt that he would deserve the extremely severe punishment that I would certainly have awarded him.'

By now, Mike and the *Daily Telegraph*'s man in the Congo, John Bulloch, had become friends. Mike said that as the Congo and Stanleyville in particular were big news, they made a deal: Bulloch would write Mike's story, Mike would check it and make any changes, and Bulloch would get it published in the *Sunday Telegraph* in Mike's name. And they would share the proceeds. 'But the payment was not great, so Bulloch said not to worry, we'll do another one. And we did. I could never have found the time to write such an article – I had to keep an eye on my ruffians. Bulloch wrote I was the funniest mercenary he'd ever come across because money was of no importance to me.'

According to Munnion, Mike made Bulloch an honorary captain and Bulloch did a lot of air travel with Mike to get the story. Bulloch also claimed to have been 'Mike's political and literary adviser'.[97]

The articles were also published in the *Sunday Times* in South Africa over three Sundays in December 1964, under the series title: 'We are the mercenaries'. In a panel in the issue of 13 December 1964, with the headline: Portrait of a leader, Bulloch wrote, 'Mike Hoare is 45 and looks rather like Viscount Montgomery. His mess is run on very pukka lines. All officers of all rank and at all times address him as "Sir". He is abstemious, though he drinks; he does not smoke, never blasphemes. The whole commando runs because the major is there. It is entirely his personality which makes men from 19 nations … give their officers and sergeants instant and unquestioning obedience. Dozens of the men I have talked to ask me if the major is going to sign on again when his present contract expires. And they say: "If he goes, we go". If the mercenaries have saved the Congo, then it is Mike Hoare who has made them, led them, and driven them into it.'

Now Mike was asked to lead raids behind rebel lines in the Stanleyville area to rescue nuns and priests, both black and white, who had been taken hostage and were literally being raped or slaughtered, or both. Such rescues were beyond his original brief, but he felt his units could not just stand by. He also committed others of his men to rescues in the Paulis area. The eventual number of priests and nuns rescued by 5 Commando is generally held to be about 2000. This was surely Mike's finest hour.

'I got a list from the Americans, with names and nationalities, where they were when last heard of, etc. Not only Catholics, there were all sorts. All around Stanleyville in a 50-mile circle. They were very dicey little operations, how we got them out. The Belgians were only too glad (that we were prepared to rescue the hostages). Will you really? – style of thing. The Belgians had been going to leave them to their fate, thinking, "They weren't forced to come here, it's just unfortunate for them".'

'I was personally involved in every one of the rescue raids (in the Stanleyville area). I led the men through enemy territory. Mercenary soldiers are not (humanitarian) philanthropists, you know; I had to go, otherwise .... (they would not have done a proper job.) At one mission we freed about 100 nuns. They had been treated badly, wooooo woo woo woo, bastards huh? You can imagine how they (the rebels) treated the women.'

On one of the rescue raids, Mike copped a bullet across the forehead, and I remember how this incident brought home to our family the risk that Mike was taking, including the immense repercussions if Mike were to be killed. But Mike himself made light of it while also milking the situation. One of the officers, Tom Courtney, later said, 'The wound was protected by the famous plaster which will go down in history as the longest-serving plaster of all time. Still, the press loved it.'

Within days of the fall of Stanleyville, the British embassy in Leopoldville asked Mike to rescue a group of British missionaries and children at Yakusu. The embassy seemed to have temporarily forgotten that they had deemed the mercenaries 'scum'. Mike mounted a patrol and, with air cover, crossed the Lindi river by ferry after a skirmish.

I was contacted by the missionary's daughter, Linda Devereux of Canberra, Australia, in 2009, and then heard from her father, Professor Jim Taylor, originally from Scotland. He wrote, 'Mine was one of the families rescued by Mike Hoare – with my wife and four children. I was a medical missionary at Yakusu hospital, a teaching hospital for medical assistants and midwives. I remember clearly the day of the rescue, when we and two European nurses (one had been beaten up rescuing the other from a probable rape and murder), and a European engineer and his wife, were all bailed up in our house.' He had just given some 17 students tea when 'the white soldiers arrived in the driveway of the mission and then Mike came to the door.'

Mike takes up the story: 'The door was unbolted and a woman said, "Major Hoare, how nice of you to come. We were expecting you!" I was flabbergasted at her composure. I almost imagined she would ask me in and invite me to have a cup of tea. They were British all right. No tears, no laughter, no suffocating emotion, no warm continental welcome, just great relief that we had come.'

Taylor continued, 'Please convey our on-going gratitude to Mike. I am now 78, have lived a useful life educating medical students at Edinburgh University and at the University of Western Australia and I have five children, all with university degrees, 14 grandchildren (one a doctor) and one great-grandchild. Without Mike's intervention, my life would have been cut short at 33 years of age and my wife and children would have been killed and their progeny would never have existed.'

On the way back to Stanleyville, Mike said, one of their own aircraft mistakenly dived on the patrol, firing some rockets, destroying a Jeep and injuring two men.

Taylor said, 'I later appeared with an Irishman on a TV programme which tried to confront Mike with two hate-filled Congolese. My response was to thank Mike and ask how they could expect us to criticise people who had saved our lives.'

In November 2007, Dave Brown, a photographer in Calgary, Canada, told me about his experience as an almost seven-year-old in a missionary family. 'My family was rescued on 30 November 1964 by 52 Commando from Poko, two hours before we were supposed to be executed by the Simbas. If this (message) could get to Mike Hoare by 30 November, that would be incredible. There have been so many unfavorable stories over the years that I wanted at least one message of thanks to get through to someone involved. Warm regards.'

On 26 November 2007, 43 years after the events described, Brown started preparing himself to mark the day of remembrance that he, his mother and two brothers hold every year on 30 November.

'Please convey my warm regards to Mike. I know there are many other MKs (missionary kids) who were children then and middle-aged adults now, who have gone on to important positions, making a difference in their world, and many of those back in Africa which was and still is their adopted home. They have done what they did because of Mike's not giving up. It was his finest hour. I'm sitting here writing to you and not a forgotten small pile of bones in a distant jungle.'

One of the mercenaries who took part in several rescues was Gary Michell, resident in Cumbria, UK, in 2008. He saw himself at the time as 'not a particularly adventurous person, just a normal person who enjoyed the military way of life'. He had served in the Rhodesian Light Infantry, and also got his wings as a para. Then, out of the air force due to dyslexia, and seeing an advert for mercenaries, he applied, lying about his age – he turned 19 in Stanleyville 1964. He was invalided out in January 1965 with blackwater fever.

'I have a helluva lot of respect for "Mad Mike". I'll always remember that he would never send his men out on a mission that he wasn't prepared to do himself. I remember one time when we had been ambushed and were under heavy fire (near Opala, post-Stanleyville), two bullets grazed his forehead and he went over to the medic and said, "Stop this oil leak", and then carried on like nothing had happened. He wouldn't leave his men.

'Once, in 55 Commando, we had to go to a very large mission to rescue some nuns and priests. We had the element of surprise and, after a big battle, we took the mission station. We found nuns who had been raped, and some were pregnant from being raped. Also, I remember walking around the mission; there was another mercenary in front of me; as he walked past this cooking pot on a fire, he suddenly swore and kicked the pot over. We saw arms, legs and other body parts spill out onto the ground. The surviving nuns told us the parts belonged to other nuns who had been butchered and cooked. It was all pretty horrific.

'We rescued about 30 nuns and priests, but there was one priest who stood on the steps and refused to leave. He said, "God put me here and God will take me away". I said "Okay, He sent me to get you", and I knocked him down and two other men picked him up and put him in the truck. Mike was NOT impressed; he said hitting him was not right – after all, he was a priest!'

Another that the mercenaries rescued was Dr Helen Roseveare, a Cambridge-qualified doctor who had given her life to missionary work at a leprosy colony at Nebobongo, south-west of Paulis. She had been there 11 years. In her diary, later published as a book, she describes the months in which she and her colleagues were terrorised and brutalised. 'The awfulness of the cruelty of a barbarous people is terrible to watch,' she said.

Of the rescue on 30 November 1964, she wrote, 'The Simbas told us clearly we should shortly be murdered. Suddenly we hear machine-gun firing drawing rapidly closer. Shouting, the door kicked open, a white man – it was all over! Near hysteria broke out amongst us. Our deliverers, some 25 brave white mercenaries, mostly Rhodesians, told us we could take nothing as the three trucks were over-full already.

'Some of the mercenaries were splaying the long grass all around the house with machine-gun fire to scare the Simbas. Five armoured Jeeps, protecting the three trucks, filled with some 135 refugees! They drove hard to cover the 100 miles to Paulis before dark, firing machine-guns at any moving object.'[98]

On the back cover of her book is a photograph of Dr Roseveare with Lt Joe Wepener, officer commanding 54 Commando, who was killed in an accidental explosion in 1966.

A Spanish nun, Sister Veronica Muguerza, is quoted in the September 1966 issue of *Argosy*, an American men's service magazine, saying, 'The rebels were cutting out the hearts and livers and kidneys from dead and dying Europeans to make a brew which they rubbed on their foreheads in the belief that it would make them invulnerable to bullets. They had almost caught up with me when I heard gunfire and saw soldiers fighting their way toward us. I owe them my life.'

A Belgian padré told *Argosy*, 'No one has done more for the Congo than Mike Hoare and his men. If one day there is peace and an end to the killing in this unhappy land, it will be because of men like them.'

Mike merely said, 'It was emotionally gruelling work, seeing the way the hostages had been abused – we could see some of the nuns were pregnant. The Simbas were unbelievable bastards. But we did it, and made a big difference in many lives. I found that rewarding.'

At this time, Hans Germani, a doctor turned journalist turned mercenary, joined Mike himself as intelligence officer/translator/doctor. 'He had been properly trained in the German Army, and had been with Denard (Commandant Bob Denard, a Frenchman leading 6 Commando), but unhappily so. I said I would speak to Denard as I needed an interpreter. He (Germani) spoke seven European languages as well as Swahili. I never regretted it. Germani was not only a good soldier, but unbelievably brave. He was also an intellectual; his English vocabulary was greater than mine; he was a bloke you could discuss other things with which made him invaluable, for example English literature.'

Lt Germani gave his impression of Mike's leadership style in his book *White Soldiers in Black Africa*, translated from the German. 'Anyone accustomed to the Belgian military units as I was, would have felt transferred into another world. There were no wild whiskers and beards, no crazy fancy uniforms, camouflaged drill-caps and daggers sticking out of every pocket. Before we departed (to save the Isangi and Yangambi missions), Hoare called an officers' conference. Everything was done politely, in a disciplined British style. No plans were discussed, nor were there long debates as with the Belgians. Hoare gave orders, allotted tasks, explained his project.'[99]

Of the actual raid, he says, 'There was iron discipline. One felt that nobody could make fun of Hoare. He addressed the soldiers in his hardest voice and roared at them whenever the occasion arose, threatening arrest and repatriation. I had to admit a quite different feeling of security from that in Protin's column (André Protin, a Belgian major). One felt that Hoare's soldiers were accustomed to battle, and already so convinced of their superiority that they could not lose their heads.'[100]

Not everyone saw Mike this way. Apparently, East Berlin Radio dubbed him 'a mad bloodhound'.

Mike describes some of the Simbas' atrocities in his book, but in a somewhat restrained manner; one gets the feeling he thinks it would not be proper to go into too much detail, nor would the reader want that. Germani, on the other hand, has no such qualms. Sensitive readers should skip the next three paragraphs.

A German sister told him about a decent and pious Congolese who was the director of an agricultural experiment station. He had been very good to his workers. 'But the rebels said that he had studied in Europe and he was a tool of the whites. So they butchered him in public during a celebration. They cut open his chest while he was still alive and pulled out his heart.'[101]

Another sister, describing events long before Stanleyville, said, 'One day they dragged us to the memorial of Lumumba. The rebels yelled with anger that all whites should be killed, especially Americans. We had to undress and lie on the ground. Then they began to dance over our bodies, hitting us with sticks and all we could do was pray, thinking it was the end. The little American (sister) lay beside the bishop, and suddenly she let out a hideous scream. The bishop turned his head and saw how a broad knife was pushed into her body and then her live body was cut open from the bottom upward. She screamed dreadfully, and then she was silent. One of the rebels relieved himself in the open, and the bishop had to eat the excrement while they beat him and the rest of us. And so it went on almost every day. We were really more dead than alive.'[102]

And, to conclude the subject, another sister told Germani, 'The worst is still to come for the younger ones (nuns) when they find they are pregnant.' 'Were they ...?' 'All of us, from the youngest to the oldest, several times a day.'[103]

Mike was in no doubt as to the nature of the rebels. He wrote, 'The savages had not moved one inch towards civilisation in the last eighty years, despite the noble self-sacrifice of hundreds of missionaries.'

He was also 'disgusted' to hear about the boiling alive of a rebel by the Congolese Army, 'but savagery begets savagery and two months later I had occasion to revise my own standards of civilised behaviour. As I stood over the tortured remains of a small boy of eight, done to death by the rebels in the most barbarous fashion, I thought back to the boiling alive episode and wondered why I had been so shocked. I then felt it was far too good for them.'

No question about it, this was Joseph Conrad's 'inner station'.

Robin Griffin, one of the volunteers we meet later, put it this way in an interview. 'The Congo was an evil place. The Simbas and Belgian mercenaries used to shoot prisoners, we saw evidence of prisoners having been eaten, there were no Western standards at all, nothing worked, many of the boys (mercenaries) were on the fiddle – selling rations, etc; it was one huge steaming jungle and we felt horribly lost a lot of the time.

'But the "old boy" insisted what we were doing was right and good. He was a stickler for shaving every day, no camouflage uniforms – it was ridiculous, he even sent guys home for wearing the wrong colour berets. But in that place, where you could become a cannibal yourself in three months if you let yourself go, he was right. He pitched the whole thing on a high moral plain, and it was just as well because the Simbas, Congolese Army and Belgian mercs, and to a lesser extent our boys, did horrible things to each other.

'It was standard practice among the blacks to tie a man's elbows tight together behind his back, and then tie his elbows to his feet, bow fashion, and leave him in the sun for days. The Congo was a malevolent wonderland where everyone was casually brutal, but I must say most of the nonsense that the mercenaries got up to was always well away from the colonel.'

Griffin told me about an event that took place in the north-east Congo. 'One of the (5 Commando) volunteers had a reputation for being a thug. He had employed a black civvie to iron his kit, and one day when some trousers came back (from ironing) he (the volunteer) said there was a 1000-franc note missing from the pocket. He took the man outside and shot him, and threw him in the river. Then, he found the note in his other trousers.'

We have seen that even the conduct of Mike himself was not above criticism, but he justified it as his way of keeping control. Griffin put it this way: 'The colonel was the best leader of men I have ever seen. He led from the front and by example. He certainly wasn't mad. He was one of the few sane people in the Congo at that time. He inspired a terrific amount of loyalty, and instilled the right sort of pride in 5 Commando.'

On 29 May 1967, in an article headlined: Death is his 'living', John Healy of the *Evening Herald* in Ireland quotes Mike as saying, 'I had good sergeants. If a man stepped out of line I usually let one of my sergeants deal with him – and you know this meant a good beating up.'

Argosy magazine wrote, 'Realising the need for discipline with his renegade lot, "Mad Mike" became a veritable martinet. Officers and non-coms felt his watchful, cold eyes on them at all times. "I was absolutely autocratic," he admits. "I made them, and if they didn't measure up, I broke them. There was no law, no authority but mine, and I used it dictatorially".'

One of the long-serving mercenaries, Lt Tom Courtney of 53 Commando, summed it all up, saying that in his opinion, 'Mike was a professional soldier; he knew very well how to lead and command respect; everyone I've met who served with him felt they were part of a fighting commando, unlike Peters and Schroeder whose men and myself felt we were part of a barroom brawl.'

Meanwhile, although 5 Commando had saved the lives of probably 2000 innocent hostages, and had liberated vast areas of the country from Simba control, they continued to attract a bad press.

The preconceived notions of Anthony Mockler, who was sent to the Congo at the end of 1964 as an 'apprehensive' special correspondent for *The Guardian* newspaper, would be typical. As he says in his book: 'At *The Guardian* the general view was that mercenaries ... were the dregs of Europe – hired killers. The reason for my apprehension was that my assignment was to track down the leader of the mercenaries, the hired killer *par excellence*, "Mad Mike" Hoare.

'It came therefore as something of an anti-climax when I discovered that "Mad Mike" Hoare was staying in Room 534 of the Hotel Leopold II where I was myself installed. His physical appearance came as an even greater shock. He bore no resemblance at all to a hired killer or a dreg from a gutter. He was short, dapper and very neatly turned out in light khaki with a major's crown on his epaulettes. He wore a beret but he carried an attaché case, not a weapon. He resembled a British officer from a good regiment, though possibly politer and more courteous than most of that class. He appeared to be in no way insane.

'That evening he took me out for a drink in a bar on Boulevard 30 Juin. He drank orange juice himself. ... He talked of his crusade against communism and told me how in order to instil the regimental spirit he insisted on church parade and football matches every Sunday for the "volunteers" ... of 5 Commando.'[104]

(Mike was often described as dapper, as above, but it was not until 2009 that I was able to confirm that he did not wear standard-issue 5 Commando uniforms – he had his uniforms made at Lerwill Pope, probably Durban's most prestigious firm of tailors at that time. Mike, however, was not at all embarrassed about this revelation, saying it was important for a leader to be smartly turned-out, to look the part, and to differentiate himself from the men.)

Another who encountered Mike and went on a rescue mission with Mike and his men was the British photographer Don McCullin. He later said of Mike, 'He wasn't totally mad, but he liked that dashing, kind of pimpernel, kind of ... name.[105] There was goodness in Mike Hoare, but not much goodness in what he stood for. He was in it for the adventure and money... Some of these mercenaries had a lust for killing Africans. I hated them in the end.'[106]

By 31 December 1964, Mike had had enough of the horror and wanted no more of the 'damnable country'. But Mobutu made all sorts of promises, and on 3 January Mike flew to Durban for two weeks' leave and to consider his options.

'Then,' Mike said, 'Horton phoned. He did not like me, and had rapped me on the knuckles for writing to him on an earlier occasion as a result of my contact with Don Rickard. Now I was well known, and he said he had something terribly important to discuss with me, and kindly asked me to put an evening aside. He came to Durban and took Phyllis and I out to dinner. I told him I had had enough (of the Congo). He said, "God, no, no, no, we must change all this. We need you."

'Three days later, he came back to me. He said, "I have been told to tell you you can name your price. We need you today. You may need us one day". Those were his exact words. I asked for $10 000 which was nothing really.

'But money was not my main concern. I needed their support in the zone. I said if I went back it had to be on a different basis, and I would have to be able to do the job, I couldn't do the job without the equipment. With the Congolese it was impossible, they would say they would send equipment, and nothing would happen. Horton said, "Name it, we'll give you everything you want".

'So I agreed to go back. They kept their side and I kept mine. They produced aircraft, fast boats, etc. That's what made it possible for me to do it all. It was absurd for us to have to rely on the Congolese Army.'

Later Mike added, 'The Americans left me entirely alone when it came to operational issues, never suggesting one strategy over another.' For his part, Larry Devlin described Mike as a 'gentleman adventurer' who was 'well-educated, articulate, a man of tremendous charm, a serious and capable soldier. Mike had dash and pizzazz. He told great stories that made your hair stand on end, and he was a man of integrity and dignity. We became great friends.'[107]

On his return to Leopoldville, Mobutu promoted Mike lieutenant-colonel. Wicks, now promoted major, is quoted in *The Daily News* of 9 January 1965, in an article headlined: Now, the crazy colonel, as saying, 'Most of the men hero-worship him – and they are all slightly afraid of him … You only get that sort of respect with a tough bunch of soldiers after a good deal of personal bravery and disregard for danger. The two main points about Mike are his extraordinary grip over the men's minds, which he has, and the extraordinary degree of discipline which then arises out of that.'

But it was not all plain sailing for Mike. In a copy of a report Mike typed to Wicks around this time, and which was among Mike's papers, he starts, 'Stormy meeting with Mobutu this morning. Upshot: Not at all pleased with 5 Commando as at present constituted. Has fired Ian Gordon categorically, no argument, nothing I could say will save him. States that Gordon has given orders to his men not to fight. Consorts with black women. Mounted a raid east of Niangara in which two men were killed and two seriously wounded, the sole object of raid to blow up safe at a certain town. Regret that evidence irrefutable.'

Now in early February 1965, Mike and Capt Eric Bridge started interviewing men in Durban and Johannesburg for the second contract. Bridge's left jab was: 'Why do you want to leave your job, your wife and your family?' Then came a right hook: 'It's not a picnic. You're going to a real shooting war. Men get killed up there.' Two hundred men signed on.[108]

Mike was still concerned about the communist threat to South Africa and was still banging that drum, for a newspaper article tells us, 'War is "a certainty" in Africa if the communists gain a hold in the Congo, says Col. Mike Hoare. The battle which the men I have recruited will have to fight will be the decisive one. If we win it, communism will suffer a death-blow in Central Africa.' The communists must lose the battle 'if there is not to be war down south'.[109]

Mobutu gave Mike command of two battalions including Congolese soldiers, their task now being to seal off the borders with Sudan and Uganda, as tonnes of communist arms and ammunition were coming in from there every day. Only ten men had renewed their contracts, and they joined the February 1965 intake who were training at beautiful Bunia, a town at an altitude of 1300 metres with a bracing climate in the north-east of the Congo.

Most likely it was here that *The Volunteer* newspaper was produced. A copy dated 19 March 1965 that has survived is almost tabloid in size, four pages, and bills itself the 'World's first "soldier of fortune" newspaper'. The editor, Mike 'Kiwi' Smith, tells us it replaces 'the Commando's earlier newsletter', the *Demain* ('Tomorrow', a cynical reference to payday), first issued on 5 February 1965, and its main purpose is 'to give our relatives back home a factual account of our movements and living conditions in the Congo'. 'Kiwi' informs us that 'liberated press, liberated ink, and liberated paper' are part of his 'cost-cutting methods', and that relatives will be sent copies from the Johannesburg office.[110]

In an article in *The Volunteer* headlined: Wild Geese Get Bad

Press, one Peter Lister writes, 'There is the subtle inference that Colonel Hoare is nothing other than a butcher ... a silent but willing party to sending men to their deaths as long as his aims are achieved. 5 Commando knows this to be a lie. The emphasis of the South African press is always on "MAD" Mike, a swashbuckling, twentieth century Cyrano de Bergerac. Hence, 5 Commando must ALL be "mad". No mention is ever made of the countless hours spent by Colonel Hoare considering plan after plan whereby he may win his objectives at the least possible cost. Nor is any space ever given to the fact that he is personally a fine soldier and an extremely able tactician. This image of irresponsibility must be destroyed. The world press and public must be instructed in the fact that Colonel Hoare leads the deadliest, most highly trained fighting force of its size on the African continent today ... Not a rag-tag rabble.'

Robin Griffin, a Hemingway lookalike and wannabe, was among the new men. He was a 27-year-old South African who had done his A-levels in the then Northern Rhodesia, been conscripted into the Federal Army and later had some local military experience. He was both a student of the classics and adventurous, and was now working as a journalist in Kitwe, Northern Rhodesia, a mere 40 miles from the Congo border.

Why did he volunteer to become a soldier of fortune? Well, had Ernest Hemingway not done so in Spain in 1938[111], and had Hemingway not got a book out of it? Certainly, Griffin admitted to signing on out of a 'sense of adventure, really; also to find out about oneself in a situation like that, although the colonel did not approve of people finding themselves, but you wonder how you will react in situations like that'.

Griffin said that most men went to the Congo because of 'women trouble'. 'I did a survey once on why people had gone up there; 80 percent had gone because of a row with the girlfriend or having broken up with the wife.' Always the joker, he added, 'The women must have been pretty awful to have made the guys prefer the Congo!'

On his arrival at Kamina, Griffin was interviewed personally by Mike. 'He was business-like. It was pretty impressive because most leaders don't bother with new people – the sergeant-major takes care of that. But he asked us what we wanted to do. I was a bit overawed, the colonel had a reputation already, "Mad Mike" and all that. I was surprised how sane he was, actually, and professional. But I was most impressed by the talks he gave us, very down to earth and straightforward. He told us as mercenaries we were there to earn our money and not get ourselves killed, but we had to earn it. He did not harp on the anti-communist propaganda. He thought the Congo had a future, we could play a big role, and possibly we could stay on. He had the idea of settling us like the old Roman legionnaires when they had finished their stint.'

Now it was time for action again. Mike called his campaign to take the key towns to the north Operation White Giant – after the rebel jungle-drummers who referred to 5 Commando as the 'White Giants'. We see the pirate in Mike when we read in *Congo Mercenary*, 'Once more I was faced with the apparently insoluble problem of transport. I had gathered every available vehicle from far and wide and lined them up on the barrack square. They were a sorry sight. I paraded the men. "Gentlemen," I said, "there lies your transport for the campaign. (Get those) vehicles ready to fight and travel a distance of one thousand kilometres. Beg, borrow or steal, but get them on the road. The alternative is marching, carrying everything on your backs!"'

About 250 men from 5 Commando struck out from Bunia on 15 March 1965. North of Mahagi, Wicks and Force John-John (Peters' elite force) were despatched by road to take Djalasiga and Kerekere, while Mike led a force of 120 of his men plus 'The Black Watch' (100 guides and scouts from a nearby town) on foot from Ambesi to Aru, a distance of some 50 km. Their twin targets were the important town of Aru and the nearby Esebi mission which was now a rebel training centre.

Germani recalled how that night, the column advanced on foot. 'Hoare was in his best mood as "nothing is as nice as a good march". Then, the sky opened. A wall of water fell down on us. In pouring rain we ran into a village, but the rebels had fled. We pressed into the abandoned houses. Everything was dripping wet. Hoare allowed three hours' rest. The freezing men fell to the ground as if dead and slept soundly.

'A few started a fire and somehow we found we had a large pot of hot tea. "One recognises a good English troop," the lieutenant-colonel proclaimed, "by the speed with which it manages to make hot tea under the most difficult conditions".

'We lay on the ground side by side. The thoroughly soaked commander-in-chief trembled with cold. After all, he was no longer so young. Some soldiers persuaded him to put at least his shoes, trousers and socks near the fire to dry.

'In the flickering of the flames I saw his sleeping face beside me. There was something innocent and wise about him, like an elderly child. Why this slim man, who could lead a comfortable life in the paradise city of Durban, with his pretty blonde wife, and among valued friends, came here to march through the night and the storm is incomprehensible. He could have led the operation comfortably, as did the high Belgian officers, from a headquarters far behind the lines, or at least from a comfortable vehicle or well-equipped quarters in abandoned villas.

'But he did not do this. He was always out in front and showed less mercy to himself than to his soldiers. Perhaps it was because this wild band of adventurers, drinkers and similar ilk loved him, although he often treated them like dogs. To the Belgians he was a mystery and magnificent.

'But how he conducted his campaign on that and the following days, how he so suddenly turned up in the rebels' rear time and again, and how he created peace in the country, confirmed what I was thinking. A hundred years ago, this little man would have become a great conqueror of the English colonial empire, a Lord Clive, a Warren Hastings, one of the Britons who conquered continents with a handful of men. It was his bad luck to have been born too late, that no England was standing behind him anymore. His campaign was a wild adventure in the service of a foreign government. History will hardly remember Hoare's march through the rain, which that night broke the main line of the rebels, as it remembers Clive's march to Arcot through the rain. And yet Hoare had approximately the same number of soldiers with him and just as many enemies in front of him as had Clive.

'He saved the Congo from communism – but for how long? He saved European hostages from a tortured death. Perhaps he did not acquire worldly glory, but he gained the esteem and adoration of all the people who lived with him during those weeks, whether they were Americans, Europeans or Africans.'[112]

On another occasion, Germani said Mike had discussed politics and literature with him, and recited English verse. 'Only now did I begin to know this strange man. He was a genuine British officer in his posture and behaviour, but also a genuine Irishman in his recurring sentimentality and his fighting spirit.'[113]

Now 52 Commando was pushing up toward Aba. Griffin recalls, 'We were driving in a long column of trucks. Tactics were to travel till you got ambushed and then get out and crawl into the ditches, and then thump the rebels. I was pretty nervous in the beginning, actually most of the time. Mike was travelling in the tentacle ... (when we got ambushed). We were all lying in the ditches on either side. The shooting was still going on. Mike shouted, "Sergeant, get out my map table." Mike put the table out in the middle of the road, put his specs on and got the maps out and rather ostentatiously went through the maps – and we all rather sheepishly climbed out of the ditches. I think it was an act, but it was pretty impressive. He was trying to show us to keep a cool head – he put things in perspective.

'He was very much the colonel in those days. We were all rather in awe of him; he was very professional and quite stern. I think he had to be to keep a grip on people, but always human as well when there were problems. He was also a bit of a showman, not a show-off, not an ego thing, but where it was necessary to make a good impression he would put on a good show for effect, to achieve his end. Very much so.'

Around this time, Mike started using a monocle, and I always assumed this was 'an act'. But no, he said. 'Glasses always get broken in action, so a monocle is the answer.' Perhaps he got the monocle idea from Brigadier Fergusson who, apparently, used to throw his up in the air and catch it in his eye – to amuse his men.

The mercenaries were mostly there for the money, but sometimes were not paid for months; this was a persistent problem for Mike. Griffin remembered how Mike handled a strike at that time. 'None of our pay had come through, so we refused to go on soldiering, and refused to go on parade. There must have been 300 or 400 blokes. Mike said he would not talk to us until we went on parade. "I've got the food and a plane ticket out of here, you can carry on as long as you like," he said. Then, Mike conducted a very strict parade, slowly marching around all the ranks, telling people to get haircuts and polish their boots, and had their names taken. Then he climbed on the back of a Jeep, we gathered around, he said he was there for the money as we were, and he told us the attempts he had made to get paid. He was confident otherwise he would not be carrying on, and would do everything he could to make sure we got our money. About eight blokes fell out and went home, and the rest of us gave him three cheers. He was very charismatic, he was a very good speaker, impressed me a helluva lot.'

It was at a deserted school in Aba, a few days later, that Mike 'became an avowed anti-Marxist'. There, an old man told him how the rebels had come and lined up all the teachers and boys. Those who could read and write were taken into the forest and massacred. Mike visited the site – some of the boys had been shot dead, others had simply been maimed and left to bleed to death. Nearby, a hospital had been wrecked and the doctors killed, one in the middle of an operation. And a mission church destroyed. 'The reality (of communism) is hideous.'

One might reasonably ask why the Simbas committed these atrocities. Germani was told the rebels believed that studying enabled one to acquire 'the evil magic of the white; school education and every other kind of higher training is like a bad spell which the whites have cast over the country' and therefore students, schoolchildren and intellectuals had to be the first to be murdered.[114] Mike said Lumumba had stirred up anti-Belgian sentiment, and had urged people to kill whites in revenge for the harsh rule of the Belgians.

In 1985, Mike wrote, 'Today when people talk to me about

communism and the growing threat to Africa, I see that scene (the school massacre) again in all its misery and I know who will be the first to suffer – the unfortunate "intelligentsia". God help them.'

Meanwhile, the 'forceful and aggressive' Mike was flattening all before him. We get a glimpse of his belligerent style in three intelligence reports from that period:

'Ugandan forces, presumably in Congolese territory, are reported to have fired on Col Hoare's column of mercenaries and Congolese Army troops just north of Mahagi. Hoare has asked Tshombe's government to warn Uganda that he will retaliate for any further attacks. Ambassador (G McMurtrie) Godley has sent a US military officer to urge restraint on Hoare.'[115] This report forms part of a CIA daily intelligence brief to the President of the United States, for his eyes only and thus top secret at that time, on 17 March 1965. The Americans were obviously tracking the actions of their man at the highest level.

Further on, the British Embassy in Leopoldville thought that after taking Aru, Mike was 'likely to move on to Aba after a pause, and may take two months to do this'. But a jittery document dated 29 March 1965 says, 'Progress of Hoare's column now indicates rebel military collapse in Eastern Orientale. Hoare occupied Faradje (beyond Aba) on 28 March and is now moving on Watsa. He is now beyond his original instructions and we do not know from whom he is receiving others. All Congolese Army HQ in Leopoldville can do is nervously endorse *faits accomplis*. Acting Commander-in-Chief [Bobozo] and (Colonel) Mulamba are reported trying to reach Hoare by helicopter.'[116]

The real reason for the jitters and the helicopter was probably that Watsa had a substantial gold mine, and that the authorities did not want the mercenaries getting their hands on the gold. However, Watsa fell to 5 Commando on 30 March, and the story goes that some South African mercenaries who had gold-mining experience quickly reactivated the mine and produced six 11-kg gold bars. One was given to Mike, no doubt to secure his co-operation. He put it under his bed, treating it somewhat like a hot potato … until it was stolen … to his relief …[117]

5 Commando completed their mission at Niangara, having taken only seven weeks to seal off the north-east.

However, Mike was soon to ruffle diplomatic feathers again. A Leo-to-Foreign-Office report dated 4 May says, 'Patrols from 5 Commando have recently suffered some casualties 4 km south of the border from rebels coming from Sudan. During one such encounter, a rebel of Uganda origin was wounded and captured. He was interrogated by 5 Commando and reported a rebel camp at a dispensary 12 km north of frontier on Juba road containing several thousand armed rebels, vehicles and a petrol dump. This seems likely to have been the dispensary at Queribe just under ten miles by road from Congo-Sudan frontier. Hoare on his own initiative and seeking no one's permission, ordered an attack on rebel camp (inside Sudan), which took place on 26 April. Some vehicles and a petrol dump were destroyed. We believe Hoare informed Mobutu too late for the orders to be countermanded.'[118]

Mike later confirmed the incursion and said there had been repercussions which amounted to 'a bit of a moan', but Mobutu then invited him to tour Orientale province with him in his personal aircraft, a DC-3 which had been a present from the American President, John Kennedy.

It would seem that administration took up a large chunk of Mike's life. In a document headed: 'Notes for General Mobutu', some of the headings are 'Hospital Board', 'Johannesburg office expenses', 'Contracts', and 'Move to Fizi?'. Under 'Recruiting Expenses', Mike wrote: 'Lt Col Hoare conducted a recruiting campaign in Durban, Johannesburg and Cape Town during Feb and March to raise 250 men for the NE Congo operation. The entire expenses for this campaign were borne by Lt Col Hoare personally and amount to approx 500 pounds. Is it possible that this sum could be refunded to him in due course?'

Now it was time for 'a 600 km dash across country, behind enemy lines' which 'sounded rather romantic'. In due course, the column got to Bili where Johannes Holte, a Norwegian, and his wife Greta were serving as missionaries. On 28 May 1965, the Holtes were marched off into the jungle by a Simba to be beheaded with a panga.

Eventually the Simba made them kneel and raise their heads, which they did, but the Simba could not bring himself to do the deed. The Holtes fled, finding their way back to their mission. Johannes Holte later told *The Natal Witness* newspaper in Pietermaritzburg, 'What a great joy. Our deliverers arrived at last. We met Dr Fleming from Johannesburg, and Mr Paterson and Commander Maiden from Durban at the door of our home. A moment I shall never forget was their leader, Colonel Mike Hoare, coming into our house and welcoming us. It was so good to hear a leader with such a gentle voice. The Lord sent Mike Hoare to save us, he was our miracle.'

Mike was certainly a master in the art of the 'calm presence' and always used it to great effect, whether it was in patching up one of his children who had a bloody foot, or, as we have seen, in keeping rescued hostages calm while at the same time getting them out pronto.

Believe it or not, the Holtes went back to the Congo, and in the early 1980s Mike heard from them; after nearly 50 years as missionaries in the Congo, they were returning to Norway via Durban. Reverend Holte sent Mike a book of devotions. Inside, he had written, 'To my great friend Mike Hoare, with my great thanks that God sent you and your 5 Commando to deliver my dear wife and I in Bili Haut, 28-29 May 1965. To God be the glory forever and ever. Your friend, Rev Johannes Holte, Missionary in Zaire, 1935-1983, 19 April 1984.'

Further on, beyond Bondo, Mike himself took the wheel of a ferry for a hazardous river crossing. 55 Commando's Volunteer Eddie 'Scribe' McCabe describes the ensuing events: 'We went downstream a hundred yards or so and then all hell broke loose. The rebels had lined the bank and as the ferry reached the closest point to their positions they opened up with everything they had. I took cover behind some drums of diesel fuel and started firing. In the middle of this, it suddenly occurred to me that if the person steering the boat were hit we would be in REAL trouble, and I moved so I could see who this was, and it was Mike Hoare. He was really exposed, a lot higher than anyone else with no cover at all and he was bowed down firing with his .45 automatic. Judging by the number of shots he fired in the time I watched him, I would estimate that he fired as many, if not more, shots than most of the men on the ferry.'

Griffin, too, remembered being thunderstruck to see Mike standing alone on the unprotected bridge with bullets whizzing past or clanging nearby. In *Congo Mercenary*, Mike chose to play his bravery down by giving it a sentimental twist.

On to Buta, but they were too late to save 38 priests from massacre and others from atrocities. By now, Mike had had enough again and told Mobutu so. But Mobutu offered him a family home in Albertville, with sentries, and command of a campaign to rid the Fizi-Baraka area of rebels. Mike accepted and flew south to 'glorious Durban' for a month's leave.

Around this time, Mike was invited by the rector of Michaelhouse to give a formal evening talk to the boys. He loved public speaking and would always prepare himself thoroughly. He arrived in the late afternoon in his beloved Rover 90, with 'Shah' behind the wheel. Shah was his sometime chauffeur and general assistant of long standing at Autoscrap – a loyal and decent Indian man. Shah once whispered something to me about Mike when we were alone that I have never forgotten: 'If the boss says, "Take this truck and drive to Francistown IN REVERSE", you do that; you don't question why, there will be a good reason and you just do it.'

My father and I walked around the magnificent grounds. Then Mike asked to see the junior dining hall where he would be speaking, saying that inspecting the venue was an important part of preparing to give a speech. Our route took us past the Founders House classroom where I would normally have been doing my prep; my classmates heard us talking as we approached and were looking forward to catching an early glimpse of the famous man through the high windows. They were to be disappointed – Mike was one of few people shorter than the height of the windows.

My main recollection of the talk is that the theme was 'Be Determined – as with determination you will eventually succeed'.

One of my school friends, Chris James, however, remembered much more and put it like this: 'Saturday nights at Michaelhouse in the sixties were invariably a bleak finale to a tiring week and a hot day on the sports field. The usual fare to tempt us from mischief was a third-rate movie played on a stuttering projector, or a down-on-his-luck musician struggling with a borrowed instrument in front of a largely philistine audience. But there was one evening that stood out above all others.

'For over two hours Colonel Mike Hoare held the entire school of 450 boys and 40 members of staff spellbound, pacing up and down the stage without a note. Like a valiant Crusader returned from the Holy Land, he beguiled us with stories of horror and heroism, adversity and adventure, barbarism and bravery. At question time a forest of hands went up, fingers clicking for attention. There were groans of despair from the staff sitting at the back of the hall, sensing that years of investment in an expensive liberal/Christian education were under threat.

'When it was sadly all over, the colonel could have filled a battalion with us zealous underage recruits for his next adventure. Such was the power, clarity, inspiration and charisma of his unforgettable address.'

And yes, at question time the liberal schoolmasters took a hostile line, asking such questions as, 'Do you enjoy killing people?' and 'Who gives you the right to go around killing people for money?'

Also around this time, I am walking with Mike in downtown Johannesburg. We are coming up behind a group of men in civvies going slowly in the same direction, and Mike says to me, 'Here, let's have some fun; those are 5 Commando men.' He shouts out an order, the men spin around and, recognising their commanding officer, react half-pleased, half-embarrassed. One or two of them are practically down on their knees, not knowing how else to show respect on civvy street, such is their admiration of him ... but he stops them.

Mike once told me that probably also at this time, he had accepted an invitation from Sir Oswald Mosley, the British anti-communist, to meet for a drink at The Edward. Later, in a written question, I asked him why he had gone to meet a supporter of Adolf Hitler. He replied, 'Sir Oswald and his beautiful wife Lady Mosley were in Durban on holiday. I am not sure how it happened but I received a card from Sir Oswald to say he would like to meet me. As I had grown up in the days when he was a world famous figure I knew all about him. I found him and his charming wife extremely interesting people. I was able to ask him all sorts of questions – he used to attract enormous crowds at the Royal Albert Hall in London.'

During the July holidays of my final year at school (1965), I flew to Albertville, on Lake Tanganyika, with an intake of volunteers. Mike was training the new men and preparing for the push on Fizi and Baraka to the north. I was shocked to see the extreme reverence with which the men treated my 'old man', whom I considered in normal life to have a list of failings to his name.

As neither the promised house nor the sentries were anywhere in sight, we billeted at the Hotel du Lac. I trained with the men in the use of the FN and other weapons, and made myself useful as Mike's (unlicensed) chauffeur. Thereafter, Mike loved to tell – as I cringed – how I had single-handedly destroyed one-twelfth of his fleet of brand new Jeeps when I had a minor accident, breaking a tie rod – there being no spares.

The promised house eventually materialised and Mike, Phyllis and baby Mikey moved in. Nearby in another house was Wicks with, at times, his wife Nanette, and their young children. Mike felt that the commander of a military unit like 5 Commando should have a spacious family home, as it would send out the 'right message to the men and to the townspeople'. It would also give him a certain distance from his men, essential in a good leader, he said.

One of Mike's favourite Mobutu tales concerned his Albertville home. 'One day Mobutu said, "I am coming to Albertville and I want to visit you and 5 Commando". In due course, his ADC got in touch with me and said they were working out the details of General Mobutu's visit. "He wants to meet you and your wife at your home. He wants an English breakfast – he has heard about porridge, marmalade, etc. Then he wants to visit the camp."

'He was to arrive at 7 o'clock for the breakfast with his entourage of ten people. Seven o'clock came and eight o'clock came, but no

Mobutu. He arrived at 9 o'clock in a cavalcade of cars. Twenty-two people got out. They came in. Someone realised the situation and said, "We won't embarrass you, we don't normally eat breakfast, but have you got any Simba beer?" I said, "What? At this time of the morning?" and he said, "Yes, that's what we have."

'But the general himself wanted porridge, and bacon and eggs. Mikey, our baby, was in his playpen in a corner. Mobutu, who loved children, went over and picked him up and gave him a big kiss, and spent the rest of his visit walking around with Mikey in his arms. When the food arrived, Mobutu looked at the porridge and said, "You actually eat this? I can't believe it." Of course, he was just kidding on. We often talked about that wonderful breakfast with Mobutu *chez-nous*.'

One of the new recruits in August 1965 was Basil Borradaile, whom I met near Eshowe in KwaZulu-Natal in 2006. He said, 'Mike had a technique which I called "intuitive interviewing". I remember he looked at my CV, asked a few questions, looked at me, then fixed me with his piercing blue eyes and said, "OK, I am appointing you lieutenant".

'Mike was a great leader and an excellent military strategist. His style was blitzkrieg, and that was just right for the situation. He took no nonsense. He gave the orders and no one dreamed of disobeying him. He insisted we shave every day and told us at O groups to pray God daily. He led from the front – I remember a 30 km march we did; the colonel was in front, he was as fit as men 20 years younger than him. He was an officer and a gentleman – with a bit of pirate thrown in. For example, I remember he once said, "There are your vehicles, find your own petrol".'

Another who volunteered at this time was Russell Richardson of Johannesburg. He had been an infantry instructor in the South African Defence Force for five years but was now retailing furniture. He told me he had joined up to get away from his wife. As a sergeant in 57 Commando with Commandant Peters, he was later in the thick of the action at Baraka, and remembered Mike for his 'iron discipline' and for the fact that he always had a back-up plan.

Mike said it was properly trained men like Richardson who had carried the heaviest load and made 5 Commando effective.

The rebels at Baraka on Lake Tanganyika were receiving vast quantities of Chinese armaments via Dar es Salaam and Kigoma. The rush was therefore on to staunch this flow. As Mike said in *Congo Warriors*, 'This, together with the influx of Cuban mercenary soldiers under the leadership of Che Guevara, posed a considerable threat to the Congolese government.'

It is now known that Guevara, the Marxist revolutionary, arrived in the Congo with a group of Cuban soldiers on 24 April 1965 to bolster the rebel cause. His base was near Baraka.

Initially Mike wanted to employ his usual tactics, but the terrain with its steep drops ruled that out. Then he considered attacking the area on foot, but soon realised his recruits would not be up to it.

'There is something infinitely romantic about a column of men striking off over the mountains led by a compass needle and the will of a determined man, and the thought died hard with me,' he wrote in *Congo Mercenary*.

He thus turned to the CIA 'navy', largely staffed by 5 Commando men, consisting mainly of an 80-foot 'gunboat', the *Ermens*, and six extremely fast American armed motor boats, and the CIA air force which consisted of twelve T-28s, five B-26s, and Bell helicopters.

One day, Mike was completing his plan for a surprise amphibious assault on the enemy's rear north of Baraka when a lieutenant-colonel from GHQ came into his office. He recommended a slow and steady overland advance that would take some seven months. As Mike later wrote, 'Under my blotter lay my detailed plan for seizing Fizi, Baraka and Lulimba simultaneously on 27 September – in exactly three days' time!'

Now, the small armada was making its way up Lake Tanganyika, Baraka-bound. Mike was on the bridge of the *Ermens* in an unpredicted fierce storm. The man at the wheel was Sergeant Ian Yule, whom we meet later.

The men went ashore before dawn in two waves, one led by Peters and the other by Captain Hugh van Oppen, a Briton and, according to Mike, a 'proper officer'. Mike and his HQ were in the next wave. Then came the Jeeps and some armoured cars.

The enemy at Baraka were extremely fierce, and their number was estimated at 2000; Mike described them later as 'very different from anything we had ever met before. We intercepted wireless messages in Spanish ... and it seemed clear that the defence of Baraka was being organised by Cubans'.

Author Frank Villafana says Guevara sent 'Aly' Rodriguez and 35 Cuban soldiers to help defend Baraka.[119]

Mike does not mention Guevara in *Congo Mercenary*. From this we can deduce that Mike did not hold Guevara in high regard – and this is confirmed in a television interview he gave in 1969.

The voice-over introduces the subject as follows: 'By sheer force of personality, Mike Hoare turned the mercenaries into a shock force which blitzkrieged its way across a rebel area the size of Western Europe. The mercenaries' toughest fight was at Baraka. Opposing them there was Che Guevara who had secretly arrived with Cuban guerrillas to reinforce the Congolese rebels.'

We then see Mike answering some questions:

Q. Did the CIA give you any warning that Che Guevara and his group were coming into the Congo?

A. Oh yes, very much so, because this, obviously, to them, with their means of information and so on, which I didn't have, meant something very serious to them.

Q. Did you notice a change when it became apparent that Che Guevara and Cuban advisors were with the Simba rebels?

A. Oh yes, immediately. When we arrived at Baraka ... the first thing that impressed itself upon me was the extent of the firepower, which was being directed upon us – which was fantastic. The Congolese rebels' tactics would be normally to get drunk on marijuana or something of that nature, and to gather in thousands and to come on you in their thousands, and overwhelm you. Now this was different at Baraka. Here we had troops responding to whistle signals, wearing equipment, carrying out manoeuvres. This went on for four or five days.

Q. Do you feel any pride in being the first man to lick Che Guevara?

A. Not a pride, because I have never regarded Che Guevara as an extremely good soldier. His showing at Baraka was less than average. As soon as the going got really rough for him, he hurled it in. That took five days. They just vanished, leaving the unfortunate rebels to collect our fury.

It is notable that in 2008/9, when the city council in Durban, controlled by the African National Congress, started renaming the streets, they chose to change Moore Road to Che Guevara Road. Of this, a Durban journalist, Gavin Foster, wrote in *2Wheels* magazine:

'Che Guevara was a failure at just about everything he did, and his sole African adventure ... was amongst the most pathetic of his grubby little escapades. He arrived in Africa puffed up and ready for battle, only to discover that he was unwanted, unwelcome and unlikely to gather a following. The locals weren't interested in fighting alongside this deeply intense, long-haired honky, and he then went into such a sulk that his own Cuban forces ended up thinking he'd gone mad. In the end, it took little effort for Durban's Colonel Mike Hoare and his 300 South African mercenaries to kick him into touch – perhaps we need a Hoare Rd in Durban.'

Guevara left the Congo after seven months, admitting his efforts had been a failure.

With Baraka in their hands, 5 Commando dashed into the now undefended Fizi on 10 October. Mike soon learned that his man, Tshombe, had been dismissed as prime minister, no doubt because he had done his job – pacifying the rebels – and was thus dispensable, and because, having employed white mercenaries, he would never be acceptable to the rest of Africa.

Undaunted, however, Mike set about freeing nearby rebel-held areas, mainly on foot. Of this he wrote, 'Of all infantry tactics, the one which never ceases to thrill me is the sight of a strong body of men making their course relentlessly across country, using covered lines of approach, and brushing aside every obstacle in their path, until they reach their objective.'

The Simba rebellion was now effectively over. Mike later said the Wild Geese under his leadership had achieved the objectives of the Congolese government. 'We put the fire out completely. It would smoulder for a while, but the fire was out.'

But in any case, Mike had well and truly 'had enough of the whole Congo scene, the problems, etc. There was no future in the Congo for the mercenary movement because of the calibre of the people, and the officers; there was nobody coming forward; even if Mobutu had said I'll give you this and I'll give you that, I could not have done it. It was incredibly difficult to get men of calibre. We had scraped the bottom of the barrel.'

What this meant, in effect, was that everyone on active service was now more vulnerable. 'I always had this extraordinary belief I could not be killed – until I stopped a bullet at Opala. "The spell has gone," I said to myself. "My luck has run out".'

Mike went to see Tshombe, who had called Mike his 'man of destiny' and who had promised Mike anything when the rebellion was ended, but came away empty handed as Tshombe was no longer in power.[120]

On 24 November 1965, Mike gave notice to Mobutu personally. According to Colvin, 'Mobutu found a spark of admiration for this resolute man. Would Hoare return, if needed? he asked. Was there anything that the colonel wanted? Hoare had reconquered vast tracts of the Congo with a few hundred men; had once held in his hand the vast opencast gold mine of Watsa, but had not been interested in that; had faced fearful hazards at only £250 a month, the pay of a Johannesburg miner. An air ticket to London, he thought, he would like as a parting gift. The General demurred and handed him instead a handsome letter of thanks. So much for a mercenary!'[121]

In part, the letter reads, 'The Congolese nation owes you a great deal, and will keep of you a living and very edifying remembrance.'

That night, in a bloodless coup, Mobutu suspended parliament and took over as president himself.

'The next day,' said Mike, 'I sat at his inaugural lunch on his left hand. I admired him to a certain date; then he got mesmerised by power and money. He did not have the rigid discipline of say an English gentleman whose forebears go back centuries, House of Lords and university; these things keep you in harness. What was Mobutu? A sergeant in the pay corps. He was a highly intelligent chap who had an opportunity to go to Belgium for some of his training. When he came back, he saw the army was a good thing to be in. He turned out to be a damned good soldier; he really understood staff and supply, etc, and the limitations of his own army. He didn't try very hard to make a Congolese army – he knew it was impossible.'

It is worth noting that Mobutu ruled the Congo as a dictator and kleptocrat for 32 years. He plundered the country into paralysis until he was ousted in 1997 by Laurent-Désiré Kabila, who, in the early 1960s had been a pro-Lumumba rebel and who in 1965 had been a Simba and had collaborated with Guevara.

Of the 1964-65 period, Hellström said: 'It is probably fair to say that the mercenaries had a major impact on history. And since the history of the mercenaries in the Congo is largely the history of Mike Hoare, it can be argued that this is a classic example of a person who single-handedly changed history.'[122]

Germani put it this way in 1967: 'Without the mercenaries, especially the White Giants of Lieutenant-Colonel Hoare, central Africa, from the Indian to the Atlantic Ocean, from Zanzibar to Leopoldville and Brazzaville, would have been under the control of Red China. A handful of white adventurers stopped the projects of Mao Tse-tung.'[123]

But there was a cost. In all, probably several dozen volunteers were killed on Mike's watch.

Mike used to tell the new recruits to look around and to realise that some of them would be killed or seriously wounded. The next day he would have a queue outside his office of men wanting to return to South Africa. He dedicated his subsequent book on the Congo 'to those who did not come back'.

Later, Yule, who told me he had been in the British Army in Korea and had joined 5 Commando because he 'missed the army', said he had had enormous respect for Mike's achievements and leadership, saying they 'must surely surpass the Duke of Wellington's victory at Waterloo and Lord Nelson's victory at Trafalgar. Mike was tenacious in battle, a fearless and courageous leader, but not without compassion for all the men in his command. His only vice was he was inclined to be sentimental.' Yule and Mike were to meet again in different roles in 1977.

Mockler said that when Mike retired at the end of 1965 he was 'the man who made modern mercenary soldiering briefly but confusingly respectable. Hoare became the *beau idéal* of the mercenary leader, quiet-spoken, quietly confident, cool, collected, charming in manner, boyish in looks, dapper in uniform, every inch the English officer and gentleman.'[124]

There is no doubt about it, Mike's achievements in the Congo made him a household name throughout Southern Africa, famous in many parts of the world, and indeed a legend in his own lifetime.

And in particular it was his pukka leadership style that stood in such stark relief when compared to the leaders and what some called the 'barroom brawl' that followed his departure from the Congo. Before Mike left, he ultimately handed over the leadership of 5 Commando to Peters, now a commandant, who, in Mike's opinion, was not the most suitable candidate.

'I didn't know at the time that Peters – he was brave, yes – but he did not have the background. He had had a helluva life; he was brought up in Yorkshire in poor circumstances which did not do him any harm of course. Later, I believe he told the CIA that Mike Hoare was stupid because he didn't know how to milk the cow that was given to him: the Congo government.'

According to Colin Baker, Professor Emeritus at the University of Glamorgan in Wales, when Mike resigned he offered the leadership of 5 Commando to Peters – who declined it. Mike thus offered it to Van Oppen, who accepted. However, Peters soon changed his mind and Mike put him in charge, with Van Oppen second in command. Baker says that by April 1966, however, Van Oppen suspected Peters was involved in some sort of fiddle.[125]

To complicate matters, around this time a group in Belgium started conspiring to oust Mobutu, the CIA puppet, and restore their man, Tshombe, who was in exile. They approached Mike who was not interested, and he phoned Peters who was on leave in Rhodesia, telling him to expect a call. The plotters offered Peters £15 000 to lead 5 Commando south and seize Elisabethville for Tshombe. He declined the offer.[126]

At this point, we can but wonder whether Van Oppen had also been approached by the conspirators or if Peters perhaps suspected he had been approached, whether Peters had told Mobutu about the conspiracy, or if Van Oppen had told Mobutu about it and the alleged fiddle – and was about to arrest Peters. Colvin says Peters did report the plot to Mobutu.[127]

Peter Duffy, a volunteer whom we meet shortly, confirmed that Van Oppen also had a meeting with Mobutu around this time, and Baker says it is a 'distinct possibility' that subsequent events occurred on Mobutu's instructions or in accord with his wishes.[128]

What is known is that on the night of 8 May 1966, Van Oppen, aged 34, met an untimely death by gunfire in Mboko, a town north of Baraka on Lake Tanganyika. Since that time, there has been considerable speculation as to the identity of the perpetrator/s, and Baker describes a number of the theories in his book.

One of the volunteers who was in Mboko that night was Duffy. When I asked him in 2009 if he knew anything about the incident, he said promptly, 'I was there. I heard the gunfire. There were nine shots. When Van Oppen was found, there was shaving cream on his face. We had stopped at Mboko for the night on our way north. The word was that a sub-machine-gun had gone off when it was dropped, but some of us did what we could to make that gun go off by dropping it and so on, but it would not.'

Another volunteer, who was also at Mboko that night, later told me that it was generally believed around the camp at the time that a junior mercenary had murdered Van Oppen at the behest of an officer.

Mike told me a senior officer had later told him he had done it personally.

Mike's solution to the Congo's problems in 1966 was the

introduction of European settlers, not contract workers, who would come to help the Congolese help themselves. A mobile fighting force of white soldiers, a sort of foreign legion, would also be required. Without them the necessary investors, administrators and technicians would not return, he said.

Later, I asked Mike if he thought he had had an effect on the world. 'Certainly on Africa, and thus on the world, but I am not really conscious of it. I have not felt, oh nobody has recognised my effort. Not at all.

'But among those of us who know, shall we say, without a doubt the Americans were really behind it (in the Congo). They achieved, largely through me what they set out to do and that was to stop the communist incursion into southern Africa. The Congo was the key and still is the key to southern Africa, largely because of its immense wealth, almost untapped even to this day.

'It's a nice feeling, to know you have made a difference. I have often thought about that. Many people feel their lives are being lived without much point, so if you have done something, it refreshes you a bit.'

10. The Schemer

'That night, I took Mobutu's ADC, Powis, to dinner and asked him if we should not ask Mobutu for a *douceur*. The following day, Mobutu ... he had a box under his table, it was thick with $1000 notes. He gave me $30 000.' – Mike Hoare

Now, in early 1966, Mike started work on a new project: 'the book'. He had always been a keen reader and knew his Shakespeare. He enjoyed writing and had written stories, articles, long detailed diaries, lengthy letters, and even a bit of poetry. Among his papers were five typed pages entitled, 'Notes for an article on Shakespeare as a seaman' – with extracts from, for example, *The Tempest*, and his comments. In short, he loved the milieu of words and paper, and was to have eight books published in his lifetime; he turned out to be an excellent non-fiction writer.

Mike had bought a house in Link Road outside Hillcrest, half-an-hour by car from Durban; he named it *Baraka* after the town on Lake Tanganyika where he had led a beach landing with 200 men. However, in Arabic *baraka* means a sense of divine presence, charisma, or blessing; Mike knew this and was, no doubt, in his own private way signalling his gratitude to God that he had survived the utter horror of the Congo.

It was a spacious home, and in pride of place was a large portrait of Phyllis that Mike had commissioned from an artist named Paul Wiles in the late 1950s.

What Mike loved about the house was that the study was

completely separate from the domestic scene – it afforded him the quiet space he demanded to write up his experiences in the Congo. He armed himself with the latest electric typewriter – a 'golf-ball' type – and reams of paper, and started typing. Every time we (the older children) visited, he would read us his latest Chapter One and ask our opinions. One non-starter, I recall, dealt at length with his feelings of guilt as he prepared to depart for the Congo … leaving his pregnant wife behind.

After struggling with Chapter One for days, he found a style and a voice – and then the words flowed quickly and cleverly; most likely, in his writing he tried to follow the advice of Bulloch, the *Telegraph*'s man in the Congo, who had advised Mike to write the book as history. As I remember it, he completed the substantial manuscript in less than six months, and posted it off to a London literary agent named Lewin.

Said Mike, 'Lewin tried Cassells, who said "As a story, it is riveting; as history, it lacks a lot – it is history as written by James Hadley Chase". Kimber said "No, not serious enough". I told Lewin I could not write it any other way.' Lewin came back with an offer of £500 (advance against royalties) from Robert Hale Limited in London. The three-page agreement was dated 9 November 1966.

The obvious title for the book was *Congo Mercenary* but Mike resisted it; there was, after all, something distasteful about being a mercenary officer – was there not? – and Mike was already trying to distance himself from it. He proposed instead some bizarre titles, none with the word 'mercenary' in the title – for example, *Vol Sudaf*.

On 28 August 1966, Mike and Phyllis's second son was born in Pietermaritzburg. The baby was named Simon, either after Mike's beloved Irish uncle or after Simon Nari – or both. His godfather was Mike's good friend, Prof Harry Grant-Whyte.

Around this time, Mike got a call from Lewin. 'He said, "I don't think you are going to be interested, but have you heard of a British television broadcaster called David Frost?" I had not. Lewin said, "He is very well known here. To be invited onto his show is generally highly regarded. It's a three-minute slot; they will pay you £50 and put you up at the Waldorf Hotel for a week and pay your airfare."

I said that didn't sound bad, but Lewin advised against it because Frost had a reputation for being highly researched and cut-throat. But I couldn't see anything wrong, and I went.'

Mike was to be on ITV's *The Frost Programme*. Frost's style, which bordered on verbal bullying, helped popularise the phrase 'trial by television'. Frost was to interview many controversial characters on his ground-breaking 'chat show', assisted by a large studio audience, many of whom were there to provide some aggression.

The interview with Mike turned out to be a cracker.

'There was someone to meet me at Heathrow that morning. The very first thing they asked me to do was sign a document. "We don't want anyone else (in the media) to get you," they explained. We went straight to the Waldorf and that afternoon I went to Frost's offices. The first thing that struck me was the vast staff he had. I had a long meeting with one of them. Eventually, he invited me to dinner with Frost that night saying, "Frost would like to get to know you before the show, and tell you what he is going to ask so that you can bone up on it."

'We meet at a restaurant in Shaftesbury Avenue, about eight of us including Frost's girlfriend who is black; that should have rung an alarm bell. Frost talks to me about the business side, and then he says, "These are the questions"; they are all written down. "Make sure you can answer them quickly as we only have three minutes. Don't stumble; know what you are going to say." The questions were innocuous.

'The next day a car came for me; we go out to Wembley where the studios are. There's a greeter there. He says, "I am going to have a drink and I suggest you have one too; it's a little bit of a trial, this, and people need to be calmed a bit." So I had a scotch, and then I hear this noise going on in the studio, and I see rows and rows of people like a university lecture room, cameras down the bottom and all the rest of it; it didn't worry me.

Now, they are singing; I subsequently discover this is the warming-up process; a bloke in the front is getting the audience hyped up, and they have to answer immediately to the questions

– and the questions are provocative. "Are you in favour of South Africa? Nooooooooooo!" That type of thing.

'Anyway, in the waiting area is the MP from somewhere who is so delighted he has this chance to be going on the show for five minutes, and someone else pretty famous; but they're all (to be) after me.

'I sit down. Frost starts asking me questions, but none of them are the questions he has given me! I thought I must put a stop to this. So I say it's all very well for you in the security of Wembley; how many of you have been to the Congo? Can you imagine what it is like in Stanleyville? How many of you have read Conrad's *Heart of Darkness*? That's the Congo. I started telling them about that. You know what happened? (My slot) went for 30 minutes. The people (guests) who were waiting could have killed me.'

In his book *David Frost: an autobiography*, Frost says, '..... because of what he had to say, Hoare became the only guest. It soon became clear that the other items in the programme must be dropped, and I was loath to interrupt the dialogue even for a commercial break. I recalled while I was on the air that the minimum permitted length for a segment on independent television at that time was four minutes. And that was how the programme came to run: a first half of twenty-nine minutes, and a second half of four minutes, all with Colonel Hoare.'[129]

In his introduction, Frost describes Mike as 'one of the few men who have become legendary figures in their time – though the legend varies a little depending on whom you speak to about him'[130]. Mike outlines the philosophy of living dangerously, but soon Frost is digging into one of the trickier issues around mercenary soldiering: how to keep discipline among the men.

A *Sunday Times* report[131] quotes Mike saying to Frost that if there was a trail of blood outside his office, it meant the regimental sergeant-major had dealt with the offender. Frost quotes Mike as also saying, 'At my level it was a question of personality and a grip on the men and perhaps, I hope, respect.'[132]

Mike takes the line that savagery begets savagery, and admits that in the Congo his standards dropped lower and lower. He tells in the context of keeping discipline, how he came to shoot off the soldier's toes in Stanleyville.

According to the *Sunday Times*, Bloke Modisane, a black South African writer and a member of the audience, then 'asked, "If he was a painter would you have cut off his finger? If he was a singer would you have cut his throat? How far can this thing be carried?" Colonel Hoare told him that as an African he should know extremely well how far it could be carried. Modisane: "Yes, I can claim that I am uncivilised, I am savage, I do not belong to the group of the civilised" (laughter and applause).' The inference was that Mike, who would obviously claim to be a civilised man, had behaved in an uncivilised manner.

But decades later Mike said, 'I got the impression I was being set up. He (Frost) wanted to show the iniquity of a man that could lead mercenary soldiers, a paid killer; he came off second best, it went right round and bit him in the arse.' This comment was followed by much laughter. 'Someone later told me I was the only man who had got the better of Frost. Frost had a preconceived idea of what I was, and I was nothing of the sort and he couldn't handle that. I thought Frost was antagonistic.'

Mike said the media would not leave him alone after that – which no doubt was his real motivation for going on the show, and which no doubt boosted book sales enormously; Mike later said in the end the book had sold several hundred thousand copies, giving it more than bestseller status.

One of the journalists who contacted him in London after the show was Judith Hare, Countess of Listowel, who had written several books including a recent semi-official history of Tanganyika. She was most anxious to read Mike's manuscript and later 'insisted' he make certain changes.

Post-Congo, Mike was a popular figure, even a hero, among the majority of white folk in South Africa. Some saw a role for him in 'saving the country' if 'the situation in Africa got out of hand'. One such was 'Ex-Alemain' whose letter to *Scope* magazine was published in their 16 December 1966 issue. He wrote, 'In the Congo, Hoare's small force achieved what battalions of United

Nations couldn't. So why doesn't South Africa recognise his value and offer him ... an appointment in some sort of advisory capacity to the South African Defence Force?'

Meanwhile Tshombe had left the Congo in December 1965 after Mobutu had made 'menacing remarks'.[133] His timely departure was vindicated when in June 1966 Mobutu had former acting prime minister Evariste Kimba and three former cabinet ministers publicly hanged for conspiracy in front of 80 000 people.[134]

'Post-Congo, I did not make very serious attempts to find work as a mercenary leader. It was always other people trying to find work and putting me forward as the leader. One day, Gino Tozzi, who had been a kind of quartermaster in 5 Commando, persuaded me to go and see Tshombe in Majorca, Spain. Tshombe apparently wanted me to lead a group and invade Katanga and put him back into power.'

Mike met Tshombe at a hotel. 'One of his aides made sure I was "clean" and then left us alone. We discussed the political situation in the Congo and the way things were going in Katanga. Then he came straight to the point. "Mike," he said, "my people need me, they want me to come back ... desperately. Can you help? Can you suggest any way that I might return?"

'He said, "Perhaps if you could lead an invasion ... we have the money ... we might ..." I looked him straight in the eyes and said "No!" He was shocked. I went on, formally. "No, *M'sieur Président* ... not that way ... nor any other at this time. With respect sir, you must wait ... at least a year ... maybe several years ... the situation in the Congo will change ... meanwhile your people will organise themselves internally ... they will rise when all is ready and the time is right ... and that will be the moment for your return".'

Meanwhile, after the book was written, Mike's thoughts turned to the rehabilitation of the Congo. Peters was to complete his tour of duty on 13 March 1967,[135] with Schroeder, then aged 24, taking over.

Said Mike, 'I had been in constant touch with Mobutu, and he indicated I was in his future, not necessarily in a military role, though. I felt I was not finished with the Congo.'

Then Mike got a message that Mobutu wanted to see him, so he flew to the Congo for a week. The National Archives in Britain holds a copy of a report dated 28 February 1967, written by Peter Mennel of the British Embassy in Leopoldville, by then renamed Kinshasa. According to Mennel, Mike, who had visited the embassy the previous day, said he had come to Kinshasa at President Mobutu's invitation to receive a military decoration.

The medals Mike received in recognition of his services to the Congo were *L'Ordre National du Zaïre*, Officer class, and the *Croix de la Bravoure Militaire avec Palme.*

Mennel's report continued, 'He thought the whole of 5 Commando should be disbanded and a much better type of man recruited in its place.' With this in mind, Mike was going to submit to the President an outline of a two-pronged plan to encourage the economy of the North Eastern and Eastern Congo and to free the Government from fear of internal or external coups. Mike would head up the new mercenary commandos. He left a copy of this 'agenda' as he called it. (See Appendix B.)

Clarke says Mobutu disbanded 5 Commando in April 1967, the last planeload of mercenaries arriving in Johannesburg on 24 April.[136]

What Mike said of all this was, 'I went up there (Leopoldville), but Mobutu had gone through 180 degrees; he had changed his mind about how to run the Congo; it didn't include me. I said I had gone to a lot of trouble and expense going there, I had done this and done that (planning the rehabilitation).

'That night, I took Mobutu's ADC, Powis, to dinner and asked him if we should not ask Mobutu for a *douceur*. The following day, Mobutu ... he had a box under his table, it was thick with $1000 notes. He gave me $30 000 (about $225 000 in 2018 terms). And he said, "When you see a house you like, let me know and I'll buy it for you." He was very fond of me, as a matter of fact. Well he might be!' But he never did buy a house for Mike, nor did Mike care.

Then, 'unfortunately, something got between Mobutu and me; I lost touch with him. No-one answered my letters after that, and I lost touch with Powis as well. It was a terrible disappointment to me, as

I had worked long and hard on the (rehabilitation) plan.' Mike was not sure who had 'wrecked' his plan but was of the opinion it might have been Schroeder.

Mike had a similarly low opinion of Denard, describing him as a 'very good corporal' and a 'lackey of the French government'. His opinion was also no doubt informed by what Mike perceived as Denard's foot-dragging when it came to any actual fighting.

Toward the end of May 1967, Mike paid a visit to his Uncle Simon in Rush and apparently gave a press conference at his house, *The Trees*. Mike always kept a special place in his heart for his uncle, and his cousins Eithne Jones, Desmond Hoare and 'Malla' Hughes. Mike later presented a copy of his first book to Simon, inscribing it in uncharacteristic fashion thus:

To my uncle Simon
- the man who gave me love when I most needed it
- and made me proud of my Irish blood
With gratitude and admiration
Michael
Grenoble, Aug 67.

Around this time, Mike realised that to better his chances of getting soldiering work in Africa, he should improve his schoolboy French; he thus registered in June 1967 for a three-month course at Grenoble University, France.

But soon Mike had to interrupt his studies when a CIA agent came to see him. 'He wanted me to do a job. I said I had paid a lot of money for the course, but they said no, no, this is much more important. I was enjoying the course, so I was rather annoyed with them. I had to go to Brussels and London, and missed three weeks of the course.'

Mike always refused to divulge the nature of this interlude. It may, however, have had something to do with Tshombe who, as we know, was plotting a return to power from Europe at that time. As Mike said, 'Very shortly after (Mobutu's coup in November 1965), Mobutu brought charges of treason against Tshombe, which forced him (Tshombe) to leave the Congo in a hurry.'

Then, in July 1966, there was an unsuccessful pro-Tshombe revolt of mainly Katangese soldiers in the Congolese Army in Stanleyville; and on 13 March 1967 Tshombe (*in absentia*) was held responsible for the Stanleyville rebellion, tried by mob decision in a Kinshasa stadium and sentenced to death.[137]

Lt Tom Courtney, who served from August 1964 until the end, later wrote, 'After completion, I went with Tshombe and a few other guys to Majorca; we stayed quite a while there while the planning was under way to re-install Tshombe and boot out Mobutu, a doomed mission – one couldn't move ten feet in Majorca without a CIA tail; I'm not sure to this day whether the girls we took out were not CIA plants. The writing was on the wall for Tshombe; the CIA wanted Mobutu even though he was a despot. Tshombe always carried a briefcase with half-a-million dollars in it, even took it to the toilet.'

As we have seen, 5 Commando was disbanded in April 1967, and, as Hellström says, 'When rumours spread that the other mercenaries would also be sent home, two of the leaders – Bob Denard and Jean Schramme – decided to act. They likely conspired with Tshombe to take power in a coup, after which the mercenaries would be allowed to stay indefinitely. But Tshombe's enemies got wind of the coup and he was kidnapped and held prisoner.'[138]

Mike's version of the kidnapping on 30 June 1967 was, 'Tshombe was in Madrid as a refugee from the Congo. He had the Bank of Katanga in his pocket (and) he was buying land. One day he was invited by a well-known firm to examine some land for sale; he was to come to Palma and then the agent's light plane would show him the area from the air. Hook, line and sinker, he fell for it. Someone took out a pistol in the air and said now we are going to Algeria. In Algiers, an Air Congo aeroplane was waiting to take Tshombe to Kinshasa where he would be forced to walk the length of Avenue Trente Juin in chains, jeered by the crowd, until he reached the statue of Leopold II when he would be beheaded with a sword.'

To complete the picture, on 5 July 1967 the pro-Tshombe revolt in Stanleyville went ahead anyway. Schramme (a Belgian settler, and leader of 10 Commando) and Denard led a mutiny of the French-speaking mercenaries. A week later, the mercenaries withdrew to

Bukavu, where they holed up until forced to retreat into Rwanda and internment in November, finally being repatriated to Europe in April 1968.

Meanwhile, as the Six-Day War between Israel and her Arab neighbours had just taken place (5 to 10 June), Algeria now decided to use Tshombe as a bargaining pawn against Israel with Mobutu, and kept Tshombe in jail for the moment. Mike was seriously concerned for Tshombe's life. He was thus moved, on 21 July 1967, to pen a letter to Lt General J-D Mobutu, President of the Democratic Republic of the Congo. His plea, with assistance from Shakespeare, was nothing if not eloquent:

'Great General,

'Hear the voice of your servant. It is the voice of hundreds of thousands of Africans, black and white, who know and admire both you and your adversary, Mr Tshombe. We beg you in the name of Christian charity to spare the life of your enemy Moise Tshombe. By showing mercy, Great General, you will by no means be showing weakness, but will demonstrate that strength and courage and soundness of judgement for which you are so justly famous.

'Permit me Sire, to point out, with great respect, that the summary execution of Mr Tshombe, however justified that may or may not be in law – and which is in no case our affair – must surely spark off a hideous reaction throughout the Congo and cause the deaths of many thousands of innocent Congolese – Congolese whose welfare I know to be your first and constant consideration; the execution of Mr Tshombe could well arouse the sleeping dogs of rebellion that have lain dormant in your country since December 1965; the execution of Mr Tshombe could be the lynch-pin on which the whole fate of the Congo will hang.

'The world awaits your decision: we pray God it may be tempered with mercy. Be great, Great General, sweet mercy is nobility's true badge.

'Your sincere friend and humble servant, M. Hoare.'

Tshombe remained in jail, and at one point in the hospital in the jail. 'I can remember him saying to me years before, "If ever you are taken prisoner, the place to go to is the hospital; the hospital you can get out of, the jail you cannot get out of." I later heard he had been taken desperately ill, so I realised (he had contrived a way to get into the prison hospital).'

Around this time, a curious incident took place. One day, Mike got a cable from Colonel Hubert Fauntleroy Julian, nicknamed 'The Black Eagle', whom Mike had first met in Leopoldville in 1964.

'The telegram says: "I am in Brussels. I have a very interesting proposition for you. Are you interested?" I replied. He then phoned: he had got someone to advance $3 million for the rescue of Tshombe, and was I interested? I said yes, certainly. I said I would wait there till I heard, but I never did. It was the sum of money that was of interest because if there is big money behind it, you can always get someone out with money, not in any other way – you have got to bribe somebody.'

Nigel Osborn, who had qualified as a pilot in the Royal Navy after serving in Katanga, corroborated the existence of this rescue plan, saying 'Mike contacted me to see if I was interested in flying to Algeria where Tshombe had been imprisoned.' And in 2010, Mike said a Belgian who had served as a mercenary soldier in the Congo had been behind this move to free Tshombe, but it had not come off.

Of Tshombe's death in jail in Algiers on 29 June 1969, aged 49, Mike later wrote, 'There is some reason to believe he (Tshombe) may have been poisoned. I heard this from a very high level later on. No one was that surprised; they all said if you play high stakes that is what happens.' Mike wondered aloud who stood to benefit from Tshombe's death, and answered his own question saying, 'Tshombe alive was a constant threat to the stability of the Democratic Republic of the Congo and the Mobutu regime.'

Congo Mercenary was published in London in August 1967 while Mike was in Grenoble. He was annoyed with the treatment Hale had given the covers of the book. Presumably for aesthetic reasons, they had flipped the original image of a soldier firing a bazooka. The back cover thus showed the bazooka on the mercenary's left shoulder, which was incorrect.

The book is fast-paced and surprisingly well written, and tells from the commander's subjective point of view how 5 Commando restored law and order to the Congo. It is impossible that Mike did not know what the men were getting up to at times, for example looting, but he tends to ignore that side of mercenary life, preferring to paint his men for the most part as clean-cut lads out getting a good job of work done.

According to Mike, *The Guardian* newspaper reviewed *Congo Mercenary* in 1968, saying it smacked of a *Boys Own* story. They were referring to Mike's youthful writing style, such as the typical: 'By Gad, Alistair, you are right ... we leave at dawn!'

Mockler refers to *Congo Mercenary* as Mike's 'generally anodyne memoirs', whereas the *Yorkshire Evening Post* says, 'His book, knuckle-hard and exciting, is a chronicle ...'. The *Daily Telegraph* said, 'This well-written and well-illustrated book gives an accurate and useful account of the military response to the rebellion.'

Sales must have been brisk, for Hale reprinted the book in both September and November 1967, and in January 1968, February 1969 and July 1971. In 1985 *Congo Mercenary* was in its ninth (hardcover) reprint.

After Grenoble, Mike went to Paris and took a flat in the lively Latin Quarter for six months. It was opposite the Pantheon at rue de la Montagne 19. 'I sent for Phyllis straight away, and said "We are going to enjoy life now". I was in love with the place, the most marvellous in the world.'

Around this time, France, South Africa and Portugal were providing the self-proclaimed Republic of Biafra, a secessionist state in south-east Nigeria, with assistance. Probably in the second half of 1967, Mike was approached to help Biafra by Roger Faulques, whom Mike had met in Katanga. The legendary Jack Malloch flew him from Lisbon to Port Harcourt via Principe.

Mike later wrote, 'I met with General Ojukwu at Aba, his GHQ at the time, and discussed the possible employment of 500 mercenary soldiers, whom he needed, he said, to support his army. The General was unaccountably anxious to employ South African mercenary soldiers, something that I suggested, in the circumstances, might not be wise. But he was adamant. Then (after I had spent a few days waiting at a hotel) he told me that he had engaged 80 French mercenaries under the redoubtable Roger Faulques, so that really my journey had been doomed before it began. But I was not greatly disappointed.'[139]

Then, John Peters took Mike to meet the Nigerians and thereafter Mike wrote in an article published in *The Times*, 'From a purely military viewpoint, I was convinced that a small well led force of white soldiers would have little difficulty in pushing the federal troops back over the Biafran frontiers. But what then? In my view the last thing that is required is the intervention of mercenary troops on either side. Personally I intend to take no part in it. I am totally convinced that such an intervention would aggravate the situation and lead to an alarming escalation.'[140]

However, the Wild Geese Club held a reunion in Johannesburg on 24 November 1967, the three-year anniversary of the liberation of Stanleyville. In a report headlined: 'Mad Mike' recruiting for Biafra, we read, 'More than 1000 mercenaries in South Africa were waiting to join Col. "Mad Mike" Hoare to fight for Biafra, a former captain from 5 Commando said last night.' And, 'Mercenaries last night said Colonel Hoare was recruiting for Biafra while Col. John Peters was recruiting for the federal forces.' Mike was reported to be in Durban and did not attend.[141]

Once, around 1967, Mike was invited to dine at the Savoy Grill in London with the ex-king of Buganda (part of Uganda), Edward Mutesa, known in the West as King Freddie. He wanted Mike to help him get his kingdom back, but the negotiations collapsed when it became apparent that payment could only be made post-coup.

Mike knew more than anyone that life was for living. I distinctly recall him saying many times when I was a teenager, for example while reading a newspaper, 'Look at this! A bloke younger than me has died of a heart attack.' And he literally would go out and buy himself a new jacket, or take us children out for a meal, usually to The Edward's classy *smorgasbord* restaurant, where you could serve yourself as much as you liked. And on every single visit, he would pretend to us that the manager had told him to ask us not to help ourselves to so much food!

On one memorable occasion after lunch, as we made our way from the restaurant toward the hotel's foyer, a grand oval space with a marble floor, he looked around mock-surreptitiously to see who was watching; he then danced across the foyer in a series of heel-clicking elevated cabrioles. And then we all laughed ....

In July 1968, probably for the sheer joy of living and because he knew he was going away, Mike invited Tim, Gerry and me to drive to Johannesburg with him for a few days of fun. We stayed at the luxury Park Royal Hotel, Mike doled out cash for new clothes, we had fancy meals together every night, and we played tourist.

Meanwhile, in 1968 Mike got it into his head to take his young family, and daughter Gerry, then aged 15 and still at school, to go and live on the island of Corsica. Why Corsica? It would have had something to do with the fact that it was French, which he always found appealing, and later he said that he wanted to bring up the two small boys speaking French; it was also off the beaten track, something else he always found attractive. And, though he never mentioned it, was Algiers (where Tshombe was in jail) not within striking distance of Corsica?

They chose to live at Saint Florent, a village on the north coast. Perhaps it was because from there Mike could see the sheltered bay where, he said, in centuries past British war fleets had had occasion to come in under sail and to anchor.

Mike was a dreamer of dreams, and now took steps to make his current one come true. Visiting the nearby port of Bastia, he met a Belgian who, it just so happened, owned a large sailing yacht which was moored on the Rhone River on the mainland, and yes, she was for sale. Her name was *Karen*, and she was a Baltic trading vessel of some 30 metres in length.

As Mike and Phyllis were by now tiring of the 'dead' Saint Florent, Mike found accommodation in Tarragona, Spain, and the family flew to Nice to join him. On the drive to Tarragona, Gerry recalled, they all stopped to examine *Karen*. In due course, apparently, Mike paid for the fuel tanks to be filled and on the agreed date, Mike returned to take delivery. But Karen was not there.

One could ask how Mike supported his lifestyle post-Congo.

The Americans, he said, 'were very good to me after I left (the Congo). Two years after I left, I was in possession of some information; I warned them of a danger that could happen to their aircraft, so they moved the aircraft. Soon after, that site (Albertville) was bombed but nothing was lost. They were very very grateful for that.

'Then, in 1969, they got in touch and said, "Is there anything you would like?" I said I would like to go to America. I had never been to America. They said they would arrange it. I went to Washington. They said, "Because you are a foreigner, we can't give you a medal, but we will show you our appreciation." There was a big gathering of officials.'

Returning to Durban from Spain in early 1969 or thereabouts, Mike took a flat on the beachfront and sold a share in Autoscrap to his close friend Dickie de Gale. He also rented an office in Salisbury House in downtown Durban and most likely it served several purposes: a bureau for handling enquiries regarding mercenary work – also called 'skulduggery' – and the study that he did not have at his flat for managing his investments.

Now Mike was asked by a television company to do an in-depth interview about the mercenary scene. They paid him a sweetener of £2000 for his trouble.

Mike is interviewed at the helm of his yacht while sailing off Durban in a big sea, in his office, and having a beer on the sundeck of the Point Yacht Club with his former intelligence officer, Sergeant Graham Paterson, and some sailing types; they all laugh a lot and Paterson cannot resist ribbing his former commanding officer by telling the world how Mike used to have his uniforms made by tailors Lerwill Pope.

In view of subsequent events, the following dialogue is notable:

Q. Have you had many job offers?

A. Yes, most have been a little on the crazy side. We have an interesting situation in Africa where 30 well-trained ruthless soldiers could overthrow a government, and they see the opportunity for coups, and they approach me from time to time.

Q. Do you have a mercenary force available?
A. Yes, I could raise 100 men in seven days and 1000 men in six weeks. I maintain a register. I receive 30 to 40 letters a month from all over the world. Something is coming up fairly soon.

Around this time he became aware that his handwriting had degenerated to the point that even he could no longer read it. This called for action. As was often the case when something new came up, he would buy a book or get a book out of the library on the subject. He loved books and many times he said: 'In a book, you can buy the sum of a man's knowledge for almost nothing.' And so it was that he chose the italic hand, and taught himself to write in that style – which he maintained for the rest of his life.

It would appear that early in 1970 Mike got restless and started scouting around for something else to do. One day toward the end of January, he suggested I drive him to Lourenço Marques (LM), the capital of Mozambique. Mike was trying to float a business deal. The following day Mike had an appointment with a government minister, most likely the minister of tourism. Mike wanted to base a large yacht in LM and run sailing charters from there to nearby islands such as Inhaca, Bassas da India, Europa, even the Comores, but the idea came to nought.

Another indication of restlessness was his application at that time to emigrate to Canada. He even went to Pretoria for an interview, but in due course the Canadians replied, Mike said, saying he was 'not suitable for immigration'.

Mike found this annoying and lacking in gratitude, as, after all, men under his command had risked their lives to rescue Canadian missionaries post-Stanleyville.

And indeed, he received a letter of thanks addressed to him personally at the *Quartier général*, Congolese Army, Leopoldville, dated 7 January 1965 from three sisters of the *Congrégation des Filles de la Sagesse* in Montreal, Canada, who had been rescued. Their names are given as Thècle de Marie, Marie-Gaston, and Yvonne du Bon Pasteur. In French, they said they were writing 'to express all the recognition that we owe you, you and your intrepid army whose valiant intervention enabled us to regain our freedom which had been so dangerously compromised. Your encouragement on our arrival in Stanleyville was precious help, and we, more than once, thanked God to have found in you a protector and a friend.'

Then, on 21 August 1970, Mike wrote to an overseas friend from Durban: 'Good trip out east. Spent some time in Phnom Penh, Bangkok and Vientiane. Also Singapore where I concluded a deal which will base us all there for one year, with an option of two more back in the UK. I leave here on the 27th and Phyllis with the kids on the 15th Sept. My address will be: c/o Coastal Surveys Ltd, 124 Stamford House, 39 Stamford Road, Singapore 6. The job has to do with navigation for oil survey ships and should be interesting.'[142]

At the time, Mike maintained that he had got a job as an accountant in Singapore, but this did not square, for example, with his sudden need to play a lot of squash with me and get fit. My gut feeling was that the 'accountancy' post was a front for his preferred type of work, but I never confronted Mike when it came to matters of this sort as I knew from past experience that he would never 'talk'.

Cut to Coastal Surveys where Neill G Hunt is working as a SHORAN operator (SHOrt RAnge Navigation, a type of electronic navigation system used in the oil and gas exploration industry at that time.) It is Mike's signature that is on his subsequent employment agreement dated 28 November 1970. The general manager, none other than John Peters (JP), was at that time 'up north with a concubine', according to Hunt. Another ex-Congo hand at Coastal Surveys was David Gough.

Hunt said, 'Mike Hoare was employed at Coastal Surveys, but he was basically using Coastal Surveys as a base to venture into Thailand and other territories. He was on the books as an accountant to enable him to stay in Singapore. The Singapore government were not too happy about having both Mike and John on the beach at the same time. When Peters went on trips, Mike took over the reigns in Singapore. I found Mike a thorough gentleman.'[143]

Another who remembered Mike at Coastal Surveys was Susan (surname withheld), the receptionist. She said, 'JP recruited Mike, whom I remember as a gentle man sitting at his desk with his eyeglasses down his nose studying his large accounting ledgers at back of office. He wrote up the books with a pen that he dipped into an inkwell. One day (toward the end of September 1970), I was on my way out of the office at 5 pm, when I ran into a commotion in front of the office on the street level. I saw John Peters and Mike Hoare struggling with some paparazzi. I saw JP throw a camera to the pavement. I just ran.'[144]

A newspaper clipping datelined Singapore confirms that Mike had 'surfaced in Singapore on a mission he refused to discuss'. It quotes *The Straits Times* as saying, 'Rumour has it that (Hoare) is recruiting mercenaries to fight for the Lon Nol Government in war-torn Cambodia. Hoare was quoted as saying: "I am not here for any bloody soldiering or recruiting any damned mercenaries. I have nothing to do with that, and I don't want to talk about anything." Asked why he was in Singapore, Hoare retorted: "Why don't you mind your own bloody business?"'[145]

However, a cutting from a South African newspaper tells us 'Col. Michael "Mad Mike" Hoare has placed 20 of his former mercenary officers on a 24-hour standby for combat in the Far East. The first 20 men will be the spearhead of perhaps 5000 mercenaries – many of them from South Africa – who will fight in either Thailand or Cambodia. The colonel will be the commander of the fighting force. The mercenaries' major tasks will be to patrol the Thailand-Cambodia borders where the bulk of the Thai Army is already operating against Communist guerrillas.'

Hunt again: 'I am aware that Mike was visiting Thailand on a regular basis and was believed to be negotiating for finance and military back-up for a small force of upwards to 5000 to enter Cambodia.

'In my personal opinion, if this had come off I would say that at least two million lives would have been saved from the Khmer Rouge. In my own mind, I find that an operation would have been very successful as the amount of seasoned troops that were available from the USA and Australia, Korea, Thailand and the Philippines would have filled the ranks in a very short time. I believe that Mike left Singapore after negotiations broke down for a private army group to move into Cambodia.'

Mike never had any trouble in keeping his mouth shut when necessary, and always refused to discuss his activities out of Singapore, whether formally or informally, once saying he was 'bound' not to discuss the matter.

The only story he ever told me about Singapore concerned an Englishman having breakfast at the table next to his at a hotel, who very politely asked the waiter, er, if there might be, er, by any remote chance some, er, marmalade; when the 'marmalade' arrived, the man proclaimed: 'Oh, horrors!!!' Mike would laugh heartily at this punch line which is in regular use in our family today .... And we came to realise that Mike was amused that, after the real horrors he had been through in the Congo, someone could think of Singapore marmalade as a horror.

But for all his secrecy, it is Mike himself who leaves some blatant clues in the first chapter of the early drafts of a manuscript that was titled *A Spirit of Adventure*, which was eventually published, with substantial changes and without reference to Singapore, as *Mike Hoare's Adventures in Africa*. The chapter opens in Singapore with Mike looking for a way out of his humdrum job. He decides to 'offer his sword' to Lon Nol, the prime minister of Cambodia, a country that is being threatened by Vietnam.

Mike said he flew to Cambodia but in due course the Cambodians said they did not want his help. Mike, however, told them he was on his way to Vientiane, Laos, where his friend Larry Devlin (ex Leopoldville) and a group from the Congo were now based. Mike said he got Devlin to visit Phnom Penh and there was a meeting of minds.

The notion that the Wild Geese might fly again, this time for action in Cambodia, is supported by a report in *The Natal Mercury* of 26 June 1970, which is headlined: Mike Hoare turns up in Phnom Penh. Part of the article reads, 'There have been rumours of mercenary recruiting, at astronomical salaries, and speculation was fanned by a hint at "future developments" by Colonel Hoare on a television programme screened early last month.'

It seems that in the end Mike did not recruit any mercenaries, and left Singapore. Whatever, the fact remains that for the rest of his life he never did a regular day's work.

Mike's fire for mercenary soldiering was still smouldering in 1973 when Mobutu let it be known that he would like to meet Mike again in London.

'Mobutu had spent two nights at Buckingham Palace as the guest of the Queen, and then moved to the Claridges Hotel where he was hosting a party for 600 people. There were eight people who had been specially invited and whom Mobutu particularly wanted to talk to. We had to be there at 6 pm. We all lined up, ready. Mobutu came in, supported on either side by huge chaps; he was drugged to the eyebrows. I was first in the line; he could not hold a conversation and left without talking to any of us. It was the biggest disappointment of my life.

'I got all sorts of reports through the CIA of what was happening to him, and how he had been taken over by – I suppose you could call it – the Mafia in a way, oh dreadful. Then he started making errors – allowing his wife and her friends to use (commandeer) regular airliners for their shopping expeditions in Brussels.

'He was wrecked by success, like all of them. He had control over the purse. Mobutu is on record as saying, "Yes, perhaps I did pay myself $220 million last year, but what would you pay someone in command of so many million people?" The real trouble was, and we can never prove this, but I saw it, he got into the hands of some unscrupulous bloody Lebanese.'

In April 1974, there was a left-wing military coup in Portugal and autonomy for Mozambique was imminent. A transitional government was established. In June 1975, Mozambique became independent from Portugal under the rule of Frelimo, a Marxist party. An opposition anti-Marxist group, Renamo, sponsored by Rhodesia (and later South Africa), then waged an armed struggle against Frelimo.

Of all this, Mike said, 'It was blown up by the political parties to be a war. It could have been stopped *ab initio* with 100 men (mercenaries) in 1974, but everybody got into the act.' In essence, this is what he told the Monday Club, a group of conservative Conservatives, when he addressed them at the Houses of Parliament buildings in London, he said.

It turns out Mike did take steps to stop it *ab initio*. According to an article in the *Observer* newspaper dated 4 August 1974, Mike had recently 'arrived secretly in Malawi to help to raise a white-officered black army to take over the role of the Portuguese Army in fighting Frelimo. Hoare's backer is reported to be Senhor Jorge Jardim, the maverick Portuguese tycoon who owns newspapers and other enterprises in Mozambique.

'Col Hoare's name suddenly appeared last week when advertisements were placed in the *Rhodesia Herald* (Salisbury) urging former members of the notorious 5 Commando to "report for a reunion". Hoare yesterday denied any involvement in raising a new mercenary army. However, one of his former colleagues in the Congo told us in Salisbury that the call for a reunion was "a call to arms and action".'

Meanwhile, after the Portuguese pulled out of Angola in 1975 – 'an absolute disgrace' – civil war erupted. Three nationalist groupings now contended for power: the West-inclined FNLA and Unita, and the Marxist MPLA. Russia declared its support for the MPLA and started sending arms and ammunition. Cuba sent 3000 men to help the MPLA.

Interestingly, the Wild Geese Club chose this time to have another reunion. A newspaper reported, 'Sixty ex-mercenaries stood to attention in a guarded Johannesburg club last night when former mercenary leader Colonel "Mad Mike" Hoare arrived at a dinner to celebrate the capture by 5 Commando of Stanleyville, in the Congo, ten years ago.' And yes, there were 'plenty of rumours about moving into Angola'.[146]

Eventually it was Mike himself who set the record straight on Angola. Writing in his epilogue to the US paperback edition of *Mercenary*, published in 1979, he said, 'I was approached early in the day by Colonel Santos y Castro, an officer in the colonial army. He begged me to provide him with 100 men, sufficient he claimed, at this stage, to secure Angola for the West. I was all in favour of it. However, the South African government had made it clear to me personally that any mercenary recruitment in South Africa would be regarded as illegal, even though their sympathies rested with the western-inclined groups.' In early 1976, Mike told the men to stand down.

Around this time, Mike had an office on the 8th floor of Tuition House in downtown Durban. A letterhead that has survived describes it as: Hollards, business brokers and consultants; and there is evidence that he did do some business broking.

It was in the same office, Mike told me, that he also worked on a scheme to provide a force of Wild Geese to protect the strategically important Benguela railway line from Dilolo in the Congo (then called Zaire) near the Angola border, to the port of Lobito in Angola; this would enable the mines in Katanga and Zambia to export their copper securely.

Trains were regularly coming under fire from MPLA and Unita fighters and Mike's men would not only ride shotgun on the train, but also do patrols along the route to prevent sabotage of the track. It would be a massive undertaking.[147] The scheme did not get off the ground.

Also around this time, Mike clashed with a Durban newspaper. Peter Duffy later told me he was on photography duty one day when he received a message from Graham Linscott who was news editor that day. Linscott had seen a story on the wires from one of the agencies, quoting an unnamed MPLA official that Mike and a group of mercenaries were on the border of Angola and were about to go in. Duffy said he had advised Linscott that he had had a drink with Mike in Durban the previous day, and the report was false.

Linscott later said he had also sent one of his colleagues, Derek Taylor, to track down and speak to a security policeman named Martin Dolinchek, whom we meet later, about the agency report. 'Dolinchek confirmed that Mike was in town and said the agency story was complete nonsense. We told the subs desk the story was a non-starter, and that Mike was at home in Durban.'

Mike was livid the next day when he read the story in the comfort of his home in Westville. Quite likely that day marked the beginning of Mike's hatred for the press.

In Mike's line of business, an obvious prospect was Rhodesia. An old photograph shows a poster for *The Natal Witness* newspaper, dated 13 December 1965, proclaiming: I'd fight for Rhodesia – Hoare. The article itself quotes Mike as saying he was 'wholeheartedly in favour of UDI and that if ever he was asked, he would fight for Rhodesia'.

Then, in the mid-1970s, after the Portuguese pulled out of Angola and Mozambique, the Rhodesian government and its military found itself increasingly exposed to communist-backed insurgents. Seeing an opportunity to assist the Rhodesian military in their civil or bush war, Mike approached and then met with Rhodesian Ministry of Defence officials in March 1976 and tried to sell them the idea of what was essentially a mercenary force.

In summary, Mike called for a force 'to counter any threat by Cuban and Russian forces to Rhodesia'. In the style of the French Foreign Legion, and with the same mystique, the unit would be part of the Rhodesian Defence Force and 'a symbol of resistance against Russian imperialism in Africa'. Its men would be 'crusaders against the evil forces of communism' and would be 'bearing arms on behalf of the West'. It would be called the International Brigade or perhaps the Rhodesian Foreign Legion, and would be based in a remote part of Rhodesia. Mike suggested the official language of the unit might be French. [148]

Once again, Mike's proposal did not find favour. However, an undated document summarising the 'national military strategy for Rhodesia' and entitled 'Strategy: courses of action to be adopted until September 1978, draft', says in part, 'The employment of mercenaries to be examined along the lines proposed by Hoare.'[149]

As we have seen, Mike was always open to further employment as a mercenary leader, with certain conditions. His views on the future of mercenary soldiering are also reflected in the 1979 epilogue mentioned above, as follows:

'In 1961, I thought we might be on the threshold of a golden age of mercenary soldiering, similar in many ways to the *condottieri* of the Middle Ages. Not that I saw myself as Sir John Hawkwood! But I really could see a role for a well-led and well-disciplined force of mercenary soldiers, professional in every respect, offering their services to legitimate African governments – perhaps it would be wiser to say well-established *de facto* governments – to be used in support of their regular forces. But the vision has faded.'

In 2006, I asked Mike if mercenary soldiers still had potential. 'Yes, more than ever, but subject to certain conditions. A good example is Colonel Spicer, who started a professional unit (for Sierra Leone). They can do it quicker than any regular unit, when you consider that to put a regular unit in the field, you have got to have almost an act of parliament. These things are not done overnight. Then you've got all the little jealousies, who is going to be in command etc. If you have someone who is being paid and who has a coterie of good officers around him, you'll get the men all right, but you'll have to pay. And, in the long run you are paying a fraction, an absolute fraction, of what it would cost a government. I'll give you an example: a mercenary soldier signs a contract which says if you lose a leg you will get £20 000 or whatever it is. Governments don't do that; they are responsible for you forever after.'

So what happened on the mercenary scene next? According to the Tim Spicer entry on Wikipedia in 2016, Spicer became chief executive of Aegis Defence Services, a private military company (PMC) based in London. In October 2004, Aegis won a $293 million three-year contract in Iraq outsourcing, among other things, intelligence for the US Army. Wikipedia quoted *Guardian* journalist Stephen Armstrong as follows: 'Spicer is effectively in charge of the second-largest military force in Iraq – some 20 000 private soldiers. Just don't call him a mercenary.'[150]

And, according to the Wikipedia PMC entry, in 2003 the industry was worth more than $100 billion a year.[151]

11. The Yachtsman

'Look out!' he yelled again. The ship staggered as though a block of flats had fallen on her deck, everything went black except for a shaft of green light where hundreds of gallons of water poured down the hatchway to flood the saloon. – Mike Hoare

The sea was in Mike's blood and sailing was one of his great loves. He once said he was 'addicted' to it. Certainly his father would have told him stories of his life at sea under sail. As a child, Mike did some dinghy sailing with his uncle Simon Hoare in Ireland. In the 1950s, he enjoyed sailing a Sharpie and a Graduate in Durban harbour; on weekends, we sometimes used to sail from the yacht basin to the beach at Salisbury Island where we would make our base for the day and he would teach us children how to sail on the clean, shallow waters, with flocks of flamingos not far away.

In April 1956, he took a passenger ship (*mv Kampala*) to the Seychelles where he was to spend his annual holiday. He had a secondary purpose too: to use the picturesque islands to see whether he would be able to make the grade as a professional documentary filmmaker, and to this end he took along his Paillard Bolex 16mm movie camera. On viewing the footage he came back with, we children were cruelly frank: don't even think about it!

The holiday itself sounded idyllic. He rented a cottage at Glacis beach on Mahé Island, and kept a 25-foot sloop, *Miranda*, anchored 50 metres off. Daily, he would swim out to the yacht and go sailing – and even fishing with handlines, though later he would disdain fishing from his yachts, saying it was 'not proper' to fish from a sailing vessel.

One day, he set sail in *Miranda* for St Anne's Island some 12 miles distant, taking two Seychellois lads as crew. Then, about three miles off Mahé, at the very moment they were changing shifts at the helm, a ferocious wind came out of nowhere and flattened the boat. It sank to the bottom, with only a foot of the mast protruding above the water. They clung onto it, but as these waters were shark-infested, they knew they did not have long. They screamed for help, to no avail. Their situation was becoming desperate. Mike thought that if somehow they were saved, he would give their rescuers everything he had. Now it was dark, and the three were shivering from both cold and fear. Later that night, a group arrived in dugouts and rescued them – one of their number had been on a hillside earlier and had seen the sail disappear. Mike consulted the village priest about his now dwindling resolve to give away everything he possessed, and allowed himself to be persuaded that whatever amount he gave his rescuers, it would be drunk; all he had to decide, then, was how many days the party should last. They arranged a party which would last for three days – and it did.[152]

Most likely it was in 1963 that Mike started getting excited about a 35-foot gaff-rigged cutter named *Colin Archer* that was in Durban harbour. A remarkable young Durban man, Donald Shave, had sailed her single-handed from Plymouth (UK), via Rio de Janeiro and Tristan da Cunha to Cape Town, encountering 60-foot waves at times; and then on to Durban with his brother John as crew, arriving there in early 1958. The voyage from Plymouth to Durban had taken about 15 months[153] and must have been hellish in an open cockpit, for Shave tied up at the international jetty in Durban's yacht basin and never set foot on *Colin Archer* again. Mike, however, was smitten. Giddy with romantic notions of palm-tree islands, white beaches, turquoise water and buried treasure, he had to have her.

A beamy double-ender, she was massively constructed and displaced 17 tonnes. She drew nearly two metres and was distinctly on the slow side, but Mike loved her with a passion in spite of the heavy tiller, somewhat spartan layout below decks, and the enormous amount of upkeep that she required. The main thing was that she was made of wood. Mike, forever a traditionalist, could 'not abide fibreglass boats'. A brass plaque I once bought for him summed up his attitude exactly; it said: 'If God had meant us to have fibreglass boats, He would have given us fibreglass trees'.

The yacht was built in 1937 by Emanuel Moen and Tor Nilsen Sauvik in Risør, Norway, and named after Colin Archer, the legendary Norwegian naval architect of Scottish descent who was famous for his pilot boat designs.[154]

For several years, Mike kept *Colin Archer* at the unfashionable Bayhead end of Durban harbour, most likely because it was handy for both his flat and Autoscrap, and because we could get stuff on board easily from the jetty where she was moored.

It was here that he met the non-conformist Australian sheep-shearer, Tom Harrison, who had his tiny yacht moored nearby. Most people would have written the scruffy Tom off as a bum, but Mike quickly recognised he was a skilled seaman, and was soon to give him a role on the rivers of the Congo … to their mutual benefit.

In some typed notes dated 25 April 1964, Mike describes an evening spent with Tom. 'Entertained Tom to dinner. He sailed a 20-foot yacht, *Sundowner*, from Darwin to Durban single-handed. A small talk with Tom and you realise he is an exceptional man. His background is typical working-class Australian; hard as nails, no veneer of culture. He carries with him innate good breeding. No swearing; the emphasis is in what he is saying, not how he says it. He is a man. A loner. A moderate drinker and a hard worker. He made his own adventurous path for himself with his own two hands. I like Tom.' Mike also records Tom's answers to a host of sailing questions, mainly to do with storm tactics.

Whenever referring to *Sundowner*, Mike would joke that she was 'so tender you had to part your hair down the middle before you went on board'.

During this period, Tim and I spent almost every weekend on *Colin Archer*, helping with the upkeep and of course sailing. Initially, we sailed only in the harbour which was plenty big enough to get into trouble. My memory is of *Colin Archer* permanently heeled over at a wonderful angle, the scuppers awash as we 'sped' across the bay. I never knew Mike to call for a reef in the harbour.

Heading toward our mooring late one afternoon, we noticed a launch had grounded on a sandbank near the sugar terminal, and the crew were signalling to us frantically. Although *Colin Archer*'s auxiliary motor was only a 40 hp Perkins diesel, Mike was keen to do the right thing, so we dropped the sails and approached under motor. In assisting, we got stuck as well – and stayed stuck for the night, keeling over onto the sandbank when the tide went out. The next day, Mike arranged with a nearby boatyard to send two workboats to pull *Colin Archer* off at high tide.

Mike learned a lot about bluewater sailing by actually doing it, from Harrison, and of course from books. *Cruising under sail*, and *Voyaging under sail* by Eric Hiscock were his nautical 'bibles'. From these and other books he learned splicing, knots, ropework, and even sail repair. Mike loved making his own canvas buckets and ditty bags. The end of every rope on board was immaculately whipped, the tiller boasted a Turk's head, and there was a light line with a 'monkey's paw' on the end – all done by Mike.

Around 1968, he moved *Colin Archer* to the more fashionable yacht basin and joined the nearby Point Yacht Club.

Then we started sailing offshore, and we youngsters would sometimes trail a warp behind and dive in, only to grab the warp and enjoy the sensation of being dragged through the clear water.

Although *Colin Archer* was a sturdy cruising boat, Mike decided to join in the offshore races on Sundays – for the fun of it. This stretch of coast is generally acknowledged as the worst in the world for sailing, and consequently these races took their toll on both equipment and crew. Sea-sickness was a problem for many of us – but not Mike.

The post-sailing sundowners were memorable. We would usually gather around the saloon table and have a few beers, though Mike's life-long preference was always Scotch whisky and water, no ice. My great friend Nick Ringrose, a regular crew member on race and other days, recalls how especially in winter, we would sometimes finish off with coffee and 'Phyllis always added a tot of whisky to make it that much "warmer".' As we went home, the chafed hands, browned skin, exhausted bodies and now glowing cheeks were a reminder that we had challenged the elements that day – and got a lot out of it.

Then, the races got longer. One was an overnight race up the coast and back. We took a large crew including my friend Chris Bird. Of that occasion, Chris said: 'I will never forget that amazing race. We came last due to torn sails, but what an experience! I was allocated cook. That evening, I went down below to stir this potato and bully-beef concoction; but with the pitching and yawing of the yacht, combined with the sickly sweet smell of the meths stove, I was soon back up on deck, lying over the side, and just retching into the ocean!'

In early 1969, Mike decided to take part in a 12-yacht race from Lourenço Marques to Durban, a distance of some 300 nautical miles. It was the Vasco da Gama Race. He took along Des Willans, an experienced yachtsman and a 'fearless' soldier ex-Katanga, as the skipper. History does not record their finishing position ...

Yachtsmen in Durban have always bemoaned their lack of sailing destinations, and summarised it by saying that when you leave the harbour you have two options: turn left, LM; turn right, East London.

So in March 1969, as he had already been north, he opted to sail to East London, some 260 miles south. Summarising what Mike wrote later[155], his crew was Bob Sims (his brother-in-law) and John MacPherson, both 'tough babies' in their own ways: Bob, wiry, energetic and resourceful, and John, an imperturbable tower of strength. After less than a day at sea, they were hit by a furious gale from behind, and only by trailing a long warp and every other rope on board behind could they slow Colin Archer down to a safe speed. Meanwhile, water was getting into the boat, keeping one of them busy on a hand pump. They had now been pushed into 'freak wave' waters; the Admiralty chart at the time described the danger as follows: 'Abnormal waves up to 60 feet high (18 metres), preceded by a deep trough may be encountered in the area between the edge of the continental shelf and 20 miles to seaward of it.'

Now they were cold, wet, hungry, exhausted, most likely unsure of their position ... and in peril. Mike described the situation thus: 'Huge green hills of water roared up astern, their crests toppling over in a mad rush downhill to explode beneath our keel with a muffled roar of frustration, spreading a brilliant white carpet of foam around us. One moment we were cowering in the trough between two enormous waves 200 yards apart, waiting breathlessly for the lift of the sea which would take us 40 feet up to the crest of the advancing wave, from which we could glimpse a vast disordered sea, waves plunging everywhere in endless confusion; the next moment we were hurtling downwards, pointing our bowsprit into the trough at an alarming angle, racing ahead of the angry white crests.'

It was time to fight if they were to survive. 'We fought, all four of us, not least the gallant little ship, aided I have no doubt whatsoever by He who guards those in peril on the deep.'

But more was in store.

'It was just a little before dark on the second day of the storm. John was at the helm again, Bob and I prostrate in the pilot bunks below, wet and utterly exhausted by the motion. Our nerves were bar taut with the incessant caterwauling of the wind in the rigging. Suddenly there came 15 seconds of absolute silence, laden with unimaginable menace. "My God!" we heard John shout from the cockpit, and then the ship pitched forward. I thought she was going straight to the bottom of the sea. "Look out!" he yelled again. The ship staggered as though a block of flats had fallen on her deck, everything went black except for a shaft of green light where hundreds of gallons of water poured down the hatchway to flood the saloon. The cabin table, bolted to the sole, was uprooted and thrown bodily on my bunk, and the air filled with a fine spray like that at the bottom of Victoria Falls. The ship was flung on her beam ends, scattering some of her lead ballast in all directions, but after an age slowly righted herself. There was over three feet of water in the cabin. We clawed our way above to see if John was still there. He was, thank God. "Sorry about that skipper," he said, waist deep in water, the ship freeing herself like a surfacing submarine.'

Bob and John decided to, er, rather fly back to Durban from East London, while Mike got on with repairing the considerable damage.

Ten days later, he left for Durban on his first – and last – solo voyage. Summarising what Mike later wrote,[156] heading northward he kept close to the coast to avoid the Mozambique current which flows southwards further out to sea at 3.5 knots. At the same time he would benefit from a weaker counter-current which flows northwards.

He soon settled into a routine, but, not having any self-steering gear, had to heave-to when he wanted to sleep. Now, on the evening of the third day, off the aptly named Wild Coast, another problem became apparent: all the cargo ships that were sailing north were also taking advantage of the inshore counter-current. Lighting his paraffin navigation lights, he spotted a huge tanker astern, but some distance away. A little later, when he realised that the tanker was bearing straight down on him, he started his engine and took avoiding action. The tanker roared past not 50 metres from *Colin Archer*, pushing up a huge bow wave and throwing Mike on his beam-ends, breaking the gaff boom. Mike was obliged to remain at the helm the rest of the night to avoid the ships that were overtaking from astern.

Now, Mike had not slept for three nights, but he could not heave-to and sleep because he was in a busy shipping lane. He also could not anchor, fearing he would not have the strength to get the anchor up again. Two days later, he was totally exhausted and, worse, he was hallucinating. At one point he realised there was a man on board wearing a Norwegian fisherman's cap. Mike thought it was Colin Archer himself. Later, in the middle of the night, thinking he was in the Dutch canals, Mike approached some rocks at Scottburgh and was preparing to throw a line when a voice said, 'Helm down'. Mike escaped at the last moment. Now he was being drawn toward a lighthouse and was almost on the rocks when the voice spoke again. He headed out to sea and crept up the coast. On the seventh night, and still hallucinating, he entered Durban harbour. A fisherman in a small boat had to lead Mike to the yacht basin and helped him moor. Mike collapsed.

Rob Griffin, ex-Congo and now a senior reporter on *The Daily News*, used to gleefully relate how he was sent to interview Mike on board *Colin Archer* the next day. 'The boat was a complete shambles. There were sails and ropes lying everywhere, and below-decks there were dirty plates, and half-eaten food scattered among the charts and wet-weather gear. I was shocked to see my former commanding officer, the stickler that he was, unshaven, worse for wear and with his hair all over the place. This was NOT the Mike Hoare that I knew.'

Mike surmised that if a certain American magazine were to have covered his escapade, it would have headlined the story: No Chichester[157] he, and always said that it was only thanks to the stranger on the deck that he had survived.

In August 1970, as other adventures beckoned, Mike put *Colin Archer* on the market. John Vigor, who had been with him on safari in 1959, was a potential buyer. Later Vigor said, 'Mike took me offshore on a very rough day and the boat was thrown on her beam ends by a particularly heavy sea. The starting battery for the engine spilled all its acid into the bilges and when we tried to enter harbour the starter wouldn't work. I remember (Mike) simply filling the battery with plain water and saying: "That should be good for one start, anyhow," and damn me if it didn't work. I thought for a man supposed to be an accountant, he knew a helluva lot of practical tricks. I'll never forget that little outing in the Scandinavian double-ender.'

Mike moved to Singapore later that month, and Phyllis and the children followed a few weeks later. In early 1971 they left Singapore and flew to Denmark to look for a Baltic trading yacht. There, Mike received news that such a boat was to be found in Ibiza, Spain.

At that time, and having graduated from university, I was working as a reporter on *The Natal Mercury* in Durban. Out of the blue, I received a letter from Mike which, in effect, said: I have bought a 100-ton Baltic trading yacht and I invite you and Tim to join us; we plan to sail as a family around the western Mediterranean during the summer and autumn. *Sylvia* will be in Villajoyosa, near Alicante, Spain. The sooner you can get there, the better.

I found *Sylvia*, a ketch, anchored in the middle of Villajoyosa's little harbour, all 22 metres of her, with a bowsprit of nearly 6 metres in addition. She was massively built of oak and had huge bluff bows, the better to carry her cargo. With her 5.5-metre beam and 2-metre draught, I surmised she would be another slow boat but she had adventure written all over her. The hull and topsides were painted black, with the strake and the rail picked out in white.

On board were Mike and Phyllis, the boys Mikey and Simon aged 7 and 5 years, and Tim. Granny Sims, now called 'Gina' (as in Winner) and still very active, was to join *Sylvia* in due course.

Sylvia had been built in Denmark in 1898 to trade under sail in the Baltic and had done so until sold in 1967, although in 1953 a Grenaa engine and a roomy wheelhouse had been added. An English owner had converted the cargo space into a large saloon and, believe it or not, a spacious bathroom with an actual bath and actual hot water. There were also three double cabins, which when added to the four bunks in the foc'sle and the two berths in the captain's cabin astern, meant she could sleep 12 people.

A closer inspection revealed *Sylvia* had not been well cared for, but she was now at least fundamentally sound below the waterline, having just spent six weeks on the slip in a local boat yard.

The engine was extraordinary: a massive single-cylinder diesel thumper that idled at about 100 rpm. Starting her was a major performance: first, the massive exposed flywheel had to be rotated until positioned 'just so' before starting; then, a large saltpetre cartridge had to be rammed into a primitive kind of glow-plug, lit like a firecracker, and screwed into the cylinder head tightly and quickly. Worse, the force required to get the flywheel turning came from a large compressed-air bottle; if she failed to start after several attempts, you were just about out of air, and just about to have an emergency.

Curiously, sometimes the motor started up going the 'wrong way' and had to be starved of something or other until, at the very last moment, a jet of fuel was pumped in by hand and, on a good day, she would now be turning the 'right way'. The variable-pitch propeller was controlled from the wheelhouse by a brass wheel that required about ten onerous revolutions to get from forward into reverse.

Evidently, *Sylvia* was an old wooden boat that had been properly

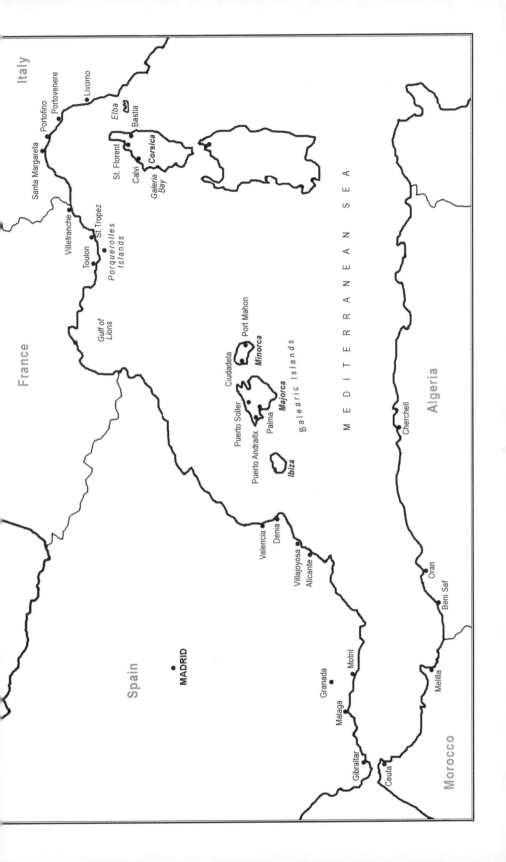

built in the Baltic tradition, and while she would not have appealed to many, Mike loved her from stem to stern because she was 'solid and dependable'. Mike was in his element: he had the Mobutu money in his pocket, offspring from both batches around him, and endless cruising in the Med stretching ahead.

Naturally, Mike was the captain, and Tim and I were the crew; Mike insisted that the Spanish for 'crew' was '*inferiores*' and reminded us of this regularly. However, we gave ourselves more suitable titles: Tim, being a mechanical whizz, became Chief Engineer, and I, being first-born, was First Mate. On occasion, we would conspire and overrule the captain as, being young, we knew everything about bluewater sailing. Later, Mike used to laugh about *Sylvia* being 'the only boat in the Med with four captains' (Phyllis being the fourth).

Sylvia was gaff-rigged on the main mast, but not on the mizzen at that time. Referring to books by Harold A Underhill, Mike painstakingly designed three new headsails and a gaff mizzen sail, and took his drawings to Valencia to commission a sail maker of the old school to make up the sails in traditional canvas. No fancy terylene for Mike.

Sylvia boasted two anchors, one heavy and one light, and an anchor winch on the for'ard deck that was as big as a small car. It had two long arms that were operated by the *inferiores*, one pushing down as the other pulled up, alternately. Mike claimed he needed 'to keep a lookout', and thus found himself unable to assist with any anchor work.

We spent a month or more in Villajoyosa and Alicante, getting *Sylvia* shipshape, for we were about to embark for Gibraltar. As most of the ports were about a day's sail apart, we usually sailed for a day and then spent a few days in port, enjoying whatever was on offer. For example, from Motril Tim and I rode on one of Sylvia's scooters to the Alhambra at Granada.

In Malaga, trouble was awaiting us. No sooner had we tied up than an armed sentry was posted at our mooring – we were under arrest. Mike reported to the local police, where he learned that *Sylvia* had left Motril two years previously without paying her mooring fees, and that it was the boat that was responsible for the fees, not the owner. Mike had no choice but to pay. He recorded his frustration in *Three Years with 'Sylvia'* thus: 'As I went down the marble steps after this piece of bureaucratic bullying, my mind dwelt warmly on the events of 1588. "Sir Francis!" I said to myself, "thou shouldst be living at this hour: *Sylvia* hath need of thee".'

Around this time Tim and I decided that, no matter what the nominal captain said, the light anchor would suffice under all conditions – and it did … until *Sylvia* dragged badly one stormy day while we were all ashore in Gibraltar some months later. That was the day we got a terrible shock – imagine returning from a family shopping expedition and finding your ship not where you left it, but being blown gaily in the direction of America. That was the day Tim and I realised we still had a lot to learn about sailing.

After stocking up in 'Gib' with essential duty-free stores such as Ballantine's whisky, we cruised along the North African coast stopping at the Spanish enclaves of Ceuta and Melilla in Morocco. Then, at Ghazouet in Algeria, we were 'welcomed' by a large delegation of customs and immigration officials who helped themselves to Mike's precious scotch. They then announced that all those on South African passports, which was most of us, would not be allowed ashore.

At Beni Saf, as the authorities were again partaking of Mike's cherished stash, I went on foot to give a bottle of gin as a gift to friends on a nearby yacht – and was promptly arrested because of some kind of ban on, yes, booze! Mike was able to explain the situation away in his adequate French, and we left for Oran, en route to Cherchell (Caesaria) where Mike wanted to visit some Roman ruins. But, after further harassment in Oran, we decided to cut our losses.

It was now time for our first proper crossing, north to the Balearics. Mike had been teaching Tim and I the principles of celestial navigation and how to use his sextant, having taught himself these things from a book in *Colin Archer* days. Soon we were able to take noon and ex-meridian sights with accuracy, assisted by his grandfather's Norris and Campbell chronometer, a stopwatch and the pips from the BBC World Service (radio). On this leg, we had to navigate in earnest and Ibiza came up right on the bowsprit.

Tim often said his best moment on *Sylvia* had been on a black night between Oran and Ibiza, standing under the stars in the bows and seeing, at a right-angle to our course, what appeared to be torpedoes coming at our bows. They turned out to be dolphins – something in the water was turning their wakes white – and they frolicked with *Sylvia* for hours as we made our way north.

After a stay in the hippy mecca of Ibiza, we left for the ports of Palma, Puerto Andraitx and Puerto Soller in Majorca; and then Ciudadela in Minorca. By now we knew how to handle *Sylvia* under all conditions, but it was especially rewarding when we came stern-to the quay in Ciudadela – a tricky manoeuvre, given the peculiarities of the Grenaa engine and the long straight keel – to be congratulated by an older British couple who were sitting at a cafe on the quayside and who had watched our docking routine with a critical eye. As Mike later wrote[158], they said 'they had seldom seen such a fine display of seamanship, a kind remark which gave me great pleasure. I issued an orange per man on the strength of it'. Mike found it impossible to vocalise his feelings for his family, preferring to 'issue oranges'.

We had already had some minor engine trouble, and on our way to Port Mahon we ran the main bearing – losing the motor completely. Not wanting to arrive at Port Mahon without an engine and in the dark, we skirted the southern coastline looking for shelter, and as we came across Cala'n Porter, the wind turned in our favour and wafted us in. My, if it wasn't an enchanted cove with cliffs all around, grottoes, and our own deserted beach.

Mike was nothing if not lucky his whole life, and in the morning a light off-shore breeze carried us out to sea, and, shifting as it did, pushed us all the way up the long estuary to a mooring in Port Mahon which, luckily again, was not 20 metres from an engineering shop and a gin distillery!

By now, we had come to see that, overall, there was not much wind in the Med, and that we would often have to motor. This, of course, thrust into glorious relief those days when we had decent and sustained winds on the beam or quarter. For example, leaving Minorca for Corsica, we motored out of the estuary directly into a fresh breeze, hoisting the flapping sails as we cleared the mouth. Falling off onto our course, and with a Force 5 pressing on our starboard quarter, we quickly set the four headsails, the main and the mizzen, and cut the thumper.

Sylvia adopted a steady heel in the moderate sea. What a picture she was! Now, in the newfound silence, all we could hear was the whoosh of the wash; all we could feel was the wind on our skin; and we could not stop marvelling at our wake rushing away behind us as 100 tonnes of sailing ship charged across that sea. Tim and I clapped the old fella on the shoulders and we all burst into spontaneous laughter. Was this not what sailing was all about? It was, bedad.

In the stillness of sunset on the third day, we made our landfall on Corsica off forested Galeria Bay, where we all agreed we had an exquisite moment: as we anchored a few hundred metres off the beach and cut the engine, the breeze turned off-shore, bringing out to our silent, rocking ship the scent of pine trees from the steep hills beyond the beach.

Thence to Calvi, and on to Saint Florent where Mike and family had spent some months in 1968; then to Bastia, and across to the Italian island of Elba where Napoleon Bonaparte spent nine months in exile in 1814, and on to the mainland port of Livorno. For some reason, as we headed north, after stopping at Portovenere, we decided to have a closer look at the famous Portofino; too late, we discovered how small the port was, and turning laboriously, almost destroyed a number of $3-million 'gin palaces'.

We thus determined to keep our 'old tub' well clear of fancy marinas, but overnighted at Santa Margareta and next tied up to a huge buoy in the bay of Villefranche from where we explored the French Riviera by train and bus. Mike described this period as the culmination of his sailing dream.

Thence to St Tropez which we visited from our off-shore anchorage before spending some days at the peaceful Porquerolles islands. The short hop to the French naval port of Toulon was to be our last for the season, for it was already November.

Mike immediately felt at home in Toulon and wintered there alone, stern-to at the Quai de Petit Rang. Always a Francophile, he adopted what he called a French style of living, buying small items fresh every day and eating his main meal ashore in the evening with the locals, in one of the many restaurants within walking distance of the boat.

During the day he worked on *Sylvia*, tackling those tasks that he could, such as painting, overhauling, rewiring, etc and even repacking the stern (prop shaft) gland. But it was hard going as many of the jobs called for more than one pair of hands and Mike was not particularly adept at DIY work. He also designed the two topsails and the square sail that he had talked so much about the previous season.

He used the opportunity to improve his French, applying himself seriously to a set of textbooks by Mauger.

He also arranged for a student who happened to be young and female and attractive, to come and converse with him in French twice a week.

Mike did not usually make friends easily, but in Toulon he drew close to a local yachtsman, the specialist physician Jacques Scarbonchi, and through him got a valuable insight into the way the French live and the local yachting scene. He also met David Lavallée, an American ex-US Navy officer who had written a book called Event 1000; Mike described him as 'that attractive combination, a man of letters and of action'.

In the European spring of 1972, Mike was ready for another season of sailing. Phyllis joined him from South Africa and I flew in from a kibbutz in Israel. The good news was the boat was 'not taking in a drop of water' but there was a substantial growth of weed and barnacles on the underside which would mean an extra-slow passage to our first port of call, Villajoyosa, for the annual slip-and-scrape.

We dressed *Sylvia* and set off across the Gulf of Lions under sail. Early the next morning, despite the good weather forecast of the previous day, we were hit by a Mistral gale, forcing us to shorten sail drastically and heave to.

Back in control, we became aware that there was a lot of water crashing around in the bilges below the floorboards. Mike started the motor so that the bilge pump driven by the engine could empty us out, but the pump would not suck; likewise, a small electric pump that Mike had fitted in Toulon.

The water was now almost up to the floorboards; worse, the motor's exposed flywheel was sending a torrent of water upward, and it came down in a spray all over the engine and the surrounding area. We were concerned that the engine would soon cut out. Mike stripped himself naked before removing and dismantling the bilge pump – but could find nothing wrong with it.

Now the water was above the floorboards and rising, but where was the leak? We searched frantically. When we could not find it, we started to think the worst and got the rubber-duck ready. Then the motor died. We were going to sink.

There was, however, still the deck pump, a massive piece of original equipment with a two-metre cast-iron handle. We were about to find out why it was nicknamed 'The Lifesaver'. We knew it would work as long as we had the strength to pull that handle down; it was reputed to be foolproof. With the wind now Force 9 and an abominable sea running, Mike and I took it in turns, sea sick or not, doing 200 strokes apiece, each stroke spewing about five litres of bilge water onto the deck and over the side.

Slowly-slowly the water level in the boat crept down. As the day wore on, the wind dissipated and eventually we pumped *Sylvia* dry and kept her that way.

As we had no more problems with leaks of this sort, we were left to conclude that the particularly big seas had caused the hull planking to 'work' excessively and let in water; and we later found a tiny crack in the old copper pipe that ran between the bilges and the engine's bilge pump ….

At sundown, as we sat in the wheelhouse sipping something therapeutic and listening to the BBC news as was Mike's almost hourly habit, he philosophised: 'This is what life is all about, my boy. Contrast. One minute you are staring death in the face, and the next you are on top of the world.'

The next day we realised we were running low on food and needed to reach Villajoyosa promptly, using the motor if necessary. Mike tried to start the motor but failed on the first few attempts. Now, there was only enough compressed air for one last go. He called me into the engine-room and together we went methodically through the pre-start checklist, and then we prayed. The motor chugged into life. We motored when there was no wind and ultimately crept into Villajoyosa, somewhat chastened. The crossing had taken seven days.

While *Sylvia* was on the slip for recaulking, antifouling, and a general overhaul, Mike hired a small car. He was upbeat about the forthcoming sailing season and one day he suggested the two of us drive up the coast to Benidorm, a high-rise seaside mecca, for lunch. There were so many British tourists there, he joked, that we were sure to find British-style fish and chips!

On the way there, though, as we chatted, it slowly dawned on me Mike was justifying the lifestyle he adopted in the 1950s, when he elected to spend months each year away from his family. His rationale went something like this: a man has only one life, and a man has to do what a man has to do; if his absence hurts his family, that is an unfortunate and unintended consequence, but a man has to do what a man has to do.

Neither did Mike ever explain, from his side, why his marriage to my mother had broken down, and I was left to assume the above rationale was intended to cover it as well.

Another time he wrote, 'An adventurer's life is hard on his family and could be regarded as being selfish. I often used to think I am enjoying myself, but there's a price – the people at home are not enjoying my absence. But, looking back, I am absolutely convinced a man is entitled to do this, even at the expense of the discomfort of his family.'

We crossed over to Palma to pick up Tim and Gerry, but as they were not due to arrive for a few days, we did a day trip to the island of Cabrera. On the return leg, we ran before a fresh breeze, prompting Mike to wish, again, that *Sylvia* had a square foresail; it appealed to the traditionalist in him. He later wrote, 'My life's dearest ambition was to see all four of my sons lying aloft in a strong blow, gathering in the foresail, arms full of rebellious canvas, feet swaying on the footrope'. In due course, and in the most extraordinary manner, his wish for a square sail was granted ...

Phyllis was suddenly called back to South Africa to attend to Mikey who had contracted encephalitis, and when Tim and Gerry arrived, Mike called a meeting and explained that he wanted to run things differently this year. The previous year, we had been a family group having fun cruising around the western Mediterranean, more or less wherever we fancied. Now (1972), there would just be us first-batch youngsters as crew, we were to be paid for doing a few hours' work on the boat a day, and we would run a kitty to cover our food. Tim and I would use our wide maintenance skills wherever needed, and Gerry would do her magic in the galley. We agreed to the generous terms. (Later in the season, we took on a multi-talented American, Gene Dewey, on the same basis for a month or two.)

The reason for this new arrangement soon became apparent. *Sylvia* was obliged to remain in the general area for the moment, as something was going on, and Mike would not say what it was. Indeed, he was always intense about visiting the post office wherever we were to collect mail and make phone calls, and once or twice had to fly away for a few days. We assumed that *Sylvia* was an integral part of some devious plan and imagined that soon we would be called to rendezvous with men in black off a deserted beach in the dead of night ...

In the meantime, when in port we took advantage of the ridiculously cheap *vino tinto* which we bought by the 14-litre carafe. As the sun went down, we would relax on the deck, fill our glasses and mellow to the sounds of Tchaikovsky or Uriah Heep, depending on whether Mike or Tim got to the sound system first.

And invariably, as we drank, Mike would recite from Keats's *Ode to a Nightingale*:

> 'O for a beaker full of the warm South!
> Full of the true, the blushful Hippocrene,'

And we would join in:

> 'With beaded bubbles winking at the brim,
> and purple-stainèd mouth;'

And Mike, after pausing to see whether we had yet memorised the next two lines, would recite them poignantly:

> 'That I might drink, and leave the world unseen,
> And with thee fade away into the forest dim:'

In Valencia we picked up two new topsails which Mike had ordered from the same sail maker. It was here, too, that we painted the topsides white, leaving nine black squares on each side of the ship to represent gunports.

Returning, we made our landfall on Majorca at Puerto Soller and, over the following weeks, slowly circumnavigated the island. Heading for Palma in a totally flat sea on the last day, we were suddenly struck on our starboard quarter by a violent and sustained offshore blast. Sylvia showed her breeding in these perfect conditions, and after half-an-hour of breath-taking sailing we calculated we were going at the unheard-of speed of 12.6 knots! Two hours later, the wind dropped completely and we motored into Palma. It was truly an exhilarating end to four months of sailing, and the crew dispersed.

Condensing what Mike later wrote[159], Mike joined the Club Nautico in Palma and prepared *Sylvia* for the winter. Moored nearby was a Norwegian double-ender owned by an American couple. They were planning to cross the Atlantic to the West Indies, but there was a problem: they could not do celestial navigation. Mike, always the trainer, rose to the occasion. He showed them how to use their sextant, how to take noon and ex-meridian sightings, and how to calculate and draw their position lines on a chart. In due course, Mike was delighted to receive a long letter from them in the West Indies – they had hit the island of Barbados 'on the nose'.

Mike wintered with the family on *Sylvia*, and tried his hand at home-schooling the boys, now aged about eight and six years old. Early in 1973, he started the process of selling *Sylvia* and advertised her in two yachting magazines. An Austrian came and spent a day at sea on *Sylvia*. Then, an American and his wife spent some days cruising with them. But they were not buyers.

Now, suddenly, they were overtaken by a dream opportunity. Mike chartered *Sylvia* to a film company who were making a film called *The Three Musketeers* starring Raquel Welch, Charlton Heston, Michael York, Faye Dunaway, Oliver Reed and the rest. A contract was signed for $350 a day, $1000 cash changed hands, Mike roped in his yachting pals Mike Walder and Jack Bunting as crew, and they all sailed to Denia on the Spanish mainland.

The production crew arrived along with a team of artisans to convert *Sylvia* into an 'Elizabethan galleon'. Walder was appointed sailing adviser and, no doubt egged on by Mike, proposed a square sail on the mainmast, and a lateen across the mizzen – and in this way Mike's wish for a square sail came true, gratis! A grand poop deck was added to the stern and lesser profiling to the bows. And now for the masterstroke: the sides of *Sylvia* were painted, in typical movie tradition, one side red, the other side black – two sailing ships for the price of one! Then the stars arrived. Mike was enchanted by his contact with Raquel Welch, and loved to tell how he had cajoled her into crawling into the engine room with him to have a look at the Grenaa ... cramped as it was in there!

The director, Richard Lester, called for some footage to be shot off the coast. Walder starred briefly as a pirate, and Mike said a few words but was never sure whether he appeared on screen or not.

Then, it was all over. Mike sailed *Sylvia* to Villajoyosa where she was reinstated to her former glory at the film company's expense. This happy ending soured rather for Mike when, in the fullness of time, it transpired that enough footage had been shot to make two films (the second film was called *The Four Musketeers*), and *Sylvia*'s time on screen in the two films totalled 70 seconds.

They returned to Palma via San Antonio (Ibiza) and Puerto Andraitx with a Swiss named Peter as crew for most of the way. Now, at the end of November 1973, a friend of Peter's named Fritz

Bühler, also a Swiss, arrived and bought the boat for $32 000. Mike said he had paid $12 000 for *Sylvia* – 'part of the $30 000' given him by Mobutu – but had spent money on her. Nevertheless, 'everything I put into *Sylvia* I got back in spades', he said.

Back in South Africa, Mike applied his mind to writing a book about his Mediterranean adventures. Ian Colvin, the journalist, had advised him to use it as an opportunity to show a different side to his personality – to get away from his image as a mercenary soldier. And he certainly did so, even though Colvin had said it might be 'as difficult as getting a hippopotamus over a stile'.

Mike called the book *Three Years with 'Sylvia'*. In terms of his earlier contract with Hale, Mike was obliged to offer them his next book. They gave him an advance of £300 and it was published in 1977. Mike told me the manuscript had originally had two more chapters: one was 'how to teach yourself celestial navigation'; the other may well have been on his experiences in *Colin Archer*. But, he said, the publishers declined those chapters as the extra pages would have pushed the book into a higher price bracket.

Mike gave me a copy inscribed in his italic hand: 'To the first Mate, with love from his Dad. Mike Hoare'. The book was dedicated to Tom Harrison thus: 'Australian extraordinary; soldier, sailor, adventurer, and single-handed circumnavigator; lost off Cape Horn in his 25-foot sloop *Sundowner*, 1967.'

'*Sylvia*' was much more than a sailing travelogue. Mike showcased his considerable ability as a writer, in the process displaying his technical knowledge of sailing and sailing ships. He also showed off his sense of humour and love of literature, sprinkling the text with French words and erudite references.

Undoubtedly, he was a man of culture, and he took the opportunity to get that across in the book along with some 'golden nuggets of truth about sailing and life'.

Even though it went out of print fairly quickly, *Three Years with 'Sylvia'* developed a cult following. In 2007, the going rate for a second-hand copy, if you could find one on the internet, was around $104 plus shipping.

Readers of the book that I have met over the years have usually enthused, nay raved, about two of the amusing stories in particular: 'the recalcitrant fridge' and 'the red and blue fire brigades'. Undoubtedly, some of the writing is spectacular. I thought the book brought out the Irish in him. Mike said an Irish newspaper had named it their 'book of the month'.

It was reviewed on the South African Broadcasting Corporation's *Talking of Books* programme by the then well-known Simon Swindell. A transcript of the broadcast says in part, 'When I was given a book written by Mike Hoare, I was afraid I was going to have a book heavily larded with bits of the war in the Congo and mercenaries. But no, the overall picture that I had right from the start and which continued to the very last page, was what a charmer Mike Hoare must be. I wonder how many times he kissed the Blarney Stone. His book is a real delight. One of the things that endeared Mike to me was the pleasant way in which he admits his own shortcomings. I enjoyed this book tremendously.'

In the book, Mike wrote: 'It is a truism that adventure awaits those who are not afraid to go out and get their share of life.' In buying *Sylvia*, Mike went out to do just that – and adventure was waiting. Some of it was of his own making as Mike was as fallible as anyone else, and of course things beyond his control did go wrong on occasion.

12. The Wild Geese

One of Mike's heroes, Richard Burton, was cast to play the Mike Hoare character.

It would seem that from around March 1974, Mike and family lived in a rented house at 15 Rockdale Avenue, Westville, and that they went to live in Villars, Switzerland, during the European winter of 1974/5, returning to a different house in Westville in early 1975.

One day in 1975, with current affairs in Mozambique and Angola keeping an 'Africa watcher' like Mike busy, he was asked to be one of several speakers at a meeting of the right-wing National Forum at Durban's Elangeni Hotel. Mike, as a famous personality, would merely be the drawcard, the organisers said; his actual views on the local political scene were of no great importance, they told him, somewhat to his chagrin.

Mike could be unpredictable and that night, 20 June 1975, he certainly was. He told the large audience how he had become an avowed anti-communist: it was the day he found schoolchildren aged 11 and 12 hacked to death by the communist rebels in the Congo because it was feared they, mere schoolchildren, would become the intelligentsia. This was met by stunned silence.

He then proposed a solution: create a black middle-class who would have something to lose in the event of a communist takeover in South Africa – he even suggested a huge increase in income tax to boost black education.

Mike said the *Rand Daily Mail*, a left-wing newspaper, had

covered the event the next day under the headline: The day 'Mad Mike' went off the right rails.

Now, probably at the end of 1976, Mike was feeling 'too accessible' living in Westville and took the family to live at Hilltop Farm near Richmond in Natal. One of their neighbours was Malcolm Spence, the 400-metres bronze medallist in the Rome Olympics of 1960. He remembered Mike as being 'a master at keeping things alive', in particular the mercenary cause and thus indirectly interest in sales of his book, *Congo Mercenary*.

It was at Hilltop that Mike received a call from Hans Germani in Salisbury, Rhodesia, on behalf of Lord Richard Gascoyne-Cecil, the son of Robert Gascoyne-Cecil, sixth Marquess of Salisbury, England. Rhodesia's capital city was named after the third Marquess. Cecil had been a captain in the Grenadier Guards and had served in the elite Special Air Service in Britain; he was now a journalist but also carried a rifle and fought alongside specialist forces, providing unique pro-Rhodesia coverage of the bush war.[160]

He wanted to meet Mike, but Mike could never understand why anyone would want to interview him, and reacted typically. 'What? Come all the way from Salisbury to interview ME? No, no, it's too far.' But Cecil and a cameraman considered the journey worthwhile and spent an afternoon interviewing Mike at Hilltop.

In April 1978, while moving into action, Cecil, aged 30, was shot dead by a lone insurgent. Later Mike made the off-the-cuff comment, 'It was a damned shame. Good bloke. One of us, so to speak.'

After a year at Hilltop, the family moved to Hilton, renting a house in Groenekloof Road. About a year later, Mike bought the *Old Vicarage*, a somewhat spartan and old-fashioned place with a two-acre garden, at 49 Hilton Avenue – the main road through the village. The new home was within easy walking distance of the post office, and Mike loved to walk there each day, sometimes several times a day, to check for letters. The house served as the family home, with interruptions, until 1989.

In mid-1977 Mike got a phone call from one of his Congo men, Ian Yule, now a film actor in South Africa. Yule said he had given Mike's name to a British movie producer, Euan Lloyd, and how would Mike like to be the military and technical advisor on a film to be shot in South Africa about mercenary soldiers, starring Richard Burton. Mike's response, he told me with a laugh, was: 'Yes how much, no comma!'

The storyline was inspired by recent events and people in Africa: A Mike-Hoare-type commander and 50 mercenary soldiers are hired by a British multinational to snatch a Tshombe-style president from a jail in central Africa where he is being held by the 'Simbas'; once the president is rescued, the multinational double-crosses the mercenaries; a sub-plot shows a meeting of minds between the black president and his white Afrikaner rescuer.

Lloyd later described the film as 'close to fact'.[161]

Extraordinarily, one of Mike's heroes, Richard Burton, was cast to play the Mike Hoare character, Colonel Allen Faulkner, and was known on set as 'R One'. The other big stars were Richard Harris ('R Two'), Roger Moore and Hardy Kruger. Stewart Granger also had a role. Likewise Kenneth Griffith. Yule had a lesser part, as did Tullio Moneta, whom we meet later and who had served in 5 Commando post-Mike.

Apparently, two of South Africa's greatest black actors, John Kani and Winston Ntshona, were initially reluctant to be in a film about mercenaries. But once they had read the script and saw it had a message in which they both believed, they changed their minds. Simply put, the message was: black and white need each other and there is no tomorrow in southern Africa for one without the other.

The $8-million British film was shot during September, October and November 1977 at the Tshipise nature resort and spa in the Northern Transvaal, just a few kilometres from the Rhodesia border. The 300-strong group of actors and technicians took over a whole camp, black and white people mixing in spite of apartheid.

The film was to be called The Thin White Line and was based on a novel of the same name by Daniel Carney, a young Irishman who settled in Rhodesia in 1963 and who served in the British South Africa Police there for three-and-a-half years. He then started a successful real estate company called Fox and Carney, but writing was his passion and he used to write at night at his kitchen table.

His widow, Sally, told me, 'Dan got the germ of the idea quite by accident. Once, at Lake Kariba airport, an elderly man who had worked there for many years told Dan the story of a distressed plane flying in at night, trying to do an emergency landing. The runway was lit up with fire-flares to guide the plane in. It had been shot up. On board, so Danny was told, was Patrice Lumumba from the Congo, the charismatic leader who had been rescued by mercenaries and flown out for his own safety.'[162]

Mike said, however, he did not like the proposed title because people would usually associate it with the well-known Thin Red Line formed during the battle of Balaclava, fought in 1854 during the Crimean War. The title was changed in due course to *The Wild Geese*.

Mike's work, he said, was to turn 50 actors into instant soldiers, and to be an authenticator. 'My duties broadly speaking would be to attend each day's shooting and to inform the director if and when any glaring mistakes of a military nature were about to be made.'

At one point, where the mercenaries are in serious trouble, Burton, who is standing on a first-floor balcony, shouts encouragement to his men who are below. No, said Mike. Get among the men, form them in a tight group around you, look them in the eyes from close up, and motivate them.

Later Andrew McLaglen, the director, told Tony Earnshaw, a British writer and broadcaster, 'Mike Hoare was with us all the time. I thought he was a very nice man. You'd think he might have been a university professor, but he had a tough inside about him. He told us some fabulous stories. We got [Richard] Burton, [Richard] Harris and the cast to listen to a talk by Hoare. I remember that whatever he said turned them off a little bit. He was saying some pretty strident words about things. I think [Burton] respected him. He got turned off by him on this one instant. Hoare was a strong character. When he had his uniform on he looked like a soldier. He always wore his uniform on the set.'

Mike remembered how he may inadvertently have upset the stars. 'One day early on, Lloyd calls for me. He says that part of my job is to give a lecture to all the actors who are mercenaries. I need to explain how they should be, how they should appear, their attitude to each other, and so on. I started preparing my talk and decided to show a tape I had brought with me: an interview I had done in the late sixties, all about mercenary soldiering.

'Come the day, the "RSM" of the film crew got the cast of 50 seated in a hall, with all the stars in the front row. I am dressed in a colonel's uniform and the RSM calls me, military style. As I march in, he calls the officers to attention, creating an awkward situation as I am really a junior member of the production team. The stars may have been a bit miffed. Anyway, I gave my talk and showed the video. Afterwards, one of the actors came up to me and said it was the best lecture he had ever heard.'

Lloyd told it thus in 2015: 'One day Mike asked me if we could gather key members of the cast and crew first thing before the day's shooting began so that he could address them. I agreed and the time was included on the daily "call sheet", issued to all the evening before. When Richard Burton saw the instruction (it was not a request!) he was incensed and said he wouldn't go ... "I'm not in the bloody army ...!" The next morning Mike began his talk about how a soldier behaves in battle and things every soldier should know. Richard B had calmed down a bit by now and popped in, curious now, to hear what Mike had to say. He was mightily impressed by Mike's thoroughness and from that moment he decided to co-operate fully.'[163]

Penny Junor recounts in her biography that Burton had initially not wanted to take the role as he did not like mercenaries, so Lloyd explained that the film was based on a real man, Colonel 'Mad Mike' Hoare. Now, Mike is giving his talk and the four stars are sitting motionless in their seats. Afterwards, Junor recounts, Burton went to Lloyd and said, "'I owe you an apology, you bastard. Now I see what you mean.' From that moment on, Richard watched Hoare's every move, and the character he played in the film was based entirely on Colonel "Mad Mike" Hoare."[164]

The *Sunday Times* of 1 September 1985 recounted the above story in a spread on the life of Richard Burton. The headline read: Tamed by 'Mad Mike' on the 'Wild Geese' set.

In due course, Mike and Burton found something in common: their love of Shakespeare. Mike had always enjoyed the set works by Shakespeare at school, for example *Richard II* and *Henry V*. He had all Shakespeare's works in his library at home, and when I was a child he often told me: 'My boy, there are only two books worth reading: Shakespeare and the Bible.' And so it was that Mike and Burton spent some of their free time together discussing their common love.

'I found him lovely to talk to. He couldn't make small talk; he was frightened of people asking him questions and then seeing his answers distorted in a magazine the next week. But I was interested in his career and his work; I had his recordings of *Henry V* and *Under Milk Wood*, and I used to listen to them at home. He told me radio was "the thing", and that he loved doing radio.

'I got more than an inkling of his greatness. I used to watch him perform on the set as I was interested in his career as a Shakespearean actor, and I used to try to steer the conversation round to that, saying it was a great shame that he had left it.

'There were times when he had to be on the set, and he had his chair, and I had my chair. You didn't approach the stars, they would not talk to you. On three occasions we spent time together, just the two of us. Though I say it myself, Burton liked to talk to me because I was different, not because I was the thing he was trying to imitate.

'Once, he told me the original script had been full of foul language, and he said, "I was told nobody had ever heard you swear in your life". I don't want to come over as a goody-goody, but it is just one of the things I don't do. Burton said he had had all the swearing taken out of the script.'

Mike's favourite Shakespearean play was *King Lear*, and he was able to discuss it with Burton, including how an actor would be able to hold the dead Cordelia in his arms for so long without getting exhausted.

Later, Mike wrote[165], 'I was reading a book about the life of Christopher Marlowe at that time. Burton paged through it and told me he had performed the title role in a 1966 production of *Doctor Faustus*. Getting to his feet he recited those unforgettable lines depicted by Faustus during his last hour on earth. On this occasion Richard Burton, the world famous Shakespearean actor, had an audience of one ... me!

'I was speechless with admiration. I then asked him if he had ever played Lear. No, he had not, he said, but it was his ambition to play Lear before he died. Sadly, he never did. He then gave me a private performance of that final heart-rending scene where Lear staggers on to the stage with the strangled Cordelia in his arms, and cries out:

"'Howl, howl, howl, howl! O you are men of stones!
Had I your tongues and eyes,
I'd use them so
That heaven's vault should crack.
She's gone for ever."'

Mike said he wept when he heard Burton had died (August 1984), and wrote to Burton's widow, Sally, with the above quotation, changing the last line to 'He's gone for ever'. Years later, Mike took the trouble to visit Burton's grave in Céligny, Switzerland; he admired the simple Celtic rock gravestone.

It seems that Kani (Sgt. Jesse Blake) was another star that Mike upset, as he took his job too seriously, almost regarding the cast as recruits. Earnshaw quotes Kani as saying, 'In South Africa blacks are not conscripted into the army. So we arrive on set and there is Mike Hoare, the mad colonel. He took an incredible interest in me. He said "Okay, don't worry. I will put you through your paces. Let's go." I used to spend an hour with him in the afternoons going through the ammo, assembling, disassembling, and he was very strange. People were saying, "Be careful. He always recruits mercenaries in reality." I was surprised when we finished the movie to get a Christmas card from him three years in a row. Then I heard that they were involved in the coup in the Seychelles. That's the last I heard.

'He was very fatherly, very caring, with a twitch of a smile on the left [of the] lip, but you were very aware you were in the presence of a very dangerous person. When he was training me he was showing me where to shoot so as not to waste bullets. He took it too serious

– he was really making a soldier out of me. It was an assignment. One time I was talking to him and my rifle was next to a tree, away from me. And he screamed at me! He said, "You are married to that rifle. A soldier never, never puts a weapon down." But after a couple of scenes the director said, "My God, you look like the real thing".'

It was on the set also that Mike established what was to become a great friendship with the legendary Bob Simmons who was the stunt team co-ordinator and who doubled for Richard Burton.

Earnshaw quotes John Glen, the second unit director on the film as saying, 'I met (Mike) when I first arrived at Tshipise. I had got lost. I found Bob Simmons with Mike reminiscing about his days in the Congo war. I stayed for three hours listening to Mike. He was very much an English gentleman, soft-spoken, understated. Interesting man. The things he told us … very hairy. I think what we did was very authentic.'

In retrospect, it is curious to note that Mike was interviewed on the set by journalist Doug Gordon, and his article appeared in the *Sunday Times* of 23 October 1977. He wrote that Mike was 'considering forming a private anti-hijacker squad. His "rat-catching" force would be non-political – essentially contracted mercenaries who could be hired by airline companies or countries.' He quotes Mike as saying, 'I would need a full anti-hijacker squad of 50,' and that the men were available. It was another one of Mike's entrepreneurial ideas ...

The post-production work was done during 1978, and Mockler described the result as 'far and away the best mercenary film ever made'.[166] The royal charity world premiere was held at the Leicester Square Theatre in London on 6 July 1978.

Later that year, Lloyd asked Mike to do a tour of America to publicise the release of the film on 10 November in 600 cinemas across the United States and Canada. Mike was contracted to spend three weeks in North America, giving interviews and thereby drumming up interest in the film.

As he said at the time, one day he was mowing the lawn at his home in Hilton and two days later, as an instant celebrity in New York, he was getting the limo treatment.

On his return to South Africa, Mike wrote a long article about his tour, and it was published in *Family Radio & TV* magazine.[167]

His very first interviewer started: 'It is well known that you are a racist. How many men have you killed?' His reply is pertinent: 'For a man who had risked his life for two years to liberate many Congolese from communist oppression, the racist remark stung. The lady had to be put right. But her knowledge of the subject was minimal and I had to educate her about the role of mercenary troops in Africa. Why we were called in by the Congolese government (to put down a communist-inspired rebellion which had engulfed two-thirds of the Congo); the principles of mercenary employment (they should be used only by a legitimate government as an extension of their own regular armed forces); and that mercenary soldiers are not gangsters (they are highly professional and well-disciplined men).'

The interviews were for the print media, radio and TV, and often he would go straight from one interview to another. Soon, Mike discovered the type of question that usually came up, and he developed standard replies, sometimes making light of it all:

Q. What makes a man like you become a mercenary soldier?

A. I like the company of strong men .... but don't get me wrong ...... I really prefer the company of weak women.

Q. You don't look a bit like a mercenary. You agree that the prototype is a big, tough braggart ready to kill for the highest price?

A. I agree that I don't look like your idea of a mercenary. And the type you describe is entirely fictional. It is the image foisted on the public by the press in 1961 – understandably, I suppose. The first mercenaries (in recent times) were recruited by Moise Tshombe for service in the army of the independent state of Katanga. They came from Brussels, mostly. They were bearded and unkempt. Their behaviour was unsoldierly, undisciplined and arrogant. They rejoiced in the name '*Les Affreux*' – the frightful ones – a pretty apt description. The press built on this image which has stuck to mercenaries ever since. I have tried for years to dispel it, with little success.

pt Mike Hoare, right, with his second-in-command, Capt Alistair Wicks, at Shinkolobwe in
tanga. 1961. *Photograph: source unknown*

embers of 4 Commando crossing a river on a ferry in Katanga. 1961. *Photograph: source unknown*

Mike's best friend Don Rickard on the beach at Salisbury Island, Durban. ±1959. *Photograph: Mike Hoa*

Before the drama and death .... Phyllis plays for the camera at Guma. 1963.
Photograph: Mike Hoare

These are the pamphlets that Mike had printed for the 1963, left, and 1962 safaris in Bechuanaland.
Photograph: Chris Hoare

Mike, left, with John Seaman in a Canadian canoe in the Okavango Delta. 1962. *Photograph: source u*

Mike at a Wild Geese Club meeting in Johannesburg in 1974. He is wearing the *'L'Ordre National du Zaïre*, Officer class' medal which he received in 1967 at a special parade in Leopoldville. Photograph: source unknown

In March 1965, Mike was sent a quote from Lerwill Pope, The Lane Tailors, Durban, for 2000 shoulder flashes; the price quoted was 45 cents each. The original sketch, above, was attached. Photograph: Chris Hoare

th Mike at a meeting of the Wild Geese Club in Johannesburg were two other veterans of both and 5 Commando, Pipe-Major Sandy King, left, and RSM Jack Carton-Barber. 1974. otograph: source unknown

Mike loved little more than telling sea stories on yachts, glass of *vin rouge* in hand, in this case in Toulon, France. 1972.
Photograph: source unknown

Mike hams it up aboard the *Cutty Sark* in London. 1978.
Photograph: Chris Hoare

Mike's yacht *Sylvia* was converted into an Elizabethan galleon in Denia, Spain, complete with poop deck and square sail on the main mast, for the making of the film *The Three Musketeers*. 197
Photograph: Mike Hoare

Mike with mother Aileen and sister June at June's Harley Street, London, flat. 1978.
Photograph: Chris Hoare

ike with his commanding officer during the early
art of World War 2, Paddy Brett, at the Old Vicarage,
lton. 1985. *Photograph: Chris Hoare*

ike, right, with his good friend, the stuntman
ob Simmons. 1978. *Photograph: Chris Hoare*

Mike in the visitors room at Pietermaritzburg
Prison. 1984/5. *Photograph: source unknown*

heers! Mike with some of the Frothblowers at his home in Hilton, celebrating his release from
ison; from left, Ken Dalgliesh, Rob Griffin (ex 5 Commando, not a Frothblower), Barney Carey, Mike
are, Peter Duffy, Aubrey Brooks and Bob Sims. May 1985. *Photograph: Chris Hoare*

Mike secretly made model sailing ships in his prison cell, using only a tiny knife. *Photograph: Chris Hoare*

To-morrow, and to-morrow, and to-morrow,

Creeps in this petty pace from day to day

To the last syllable of recorded time,

And all our yesterdays have lighted fools

The way to dusty death. Out, out, brief candle!

Life's but a walking shadow, a poor player,

That struts and frets his hour upon the stage,

And then is heard no more; it is a tale

Told by an idiot, full of sound and fury,

Signifying nothing.

13

~ daffodils,

That come before the swallow dares, and take

The winds of March with beauty; violets, dim

But sweeter than the lids of Juno's eyes..

On Cytherea's breath

THE WILD GEESE

To assist in paying the various legal fees, Mike sold cloth Wild Geese badges made two sizes, 105 mm and 60 mm. 1982.
Photograph: Chris Hoare

A page from Mike's prison notebook. Mike learned hundreds of lines from Shakespeare to maintain his sanity in prison.
Photograph: Chris Hoare

Mike, left, and brother Ben having a bit of fun, at Ben's Rorvik Avenue home in Durban. Mike usually kept loose banknotes in his shirt pocket, and here he is pretending to be protecting them from Ben's potentially probing fingers. March 1995. *Photograph: Chris Hoare*

Mike at his irrepressible best, seen here at his son Tim's wedding. 2 April 1982. *Photograph: Chris Hoare*

The Daily News

CITY LATE

Established 1878
Telephone 324324 Classifieds 324371

DURBAN, THURSDAY, NOVEMBER 26, 1981

NATAL'S
BIGGEST
DAILY

19c + Tax 1c

HIJACK!

Officials (arrowed, left) confer with hijackers at the top of the Boeing steps. On the right is a Hippo armoured personnel carrier.

Daily News
Reporters

South African suspects arrested in Louis Botha Boeing jet drama

he newspapers gave the events in the Seychelles saturation coverage. Mike was in the news gain, but this time it was for all the wrong reasons. *Photograph: Chris Hoare*

Mike visited numerous Cathar sites during his
14 years in 'Cathar country', France. 1996.
Photograph: source unknown

Mike playing grandpa with his
granddaughter Shannon Herd-Hoare.
March 1995. *Photograph: Chris Hoare*

Mike is seated with three of his grandchildren, from left, Shannon and Sean Herd-Hoare, and
Justice Hoare; back from left are Pat Hoare (daughter-in-law), Chris Hoare (son), Mikey Hoare (son),
Gerry Hoare (daughter), Radha Hoare (ex-wife), Terry Herd-Hoare (daughter-in-law), and
Tim Hoare (son). Durban, 2002. *Photograph: Chris Hoare*

Mike assembles a model of the sailing ship *Albatross*, at Miramont in France. 2001.
Photograph: Mikey Hoare

...ke's brother-in-law Bob Sims and his wife Sue at ...eir home on the South Coast of KwaZulu-Natal. ...93. *Photograph: Chris Hoare*

Mike with the CIA's go-to man in the Congo, Larry Devlin, at *La Maison Rose* in Miramont, France, in 1994. Devlin went on to write *Chief of Station, Congo: Fighting the Cold War in a Hot Zone*.
Photograph: source unknown

Mike was the published
author of eight books. 2017.
Photograph: Chris Hoare

Rob Griffin, writer, raconteur and close
friend to both Mike Hoare and the author.
Photograph: Alice Rose Ferguson

Mike and Peter Duffy, always a clown in front
of the camera, celebrating St Patrick's Day
in Durban, 2012. Mike turned 93 years old
that day. *Photograph: Chris Hoare*

Mike with his 'first batch' children, Gerry, Chris and Tim in Cape Town. 2013.
Photograph: Pat Hoare

...ke opened a parcel containing his World War 2 medals on his 93rd birthday in 2012. They are, ...m left, 1939-45 Star, Burma Star, Defence Medal and War Medal 1939-45. *Photograph: Chris Hoare*

P/189576 MAJ T M B HOARE RAC

Mike received the valuable Territorial Army 'Efficiency' medal in 2012.

Photographs: Chris Hoare

...his old age, Mike enjoyed little more than reading in the African sun. He is seen here at the ...thor's home in Durban. 2016. *Photograph: Chris Hoare*

Mike poses as explorer, pirate and Frothblower in these portraits created by the author at his home in Durban. 2015.

Mike at a small party to celebrate his 99th birthday in 2018, with, front, Terry Herd-Hoare and Chris Hoare; and back, Laurie Kaplan, ex-5 Commando, and his wife Elizabeth, Mike's niece Aideen Omara, Sue Miles, Maryse Geech, David Day and Jacques Mathen. *Photograph: Roy Reed*

Q. This must cause you some embarrassment, personally?

A. It does. I know what people expect. Usually I apologise for not being six foot six.

Q. Will the image of the mercenary as depicted in the film, presumably the real one, change all that?

A. I'd like to think so, but I doubt it. It might even add to my problems. Now I'll have to go around apologising for not being Richard Burton.

His first television interview in America was with Tom Brokaw, something of a personality, on the *Today Show* which broadcast right across the land. It was to be a four-minute interview, followed by a clip from the film, and another four minutes' talking. Obviously, interest in the film was exceptional, as four minutes with Tom Brokaw was the norm. Mike was warned before the show that Brokaw 'goes for the jugular'. He wrote:

'I sat close to Tom Brokaw in an armchair. His hand, out of camera, rested near my knee and when I ran on too long he would squeeze it. American TV gets into the guts of its presentation at once. Tom lost no time. After a short introduction, he flung his first spear ... at the neck of course, where else? "How do you see things in Rhodesia now that the terrorists control 90 percent of the country and are winning the war?" he asked. Try that one on for size! Worse still, try answering it in 20 seconds, with some pressure on your knee around the fifteenth second.

'Brokaw ended with two dagger thrusts to the aorta: "Tell me, Colonel, how many men have you killed?" I told him mildly that commanding officers do not go around killing people – they direct battles. "Is there a difference between mercenaries and a hit squad?" he asked. Mercenaries are not gangsters – they are professional soldiers, I replied. On the whole, I felt I hadn't done too well. Tom had won on points. But everybody at Allied Artists was pleased – *The Wild Geese* had had tremendous exposure.'

Then Mike was flown to Los Angeles where the major item was an interview with Tom Snyder on *The Tomorrow Show*. Tom had a reputation as a 'hatchet man', but was gentle that night; perhaps it was because he had got off on the wrong foot by 'introdoocin' Mike as the author of *Congo Missionary* (instead of *Congo Mercenary*).

Mike discovered, however, that as skilled as his interviewers were, they could not and did not know everything about everything. He discovered that an effective defence against an unfair question was to reply with an equally tough one. For example:

Q. So, you were politically motivated as a mercenary commander? You went around the Congo for two years with 500 men, making war just to further your own personal anti-communist ambitions? Is that a justification for killing people?

A. But isn't that exactly the same as 600 000 Americans going to Vietnam, a land two-thirds of them didn't know existed before the war, to carry out the anti-communist policy of the US government?

After a quick working stop at Chicago, he flew on to Toronto. In one day, beginning at 6.30 am, he did ten interviews, including two TV shows. Back in New York, the schedule became even tighter. A dinner interview with *The Daily News* film critic Kathleen Carroll was a special occasion.

Suddenly, at 11 pm, he was on Barry Farber's two-hour talk show. He was able to put across his views on the Marxist invasion of Africa. The Russians, he said, 'are flooding Africa with AK-47s, arms and ammunition and terrorist aid, all designed to gain their own political ends. The Russians and Cuban mercenaries have seized Angola, Mozambique, Ethiopia, Congo Brazzaville and many smaller nations without any resistance from the West. They are winning by default.'

Americans were leaders of the world, he said, and should lead, not just react to communist successes. He implored them to lead with money and technology to improve the living standard of millions of Africans up and down the continent and so defeat communism.

A five-minute television spot was scheduled for the next day. Jack Cafferty was the interviewer. 'What does your wife think of the things you do?' was one of the questions. Mike responded, 'When a woman really loves a man she doesn't give a damn what he does.'

Then he was interviewed by Henry Allen of the *International Herald Tribune* as they traversed Washington in a taxi. The ensuing article[168] was headlined: 'Mad Mike' Hoare: Oh the Stories ..... Describing Mike's early days in South Africa, Allen says: 'And the maps came out. Hoare has thousands of maps, loves maps, can see the ground itself when he looks at maps, and whenever his wives (he's had two) have seen him opening the maps, they knew he'd be gone for a while.'

Unusually, Mike then went on to reveal his quintessential self to Allen, summing up what we in the family all knew and loved about Mike, for he had often said things like, 'I should have been with Sir Francis Drake, out sailing, robbing the Spaniards, and when you brought the gold back to the queen of England, you knelt before her and she made you a knight. You were respectable – even though you were a thief.'

Next, Mike had a date with Joey Adams, a famous comedian in his seventies. Unfortunately, Adams got his wires crossed and concluded his introduction, Tom Snyder-style, by saying, '"Now, Mike, please tell the good people of America how you spread the Word of God throughout the Congo ...".'

Mike's last interview was with the Canadian Broadcasting Corporation. With the confidence gained from 100 interviews in 21 days, he recited *Epitaph on an Army of Mercenaries*, by AE Housman:

'These, in the day when heaven was falling,
The hour when earth's foundations fled,
Followed their mercenary calling
And took their wages and are dead.

'Their shoulders held the sky suspended;
They stood, and earth's foundations stay;
What God abandoned, these defended,
And saved the sum of things for pay.'

The poem was written in 1914 and, according to Martin Hardcastle, a Housman enthusiast, the mercenaries Housman was talking about were regular British Army at the time of the battle of Ypres; they are described as mercenaries by the Germans because they were a volunteer rather than a conscript army. One interpretation of the poem is that it is possible to be paid for fighting and still to fight in a good cause.

The tour was now over. Ted Albert, one of the top men at Allied Artists, rang and told Mike he was 'a trooper'. Mike took a cab to John F Kennedy Airport and flew east, jugular intact.

According to a newspaper cutting[169], Bantam was to release a paperback edition of *Congo Mercenary*, called *Mercenary*, on the American market in January 1979. This was in response to the renewed interest in Mike and mercenaries after the release of *The Wild Geese*. The book had a new 5400-word epilogue written by Mike, updating the reader on events in the Congo and elsewhere, post-1965.

And in Britain, Corgi, having first published an illustrated softcover edition called *Mercenary* in 1968, reissued it in 1978, and reprinted it a further four times between 1978 and 1982. It was also called *Mercenary*, but the cover had a *Wild Geese* feel, and proclaimed that Mike had been technical adviser for the film. By 1986, this edition had sold more than 100 000 copies.

In late 1978, Mike gave an interview to Malik Stan Reaves, from a journal called *Southern Africa*. In the January 1979 issue, Mike talks about the Wild Geese Club in Johannesburg. 'Basically it is a social club but obviously it would have other uses. If we knew that all the men were going to gather there every Friday, and we put out the word that possibly there was a role for them, they would all be there, and that would provide an opportunity to see who was available.'

He also described himself as a 'Pan Africanist. I view things from the viewpoint of a man who has fought communism in central Africa. I don't necessarily take a white view. I take an overall view of Africa. The basic premise of Afrikaner supremacy is baloney and apartheid is indefensible. We have to improve the lot of the average African and raise a new middle-class that has something to lose.'

In those days, Mike was a 'gold bull'. He had invested heavily in gold shares, which, by mid-1979, had 'come out of the basement' and had 'put on their burnished coat'. Selling some of the shares at a peak moment enabled him to take the family for an extended holiday in England and Europe, he said.

As was often the case with Mike, his adventures started with a vision: 'A horse-drawn caravan clip-clopping down an Irish country lane, himself leading the horse by the bridle, Mamma looking fragrant on the front seat, the childer asleep within. Shure wasn't that the quintessence of adventurous living? It was, but only in my dreams. The gipsy caravan dream faded away; what I settled for was something more prosaic – a motorised caravan.'[170]

The holiday started in London, where I was living at the time, and the family stayed with me initially. We visited the informal campervan market patronised almost exclusively by Australasians. Now, I thought, I would see the cut-and-thrust of an expert in the buying and selling of used vehicles. We came to a Ford Transit motor caravan and after asking the usual questions, we took it for a drive. She was a beauty, but a bit pricey. To my amazement, Mike gently and politely made an offer marginally below the asking price, and the deal was done.

A few days later, we drove the van down to Box Hill, Surrey, where we did a 12-km hike in the woods. Mike loved a walk in the country. He always remembered that day thereafter – it was 27 August 1979, the day the Irish Republican Army assassinated Lord Louis Mountbatten.

After a few days of enjoying the sights of London, they set off on a meandering tour that included Glastonbury, Hadrian's Wall, and Scotland where Mike looked up his old friend Jock Roger who, in the early days in Durban had lived near Mike and Betty, and who had taught Mike how to fly fish in the Drakensberg. They skipped Ireland, crossed into France and toured the Loire Valley before visiting Switzerland; they were due to visit Gerry in Italy for the first time, but suffered a minor harassment in the north of the country, and simply abandoned that leg, upsetting Gerry no end, and returned to London and South Africa.

I asked Mike how he had managed to support his family through the 1970s without working as such. Part of the answer, he said, was living quietly, and for long periods he certainly did live quietly, actively managing his investments on the Johannesburg Stock Exchange; at one point, he even tried to get a Reuters financial 'ticker' installed in his home office. 'I was also paid very well for *The Three Musketeers*, and the military adviser role (for *The Wild Geese*) was also well paid. I lived for a year on the fee for the publicity tour in North America. My life has been a succession of those things.'

By Christmas 1980, I was living in South Africa again. During the season, Mike, Mikey, Simon and I spent a week at the Underberg Hotel in the southern Drakensberg, and did a bit of fly fishing in the local rivers. Then, in the winter of 1981, Mike and I planned to do part of the Giant's Cup hiking trail in the Drakensberg. On the Friday, the weather forecast for the weekend was unforgettable: 'Cold to very cold with rain and snow'. I phoned Mike. 'Sod it,' he said. 'Let's do it.'

Early on the Saturday, a friend of mine and I drove up to Hilton from Durban. As was his style, Mike had planned the hike meticulously; he had the maps, the pamphlets, the permit, the backpack and the boots. Military style, he issued each of us with tiny super-light stoves which took a tiny block of fuel; each block was exactly enough to boil one mug-full of water. He issued our 'rations', ran through a checklist, and we were off.

Leaving my car on the road to Sani Pass, we took the trail across the veld. The weather was as predicted. After an hour, we stopped to 'brew up'; ten minutes later we were on our way again, and this became a pattern that we adhered to strictly. Mountains in the mist have immense appeal, and I recall our sense of wonder as we rounded a ridge to find a herd of about 50 eland right there. We just stared at each other in the silence; it was a special encounter. After about 13 km we came to Pholela Hut at Cobham, where we made a roaring fire and cooked up a hot meal before crawling into our sleeping bags. The next day we hiked on to Mzimkhulwana Hut and thence to the nearest farmhouse, that of my friends the Morrises, where

Phyllis picked us up. Mike summed the weekend up by saying we had taken a calculated risk in doing the walk in those conditions, but were we not immensely richer for the experience?

Meanwhile, Mike had been busy conspiring to overthrow a government. This time, for everyone involved, it all ended not just in disaster, but in catastrophe …

13. The Idealist

'The exiles had a righteous and a legal cause. And it was manifestly anti-Marxist. I decided I would give them all the help I could. Further, if they were unable to pay me for my services, I would give them for nothing.' – Mike Hoare

During the late 1970s, I became aware that Mike was up to something. He kept pitching up in London where I was living, and he would talk vaguely about exiles and a possible coup attempt, codenamed Operation Anvil. Little did I know that I would soon be ensconced at 'Coup HQ'.

The affair began for Mike at a 'glittering occasion', a formal party at the Durban home of his good friend, Harry Grant-Whyte, who was by now a world-famous professor of anaesthetics and something of a medical legend. It was on that night in 1978 that Mike was approached by one of the guests to overthrow the Seychelles government.

President Albert René came to power in the Seychelles after a coup on 5 June 1977, when the elected president, the pro-West James Mancham, was out of the country. Deryck Scarr, in his book *Seychelles since 1770*, says 'some 20 Tanzanian mercenaries' were involved, adding that Mancham had later been heard to say that '25 men with strong sticks could have taken Seychelles'.

The Seychelles islands are strategically well placed to conduct surveillance of all the countries on the Indian Ocean rim. Under the socialist René, Mike said, the Russians had started building a military base together with a long runway and underground missile silos on far-flung Coetivy Island, part of the Seychelles. The Americans, for their part, had already built a satellite-tracking station on Mahé, and a naval base on the island of Diego Garcia, further east. Mike described these events as 'globally significant' and was clearly concerned that the Russians would use Coetivy as part of their master plan to control Africa, including South Africa, for their own benefit. The cold war, of course, was still very much a factor in the late 1970s, and Reds were imagined under South African beds.

Meanwhile, the countries that formed a buffer for South Africa against the 'wind of change' that was still blowing, had either become independent (Angola and Mozambique) or were soon to do so (Rhodesia). White rule in South Africa was increasingly being challenged and the powerful but besieged apartheid government was suffering internal insurrection, trade boycotts and armed attacks from inside and outside the country; it was dubbed 'total onslaught'.

South Africa, for its part, started pursuing an aggressive policy that is usually described as 'destabilisation' – its hallmarks were cross-border raids and incursions, bombings in neighbouring states, assassinations, sabotage attacks, secret missions, government death squads, letter and parcel bombs, car bombs, airborne attacks, the funding of non-Marxist resistance groups, dirty tricks, etc.

It was against this background that a group of Seychellois exiles approached Mike. And even though Mancham had not fully committed himself to a counter-coup, the exiles asked Mike to visit the Seychelles and give a military opinion on its feasibility.

Post-Katanga, Mike had always said, 'Mercenaries should be used only in support of a legally constituted government.' Here, 'the legal President was James Mancham. The exiles had a righteous and a legal cause. And it was manifestly anti-Marxist. I decided I would give them all the help I could. Further, if they were unable to pay me for my services, I would give them for nothing,' but he 'would have expected a lucrative position of some sort in their new set-up'.

For decades, Mike's fans had all somehow used the same words when expressing their admiration of him. They would say, 'Mike was one of the very few people in the world who actually got off his backside and did something' about what he believed in. Now he was going to do it again and no doubt he reasoned his pre-emptive strike would make a difference by keeping the Russians out. Most likely, it was intended to be a strategic power play and a last hurrah all in one. In the end, however, it turned out to be neither.

In writing about subsequent events, I have drawn in places on Mike's book on the subject[171], on my interviews with him, my own experiences and on other sources.

In September 1978, Mike flew to the main island, Mahé, with an associate from his Congo days, Jerry Puren. They did a reconnaissance of the island and met up with Gerard Hoarau, the leader of an underground opposition group, the *Mouvement Pour la Resistance* (MPR). Back home, Mike devised a plan which in essence would involve 200 men who would undergo four months of training in secrecy in the Persian Gulf, culminating in an amphibious assault in 'rubber ducks' launched from trawlers. Cost: $5 million.

Perhaps Mike had been influenced by Bob Denard's landing in the Comores some four months earlier. It all looked so easy: early one morning, 46 men dressed in black landed on a quiet beach in three 'rubber ducks'. They had the president locked up and there was dancing in the streets before breakfast.

And perhaps Mike had been influenced by the make-believe world of the movies. It was, after all, only a year since the filming of *The Wild Geese* fantasy. Whatever, Mike was in no doubt that his coup would succeed.

Later that year, in London, Mike met Eddie Camille, the *de facto* leader of the exiles. Camille asked Mike to take their case to the South African government, and in May 1979 Mike met Alec van Wyk, the head of the National Intelligence Service (NIS) in Pretoria. The nub of it was: would the South African government provide $3 million toward the cost of the coup? In exchange, the new government could offer a pro-South Africa stance at the Organisation for African Unity, and various trade benefits. 'Mr van Wyk said the matter would be presented to the State Security Council of the Cabinet.' They declined.

Then, in January 1980, Mancham suddenly threw his weight behind the exiles and asked to see Mike, but insisted that a big power should be involved. Mike urged the exiles to approach America, but the exiles again asked Mike to take it up with Pretoria, and the NIS arranged a meeting for Mike with Brigadier Danie Hamman of the South African Defence Force (SADF), but at the very last moment Hamman was unable to make the meeting. Nevertheless, Mike met Mancham in London in March. As money was still a problem, Mancham agreed to approach Adnan Khashoggi, the wealthy Saudi-Arabian arms dealer. Khashoggi also declined.

Now, as Mancham lost interest, an exile in Australia, Robert Frichot, asked to meet Mike in the Seychelles on Independence Day, 5 June, 1980, to observe the march-past and assess the army's capability. One hundred and eighty soldiers took part, and, judging by their equipment, Mike described them as 'not a formidable force'.

Then, Hoarau arrived in South Africa from 240 days in jail without trial in the Seychelles, and set to work energetically. Soon he made valuable contacts with the NIS. He also got the Kenyan government to agree to recognise their regime, come the day.

Then, a shock. Mike said he became aware that the exiles were also negotiating with George Schroeder, the last commander of 5 Commando. Mike felt he had been double-crossed by the exiles, and threw it in. Soon, however, he was persuaded to 'overlook what was without question utterly disloyal behaviour on their part. It was an error.'

With the disaffected Schroeder and his group, size unknown, now out in the cold, Mike was concerned that there could have been a security breach ... with possible repercussions for his initiative. This was always a question mark for Mike.

Then some good news. Frichot had secured $200 000. But Mike said they would have to act fast for a number of reasons, and to facilitate this, came up with a plan for what he called 'a cut-price coup', $300 000 in fact, which would cover the preliminary expenses. Essentially, the plan called for 30 or 40 men who would accept payment after the coup.

In 2010, Mike said 'relatively small amounts' of money had been donated by a few Seychellois and a Durban businessman whose Berea home was the meeting place of the dissidents.

Then Hoarau chaired a meeting in Durban. On the agenda were such items as terms of payment, indemnities, diplomatic recognition, and 'that the principals involved in the financing of the operation should be made known to the commander'. The meeting did not deal with this point, but on Mike's insistence, he was given an answer later. 'It was: the South African government acting through the National Intelligence Service (NIS).'

Now things began to move. In early September 1981, Mancham gave a written undertaking that he was prepared to return as president, giving the coup what Mike called a 'basis of legality'. Mike visited Mahé again, this time with Tullio Moneta who had served as a mercenary soldier in the Congo. They met with a member of the resistance who was an importer of certain bulky goods in crates, and who had a cosy arrangement with customs; he agreed to receive the necessary weapons in similar crates. The plan was that about 100 men would arrive as tourists in small groups on commercial flights, and on D-Day (at the end of November 1981) would collect their weapons and carry out a bloodless coup.

But there were still no actual funds. So sure was Mike of his ground that he sold enough of his own shares in listed companies on the Johannesburg Stock Exchange to create a war chest. Some arms arrived from a Rhodesian source, and Mike claimed to have set up a company and bought enough of the bulky goods to fill 50 packing cases, and made arrangements for them to go by ship, to arrive at the end of October.

Meanwhile, as they were still short of weapons, Hoarau appealed to the NIS who said the State Security Council of the Cabinet would have to approve. Four days later, Mike found himself in Pretoria, face-to-face with Jimmy Claasens, the number two in the NIS. Mike quotes Claasens as saying 'The Cabinet has given it the OK and the Prime Minister himself is right behind it!'

The next day Claasens introduced Mike to Brigadier Hamman and Brigadier Martin Knoetze of the SADF, and asked them to supply certain arms and ammunition immediately. When the brigadiers insisted on seeing something in writing, Claasens responded, 'Ring Cape Town now and speak to the secretary to the Cabinet. She'll give you the number of the minute in which this instruction was authorised.'

This must have been done because Claasens left and Mike discussed his needs with the brigadiers. They agreed to supply AK-47s, ammunition and walkie-talkies, all gratis. They questioned Mike on the detail of the operation, and when it came to the final planning, and the training and familiarisation of the recruits, Mike said he had a friend who had a game ranch which he could use. The brigadiers, however, preferred the use of a remote SADF camp, and Mike accepted the idea.

Soon, an SADF truck arrived with the requested weapons and more. Incredibly, the SADF produced a delivery note and Mike signed for, inter alia, 60 AK-47 assault rifles, 240 magazines, ten RPG 7 rocket launchers and 102 rockets, 23 800 rounds of ammunition, 40 hand grenades, and 15 two-way radios.

Mike loved to tell how, while they were busy stashing the weapons in a lock-up cellar at the *Old Vicarage* 'like old-time Cornish smugglers burying their loot', an old lady and her grandson entered the property via a back gate, and, mistaking Mike for the old vicar, enquired where the confirmation classes might be ...

Then, two blows. Brig Hamman phoned to say the Seychellois importer was now under suspicion, and that route should not be used for the weapons. The next day, a friend of Mike's in 'another intelligence service, part of a foreign embassy in Pretoria' phoned with a similar warning.

Later, Mike was often to wonder aloud whether the source of this information had wanted to stop the coup attempt for its own reasons. One rumour had it that they were not keen on a potentially unstable new government in the Seychelles, and preferred the stable, if socialist, government of René. Another rumour was that the various South African agencies involved ultimately had conflicting agendas, and ultimately set Mike up to fail.

The second blow, which ultimately had far-reaching consequences, was that the SADF training camp was now unavailable.

Mike turned to his Plan B, namely getting the weapons to the islands by yacht. He found a yacht with spacious bilges for sale in Durban, apparently for about R150 000, and approached an experienced skipper who knew those waters. However, his asking price was sky high, apparently R50 000, and Mike abandoned this plan because he had insufficient funds.

David Alexander of Basutoland fame later wrote that he was 'nearly enmeshed' in the coup attempt 'as the skipper of a yacht that was to deliver certain items to the Seychelles'.[172] Indeed Alexander's widow, Mary, told me how Mike had visited David at their home during the planning of the coup, and had shrewdly brought flowers for her in anticipation of her likely opposition.

Now, toward the end of October 1981, Mike came to visit me in Durban and asked me to give a hand – the money would be excellent. I lied to my editor (sorry Jimmy!) at *The Natal Mercury* newspaper and moved to the family home in Hilton. I must have been influenced by a letter Mike sent me in February 1980, in which he wrote: 'Eschew security my boy and let the future look after itself. There are times when this course of action looks wrong but over the years I have found it gave the best results; in fact, frequently I have been saved in spite of myself when the security I sought was not available and better things came along later. Here endeth the lesson.'

Mike had received word that the island's defences might soon be reinforced, and was anxious to act soon or not at all. It was already early November. But Mike still did not have a viable plan, so he approached Gerard again. His contacts with the NIS now proved fruitful and 'from this moment onwards the guiding hand behind the final plans was that of the NIS.'

And indeed, a frequent visitor to the house at this time was a senior intelligence agent from the NIS. He was introduced as Martin Dolinchek, and Mike said Dolinchek was keeping his superiors informed on the planning process. Dolinchek later said he had met Mike in 1974, apparently after he had been told to warn Mike to stop meddling in South Africa's foreign affairs, specifically in Rhodesia.[173]

Peter Stiff, the well-known writer on war in southern Africa, confirms this. 'Dolinchek said they first met in 1974 when Col Hoare was attempting to put together an International Brigade to fight in Rhodesia.'[174]

According to Louis du Buisson, who later wrote up Dolinchek's story, Dolinchek's judgement became impaired after his first meeting with Mike. 'Mike Hoare wove magic spells with words, and Dolinchek was entranced,' he wrote. 'He (Mike) made the subcontinent come alive, and he could paint sweeping pictures of the major continental forces and the powers that controlled them. He had a vast store of knowledge, and he created the impression that he had his own agents running around every little village from Dar es Salaam to Lobito, that he had powerful allies in the great lobbies of the world, that he was in fact the nerve centre of a dynamic new force in the battle against the Red Menace.'

Dolinchek and Mike would meet for lunch from time to time, and Du Buisson describes the scene thus: 'Mike Hoare used to insist that the Ulundi Room (at the up-market Royal Hotel) was the best Indian restaurant in the world, and he should know because he was born in India. He knew all about the relative merits of Madras and Bombay, and could go on interminably explaining how to make the best chapatis or papadums. And he knew all the right things to say to the maitre d' and the waiters, so that they always flocked around his table like mynahs, twittering with delight.'

Then Mike offered Bob Sims and his fiancée, Susan Ingle, an all-expenses-paid holiday in the Seychelles and an administrative role which included setting up a safe house near the capital, Victoria, on Mahé.

The final plan, Plan C, was now as follows: Fifty men would travel by coach from Johannesburg to Ermelo where they would spend the night. There, they would each be given a holdall with a false bottom concealing an AK-47 rifle and two magazines containing 58 rounds. Thence to Manzini Airport in Swaziland. Border and, more importantly, customs formalities would be 'arranged'. From there, they would fly in a chartered aeroplane to Mahé, where they would stay in different hotels, and familiarise themselves with the area for a day or so, until called into action.

It was a variation on the theme of airborne assaults – remember two had been carried out not long before: Israeli commandos successfully rescued about 100 hostages at Entebbe airport in Uganda in 1976, and Bob Denard unsuccessfully raided Cotonou, Benin, in 1977.

Initially, the men were to have been members of a club called 'The Chauvinist Pigs', but Mike did not like this name and topped it with 'Ye Ancient Order of Frothblowers', after a charitable organisation that existed in Britain between the world wars for the benefit of deprived children. Mike added a South African touch: the men were rugby players and beer drinkers; this was their annual club holiday, and, cleverly, Mike proposed they should distribute plastic toys to the underprivileged children of Mahé; some of these lightweight toys (eg beach balls, plastic animals etc) would be packed in each holdall.

Meanwhile, Mike chartered an aeroplane to fly Gerard Hoarau and the new government in from Nairobi, Kenya, to Mahé within an hour of the coup.

One morning, as the pressure mounted, I said something to Mike about Gerard, who had been a very regular visitor to the house. I was astounded by Mike's response: 'Gerard who?' I soon realised there was something wrong with Mike, for he could not remember Hoarau at all. I took him to Pietermaritzburg to see a specialist who recommended he should take a few days off. His memory came back completely, and we put it down to the stress of the preparations.

Meanwhile, according to Stiff, Brig Hamman asked Col Jan Breytenbach, a reputed recce commander, to meet with Mike and evaluate his plans. Stiff says Breytenbach did so and advised Hamman to 'laugh it off'.[175]

Now, still in early November 1981, it was time for the recruitment. Mike ordered Moneta to start recruiting in Johannesburg and instructed Barney Carey, a senior ex-Congo mercenary, to network among the many ex-Rhodesian military types who used the bar at the Riviera Hotel in Durban as their 'local'. A central figure at the Riviera was the hotelier, Ken Dalgliesh.

In Johannesburg Moneta had rounded up a large group, many of whom were 'Recce boys' – the elite of the SADF. Mike wrote, 'They were led by Piet Doorewaard, a very correct leader who wanted everything done formally. Once he knew what was afoot he said he would have to have permission from Defence Force headquarters before his men could take part in this operation.'

Many of the group signed up, and Mike paid them each R1000 in cash. The rank-and-file were to receive a further R10 000, 90% of which was to be paid within 14 days of completion of the task, and 10% to be paid after 60 days subject to total secrecy being observed by all members of the group. 'Officers' were to receive more than R10 000 each. In those days R1000 would have been almost a month's salary for many white-collar workers in South Africa.

Now, in mid-November, I accompanied Mike to Durban to meet with some possible recruits. We parked in the motor town area, and as we were walking toward the meeting, I could see Mike was deep in thought. Then he said, 'I just don't know whether I should tell Jerry Puren we are going – he's got a bit of a loose tongue.' However, seconds later, we entered the motorcar showroom where the aging Jerry worked, and Mike invited him along in a specific non-combatant role.

Then to nearby Coastlands, a holiday block near the beachfront, where a flat had been made available. I knocked on the locked door. A stocky figure opened it slightly. 'Who you?' he asked, all suspicion. Such was my introduction to Peter Duffy, a Scot of some 40 years who had served three contracts in 5 Commando in the Congo post-Mike – 'for the adventure'; he completed his service with the rank of captain. Duffy had been educated at Gordonstoun (before Prince Charles's time), had managed a coffee estate on the slopes of Mount Kilimanjaro, played rugby for Tanzania, trained in karate in Japan, and had been a movie stuntman, long-distance truck driver, and a gourmet chef.

He was now an award-winning press photographer in Durban and, with his canny ways and cool nerve, was reputed to be the best 'sneak pics' man in the business. He was living on the Berea in a large house with countless indoor plants and in the garden he kept a large flock of geese – his memory of the Congo burned brightly.

228228228 *'Mad Mike' Hoare: The Legend*

Mike had persuaded the eternally cheerful Duffy, a 'big personality', to play a small but special role as the supposed leader of the Frothblowers, and Duffy was already playing the part, it seemed. About a dozen men were present. Many were ex-Rhodesian Army. Mike outlined the background and the plan.

One of the group was the young 'Stan' Standish-White, who had recently served in the elite Rhodesian SAS and been demobbed as a lance-corporal. He later said, 'My first impressions were favourable. Hoare was well turned out and sprightly, in spite of his 62 years. How much of his magnetism was real and how much a result of our own preconceptions matters not – he had it. Bolstering this impression were his infectious optimism and Irish gift of the gab. All those at the meeting were of a mind regarding left-wing violence and "the Commies" in general but Mike couldn't resist reinforcing this with some glib and erudite talk on what was obviously one of his favourite subjects: how the Red Menace was spreading inexorably through the Middle East and Africa.'[176]

Another in the group was Aubrey Brooks who had served as a colour sergeant in the elite Selous Scouts in the Rhodesian conflict. He had been trained to survive in the bush and had seen a lot of action 'at the sharp end of a very rough and very ugly war', serving one month on, three months off. Since he moved to Durban after the Lancaster House settlement, he had been approached half-a-dozen times to take part in a 'funny', a discreet mercenary operation somewhere in Africa, but had always declined. Now, having just been swindled out of his printing business, he was at a loose end, and the money on offer would get his life going again.

In his book *Death Row in Paradise*, co-written by Graham Linscott, Brooks describes the Coastlands meeting thus. 'Colonel Hoare was standing to one side. My initial impression was surprise at his smallness of stature. I had always imagined him to be a hefty fellow but actually he was small. Yet when he started addressing us I realised this was actually a giant of a man, a real gentleman officer who put his points across with absolute clarity and had a total grip on the situation. I had said I was interested in the operation but I wanted to know more. As Hoare spelled it out, we would be reinstalling a legitimate elected president who had been deposed by Marxist revolutionaries; we would have the element of surprise; the opposition would be weak; there would be popular support for us and the whole exercise would be over in a few weeks. I knew this was for me. When you've been on as many military operations as I have, you recognise officer quality when you see it, the way he ticks off every item, every possibility, and the way he keeps cool about it. You just know when you've got quality leadership. That's how I felt about Colonel Mike Hoare, whom I'd only just met.'[177]

Another of the group asked what turned out to be a good question: 'Route out, sir?' Mike explained that in an emergency they could fly out in the plane bringing the new government in. The man did not sign on.

The recruiting was now complete. The largest group consisted of mostly South African nationals; in this group of 26, according to Stiff, there were '13 operators including two doctors from 2-Reconnaissance Commando, six operators or former operators from 1-Reconnaissance Commando, and seven former operators from the disbanded 6-Recce.'[178] There were also some ex-5 Commando soldiers, a biggish group of ex-Rhodesian fighters, and a number of unaffiliated men.

The Wild Geese were about to fly again.

But, as Standish-White later said, 'Giving a bunch of total strangers this much intelligence and then leaving them to their own devices in a big city for a few days was highly unsound, and showed up the naïveté which characterised Hoare's handling of the operation.'[179]

An advance party of six now flew out of Durban via Johannesburg and Reunion, having checked their false-bottom luggage straight through to Victoria. I saw Mike reluctantly agree to Dolinchek's pleas to go as an unofficial observer, and he also flew off early, complete with a false-bottom holdall and a new name. As they all arrived in the Seychelles without incident, Mike felt the route had been adequately tested and was satisfied there was no risk in taking the weapons to the Seychelles in this way.

Forty-three men assembled at Jan Smuts Airport, Johannesburg, on Tuesday 24 November 1981, and travelled by coach to Ermelo. Very early the next morning, the holdalls were handed out. One of the men deemed the new plan too risky and pulled out. In Manzini, Swaziland, they boarded a Royal Swazi National Airways Fokker aircraft for Mahé. Mike was surprised when they landed in the Comores to take on a passenger, a Frenchman, as he (Mike) had been told beforehand that the only people on board would be his men. And now at twilight, Mike was leading the Frothblowers through the formalities at Mahé.

Dolinchek later recounted his conversation with Mike in the car park outside the airport building. Quote: So I said, 'Did you have a happy landing?' He said, 'My God, I've got a bunch of people who have been drinking all the way from Swaziland and I do not think they will last.' Those were his actual words to me. He said, 'We will have to do it tomorrow because that bunch will not last until Friday,' – this was Wednesday. Unquote.[180]

Meanwhile, with only two Frothblowers still to go through customs, an official found some fruit, a banned item, in the Frenchman's baggage. This put customs on alert, and they searched the next man's bag thoroughly, finding his weapon. Other versions of how things went wrong have been flighted, but the above is Mike's and it is supported by Duffy who said he was standing right there watching events unfold and going 'quack, quack' with a plastic duck in an attempt to distract the customs men.

When some shots were fired, Mike realised they had lost the vital element of surprise and decided to carry out the coup then and there (as opposed to midday two days later) even though he had not prepared a formal plan for an immediate attack.

The first objective was now to take the nearby army barracks and secure the airport. Mike and some of the men made their way to the barracks, but an armoured car appeared, blocking their way. They withdrew in the fading light, determined to attack in numbers at dawn.

Meanwhile the airport buildings were being defended by the men, but one of the mercenaries had been shot dead accidentally, and another was wounded. Sixty-five civilians were herded into a hall – this was later construed as hostage taking. Some of the men captured an armoured car, killing the commander in the process.

Now, night has fallen. One of the men in the control tower, Charles Goatley, reports that Air India flight 224 from Harare, Zimbabwe, en route to Bombay, India, is asking for permission to land. Mike replies in the negative – three times – but one of the men, Alan Mann, later told Mike he had countermanded the order. And so, in spite of the lack of proper runway lights and obvious disorder in the control tower, the Boeing 707 came in. The inference that Duffy and others drew was that for some reason the flight had not bought sufficient fuel to land elsewhere, for example Mauritius, and had to land at Mahé, come what may.

Mike, meanwhile, rang the head of the resistance, demanding to know why he and his men were not lending support.

When the plane landed, Mike sent Duffy to get the captain, Umesh Saxena. The 65 passengers and 13 crew remained on board. Mike introduced himself as 'Mr Tom'.

Both Mike and the captain want the plane to take off again, and refuelling is arranged. Now, a 75 mm recoilless rifle is shelling the runway from afar, aiming for the Boeing. Mike gets first the minister of defence on the telephone, then President René, and asks him to stop the cannon fire so that the plane can take off. Soon the shelling stops, and an hour later René agrees the plane can take off – without Mike and his men. Saxena and his co-pilot inspect the runway for obstacles in spite of the danger involved.

Now Saxena, grateful to be on his way, spontaneously says, 'Is there anything I can do for you chaps? You saved me; perhaps I can save you.'

Some of the men want to fly out with Saxena, and Mike has to concede an attack on the barracks at dawn might incur as many as 'ten killed and wounded'. This is regarded as unacceptable. The group considered and ruled out Bombay, Oman, the Comores and Mauritius as destinations. That left South Africa. 'Undoubtedly the men thought that as the South African government were completely behind us in the attempted coup, surely they would do what they could to help us on our return.'

Mike ordered the withdrawal, emphasising that no weapons or ammunition should go on board. But he himself had decided to stay and fight; he was sure some of the ex-5 Commando men would join him, as would the resistance. But, at that moment, Moneta entered the room with one of the men, Kurt Priefert ... who had a Colt 45 in his hand. Mike capitulated.

All but seven of the whole group boarded. The plane was fired on during take-off but was not hit. Soon Mike noticed some of the men had their AKs with them – Moneta had countermanded Mike's order. Then, 'Saxena came back from the cockpit with a broad smile on his face. He held out his hand. "Congratulations, Mr Tom!" he said warmly. "I cannot thank you enough for getting us out of there".' Then, incredibly, he handed out glasses of champagne to Mike, Moneta and Duffy.

Goatley, a pilot, was posted to the cockpit to make sure the plane actually flew to South Africa; this was to count against the men later.

The plane landed in Durban at 5 am on Thursday 26 November 1981. Six hours later, the men disembarked, shaking hands with the captain and his crew as they left the plane. They were formally arrested by a brigadier who announced that they would be charged with hijacking an aeroplane. Mike immediately remonstrated, saying an arrangement had been made between him and the captain. Thence by Hercules C-130 to Pretoria, and Zonderwater Prison which Mike described as 'harsh, sordid and utilitarian. In places some flowering bougainvillaea triumphed over it.'

There was no getting away from it – it had been a wild-goose chase for the Wild Geese. In addition, massive costs had been generated by the misadventure for everyone involved.

So, who was to blame for the failure? Puren, in his book published co-incidentally in the same week as Mike's *The Seychelles Affair*, was in no doubt. 'The fault for the failure of the coup must lie squarely with Mike Hoare. Cardinal errors were made in planning and execution. The second fault was that Mike failed to exercise determination and push through with the plot once the arms had been discovered. In the event, of course, it very nearly did work.'[181]

Puren also said that Mike had panicked after his return to the airport from his attack on the barracks nearby. 'I find it painful to recount the behaviour of a former Congo comrade-in-arms and a friend in civilian life, but there is no other way to describe Mike's actions except as panic. The unexpected turn of events had completely unsettled him.'[182] *The Star* of 7 December quotes three unnamed mercenaries saying something similar.

Probably, the gulf between mowing the lawn at Hilton on D-Day Minus 2, and leading 50 lightly armed men, quite a few of whom may have been drunk, into an unplanned night battle in a foreign country on D-Day, was too big a jump for a 62-year-old civilian who had not fired a shot in 16 years.

Other factors contributing to the failure would have been the absence of rockets, inadequate ammunition supply (only 58 rounds per man), the inaccuracy of the butt-less rifles, the fact that the men had done no training as a team – not even practising radio procedure – and, as Standish-White put it, that the men had let Mike's 'colourful reputation override the many unanswered tactical questions'.[183]

When I asked Mike about the 'panic' allegations, he replied without hesitation, 'I am not noted for panic in military actions. Rubbish!' Barney Carey later told *The Natal Witness*, 'Mike was in charge of his men and in control of the situation.'

Mike himself was quite clear about the fundamental cause of the failure. It was that he did not know the men, and more importantly, they did not know him; they had not had the opportunity to build up complete trust in him, whereas in the Congo, for example, his men had. 'When the chips were down and a decision had to be made as to whether we would fight or not, the total lack of cohesive thought or close understanding of one another proved fatal.'

So why did he not go back to the game ranch idea, where he could have got to know the men, and vice versa? 'The whole thing was taken out of my hands and run by … Pretoria.'

Mike admitted that he had been over-eager to carry out the coup, and this was part of the reason why the attempt had 'come unstuck'. He described a conversation he had with Moneta on the plane thus: 'Well, Colonel, what now?' 'Five million dollars and we do the job properly, Tullio. There's no future in cut-rate coups!' Tullio laughed.

'He decided to hand me his ultimate accolade. "Colonel," he said, "you got balls".'

The story was front-page news in South Africa for three weeks. Think 'saturation coverage'. *The Daily News*, Durban's afternoon newspaper, told the world what had happened in one word spread across the whole front page that first afternoon: HIJACK!

The next day's *Natal Mercury* led with: Co-operate or be killed under the strap heading: 'Polite' mercenary warns hijack plane's pilot. In the story Saxena 'said he had been confronted by a polite mercenary leader after he had been hauled into the terminal building. The mercenary leader told him: "Follow our orders and you will not be harmed. Disobey and you will lose your life".'

It was only on the afternoon of the 27th that the mercenaries started to be named. *The Star*'s page one lead story was headlined: Hoare linked to coup bid. The city-late edition of *The Daily News* took a local angle: Durban man's key role in hijack raid, which referred to Duffy. A smaller headline proclaimed: No sign of 'Mad Mike' Hoare. However, in the city-late-final edition, we read: Hoare named as the coup bid leader.

On Monday 30th, however, and extraordinarily, we read: 'Mad Mike' Hoare hunted by police. The story quotes a spokesman for police headquarters in Pretoria saying Mike had 'not been taken into custody' and was being sought. On 1 December, however, we read in the *Mercury*: Hoare in prison, according to police sources.

In Zonderwater, the men all made statements, and Mike was whisked back to Hilton for the police to remove all documents associated with the coup attempt. The police also said they would arrange for the unused weapons and ammunition to be removed from the cellar.

Then, on 2 December, Mike, Moneta, Duffy, Goatley and Dalgliesh were charged provisionally with kidnapping and appeared in a Pretoria magistrate's court; they were remanded to 7 January and had to report to the police once a week. Mike's bail of R10 000 was paid in cash by Sims's son, Leo Baxter, who then whisked Mike away in a helicopter to his mansion in Bryanston, Johannesburg.

All the other men, the number given was 39, were set free and went to ground. A furore erupted. The media weighed in. The *Rand Daily Mail* of 3 December, for example, devoted the entire front page to the subject, including a huge photo of Mike. The headlines screamed: Hoare and his men dive for cover, Release of 39 proves SA's role says René, Malan to probe use of SA dogs of war, Minister says Khashoggi put up cash for raid, and Seychelles parades battered coup-bid prisoners.

But the most memorable headline was: What law did they break? – Le Grange. In a statement that was to attain a certain notoriety and that was typical of the *hardegat* attitude of the South African government at that time, the minister of police, Louis le Grange, said, 'They only shot out some windows and ran around in the bush. You tell me what laws they broke in South Africa.' In the main story, he is quoted as saying the police 'could not find that they (the 39) had contravened any laws'.

The freeing of the bulk of the men, however, was regarded as a scandal. In a story in *The Star* on 3 December 1981, headlined: Decision could ground South African Airways abroad, the US State Department is quoted as saying that 'the South African government was a party to the Hague Convention on hijacking "which obligates the government of South Africa to submit for prosecution or to extradite persons accused of unlawfully seizing an aircraft".' The *Sunday Times* of 6 December led with: SA-world air links in danger, saying 'South Africa is facing a real threat from its Western allies to sever air links in retaliation for Pretoria's failure to prosecute the men in accordance with international anti-hijack agreements'.

And then there were the colour articles, with headlines such as: Bail just petty cash as Hoare lands in lap of luxury, He's the most caring person I've met: safari woman, Hoare – the hottest hired gun around, and John Vigor's My friend Mike in which he says Mike 'would have made a perfect Robin Hood or a gentleman pirate on the Spanish Main'.

On 15 December, the security council of the United Nations established a commission of inquiry under Resolution 496 (1981), to 'investigate the origin, background and financing of the mercenary aggression'.

Meanwhile, seven members of the group had remained on the island. Roger England, Brooks, Carey and Sims had been rounded up and badly beaten in jail. Dolinchek was detained but not beaten. Puren was arrested 17 days later, claiming he had survived in the wilds on coconuts. Ingle was arrested but released in June 1982 when all charges against her were dropped.

On 5 January 1982, Mike and all the men were re-arrested. They appeared in five courts around the country on four counts under the Civil Aviation Offences Act No. 10 of 1972. The kidnapping charge was dropped. Mike appeared in a Durban magistrate's court and his bail was upped to R20 000.

An item in the *Rand Daily Mail* the next day told why the men had been re-arrested. It said, 'Whitehall sources let it be known that it had joined other Western countries with secret warnings to South Africa last year. They made it clear that there would be sanctions against flights to and from South Africa unless the mercenaries were prosecuted.'

Ten of the Recces appointed an advocate to handle their defence, and it became obvious that the SADF was paying his bill. Mike announced he would arrange the defence of the balance of the men, at no cost to them. He set aside R50 000 for this purpose and consulted a top Johannesburg advocate who insisted that Mike should implicate the South African government by telling the entire truth; Mike was against this idea. The advocate also predicted Mike would be found guilty and imprisoned. Mike then appointed advocate Mike Hannon to defend the men and himself – and the six on the island.

During this period, I was a regular visitor at the *Old Vicarage*, and Mike and I would go for long walks in the countryside beyond the village. He would go over the events, and we would strategise his defence. Though he was loath to implicate the South African government in the coup attempt, he often repeated what the NIS's Claasens had said, namely, 'The Cabinet has given it the OK and the Prime Minister himself is right behind it!' Mike took great comfort from this and felt that it would make a difference in the trial – although of course he was not being tried for the coup attempt.

Then, in late January, the UN commission visited the Seychelles and interviewed Dolinchek at length. He told them inter alia, 'My government was very well aware of Mike Hoare's plan', and 'South Africa gave a tacit approval for the operation' and 'The government gave tacit approval to it – gave the armaments'.[184]

This stands in contrast to a statement in early February to the commission by Pik Botha, minister of foreign affairs and information, who 'drew attention to the statement made by the prime minister of South Africa on 3 December 1981, in which he had declared that the South African government had neither initiated, approved of nor known about the attempted coup'.

To assist in paying the various legal fees, Mike had some round cloth badges made in two diameters, 105 mm and 60 mm. The badges said, 'The Wild Geese' and showed a goose flying over an island, and palm trees. A display in the *Sunday Times* of 20 June 1982 advertised the badges for sale for R5 with a signed certificate naming buyers honorary members of The Wild Geese. For another R10, buyers could also order signed copies of the Corgi edition of *Mercenary*. Later, Phyllis advertised the badges for sale for $5 in *Soldier of Fortune* magazine in America; someone signed Mike's name on the numbered certificates. There was a lot of sympathy for Mike and his Frothblowers, and more than 3500 people responded.

This sympathy played out in an unusual way for me around this time. A traffic policeman stepped out of the shrubbery one day as I was zipping along in suburban Durban, and stopped me for speeding, which I was. Quickly he took out his official fines pad and filled in my car details and details of the offence, etc. Then,

Him: 'May I have your name please sir?'
Me: 'Chris Hoare'
Him: 'You mean Hoare like 'Mad Mike' Hoare?'
Me: 'Yes, that's right.'
Him: 'You are not related to him, by any chance?'
Me: 'Actually, I am. He is my father.'
Him: '*Ag*, no man! Why didn't you tell me when I stopped you? I would have let you off, but now I have filled in all the details, so I can't ….'

The trial opened in the Supreme Court on 10 March 1982 before Mr Justice Neville James and two assessors. The venue was a cavernous building which had been prepared in College Road, Pietermaritzburg.

The next day, the *Rand Daily Mail* described the scene as follows in an article headlined: Hoare as cool as ever. 'Colonel "Mad Mike" Hoare breezed through the first day of the hearing with a nonchalance that has almost become a trademark. Wearing an immaculate suit, his hair neatly groomed, he was whisked into the grounds of the court in a silver Rover only seven minutes before the hearing was due to start. He made his way through the besieging mass of photographers and reporters with aplomb and strolled calmly into the courtroom.'

Mike was 'Accused Number One'. Two of the men, both doctors, turned state witness. The main charge was that the men had 'unlawfully by threat of force or by intimidation and without lawful reason seized or exercised control of the aircraft'. All 43 of the accused pleaded not guilty. The men, for their part, contended that they had flown 'from Mahé to Durban at the invitation of the captain of the aircraft, who made the invitation because we had saved his plane from destruction on the ground by cannon fire'.

Scores of witnesses were to be called, chief among them Captain Saxena. But the Indian government would not allow him to come to South Africa to give evidence. Mike hoped this would be sufficient grounds for the prosecution to withdraw the charges. But they would not. 'It was becoming plain to us that somebody was very keen to have our heads on a platter. The general feeling among the accused was that this was (the state-owned) South African Airways, who felt their operations worldwide had been jeopardised by our action. It seemed certain to us now that the government were determined, come what may, to nail us.' Mike felt he was being made a scapegoat, and would later quote Leviticus 16:21 in this connection.

In the end, Saxena's evidence was taken on commission in the Seychelles. A lawyer later told Mike this was a 'travesty of justice'. Saxena admitted to the commission he had not mentioned a hijacking in his statement to the South African Police. He also admitted he could have escaped from the men when he examined the runway.

Mike's evidence-in-chief and cross-examination took four days. Then Hannon excused himself on the grounds that there had been a conflict of interest among his clients. As Mike's funds had now run out, he decided to defend himself, as did two of the men. The other non-Recces appointed an advocate and each man gave evidence. Mike was able to cross-examine them and got Lieutenant Nick Wilson to confirm that in his statement to the police he had said that prior to embarkation on the Air India plane, 'Some of the resistance movement and some of the guys refused to go. Colonel Hoare was one of them. We ignored him and put him on board anyway.'

There were many such light moments during the trial and during the breaks when Phyllis and some of the other womenfolk served tea and cakes. However, it had become apparent to those of us watching the proceedings closely that it was not going well for the men.

Mike presented his closing argument. He made a logical attempt to counter the charges, but, without a lawyer by his side, his address was light on legal substance. Probably, he had seen the writing on the wall.

In part, he said, 'I conclude my lord with the observation that I know I am not being tried for an attempted coup, or for my political beliefs, but I ask you to weigh my actions in the light of what I am now about to say. I see South Africa, my lord, as the bastion of civilisation in an Africa subjected to a total communist onslaught. In the last 22 years I have watched, and in many cases physically battled against, its inexorable encroachment into Africa. The catalogue of Russian conquest by default is formidable: Ethiopia, Congo Brazza, Senegal, Angola, Mozambique, Zimbabwe, Seychelles – until South Africa itself is threatened. The enemy is at the gates, my lord. The hour of reckoning is at hand. I prophesy that South Africa will fall prey to Marxist doctrine before the turn of the century unless South Africans of all races become actively engaged now in the fight against communism! My lord, I see myself in the forefront of this fight for our very existence. I see my men as a noble band of patriots motivated by the same ideals. It is my sincerest wish that South Africa will recognise us as such.'

Judgment was handed down on 27 July 1982. Nothing had

made any difference, neither Saxena's invitation, nor the fact that Mike had been forced onto the plane; neither the pilot producing champagne, nor the fact that the pilot had not mentioned a hijacking in his statement. Nor, of course, Mike's assertion that the Prime Minister himself was right behind it.

The judge said, 'Colonel Hoare's whole case depends on Saxena volunteering to take the accused with him as an act of gratitude because Colonel Hoare had negotiated a cease-fire and saved the plane. The court is satisfied that there is no truth in this version.'[185] Further, 'All the accused entered the plane as a group, most of them were armed and it seems to be abundantly clear that in acting in this way they effectively exercised control over the airplane.'[186]

The judge also said, 'It would be naïve to suggest that the NIS was not aware through Dolinchek's agency of Hoare's projected mercenary expedition.' But, 'Colonel Hoare does not claim to have had any direct contact with Mr PW Botha and the cabinet and any allegation that he has made about their involvement in the affair is pure hearsay.'[187]

Mike was flabbergasted. 'This ... came as a shock to me. I recalled clearly that the judge himself had advised me against calling any government witnesses when I had wanted to. However, he seemed to have absolved the government of all knowledge of the affair very satisfactorily, which is what most of us imagined the trial was all about.'

Mike was found guilty on three counts. Later that day, he sought expert opinion on the question of an appeal and was advised that the judge would be likely to grant leave to appeal the convictions.

The next day, 28 July 1982, in mitigation of sentence, Mike simply said: 'I did my duty as I saw it; I brought my men back and I am proud of that.' He was sentenced to an effective ten years' imprisonment. Duffy, Moneta and Doorewaard got an effective five years each, others received lesser sentences, and the remaining 34 men received effective six-month sentences. We had assumed that leave to appeal would be granted on the turn, but to our horror, Mike and the men were whisked off to jail within the hour.

The Times in London said, 'Colonel Hoare took his medicine calmly. A small dapper figure with a trim goatee beard, he appeared to the casual observer every inch the respectable chartered accountant which he has been for most of the past 20 years. A very different personality emerged from evidence at the trial.'[188]

Seven days later, the judge refused Mike leave to appeal his conviction, the basis of which was that another court would have rejected Saxena's evidence. Mike had also applied for leave to appeal against his sentence, calling it 'harsh and inappropriate', and this bid too was unsuccessful. It was the end of the road. As journalists were wont to write at the time, Mike's goose was cooked.

Now Mike found himself in 'observation', inside the 'cold, stark and forbidding' Pretoria Central Prison which had been built in 1908. Luckily, he later joked, he had had 'the finest training a man can have for prison – boarding school'.

Mike was in the whites-only section of course, and got a cell to himself, about 4 by 2 metres, with two steel doors and lavatory bucket with lid. His prison number was 1496/82. If he qualified for a one-third good-conduct remission, he could be released after six years and six months on 29 March 1989.

Early on, an old lag took Mike aside and gave him some advice. He said if Mike wanted to retain his sanity and achieve a measure of happiness while inside, he should identify a man less fortunate than himself and make life easier for him wherever possible.

Initially, Mike was allowed one 30-minute non-contact visit a month and could write and receive one censored letter a month. After seven weeks, he passed out of 'observation' and qualified for 20 visits a year and 30 letters in and out. As a hard-labour prisoner, he was told he could receive training in the trade of his choice; he chose cabinet-making, but the reality was that there was no-one available to train him.

In all, he sent me 14 letters from prison. In his first letter, dated 15 October 1982, he wrote, inter alia: 'I have lost 27 lbs (12.25 kg). Morally, the whole thing is hard to take, and in typical Celtic fashion I hit well-pronounced highs and lows. Mentally, I am struggling to maintain a sane outlook, and holding the thought that once the men are off the island ... the government will have a chance to help me.

Most days, Duffy and I work in the carpenter's shop. We are carving proteas into imbuia panels which form part of grandfather clocks we are making.

'I cannot speak too highly of Peter's wonderful spirit and moral support. He is a gem. Fortunately, I have my Shakespeare with me and as a mental exercise I learn choice passages by heart. So far, I have learned some 200 lines and realise I have the makings of a complete ham! Whenever we queue up, I mouth the lines and get a strange comfort from those beautiful words in such sordid surroundings. How about (Shakespeare's) "Daffodils which come before the swallow dares and brave the winds of March"?'

In a later letter, he wrote, 'Here's a line from my (forthcoming) book. In Pretoria Central, I am brought before a female colonel in regard to my request for a dictionary. She regrets I am not allowed one. Reason: the convicts might look up words the warders won't understand. I let that pass. May I have a book of the London *Times* crosswords then? Sorry, no. Reason: if we let you have it, all the other convicts will want one!' Later, Mike sent me his thanks for a book I had now been able to give him of the *Sunday Times* crosswords, saying, 'I do one per day to keep the brain working.' Reflecting on the inequalities of justice, Mike said, 'A man who is reasonably cultured and enjoys classical music and good books, he suffers more than a ruffian who has never read anything.'

Another job that Mike had was toilet cleaner. 'Early on, Peter (Duffy) was volunteered to clean the lavatories, which was one helluva job, of course. Peter said, "You volunteer and we'll do it together".'

As the months went by, naturally Mike had a wide range of prison experiences. If in the Congo he had witnessed extreme barbarity, here he was exposed to the cutting edge of depravity, for example, being subjected to a 'short arm' inspection to see who had been dismantling rosaries and implanting the beads into slits in their foreskins.

At that time, capital punishment existed in South Africa. It is estimated that 92 people per year were hanged in Pretoria Central during the 1960s, 1970s and 1980s – nearly two people per week, on average.[189] Mike, who was anti-capital-punishment, was moved to write this chilling description of his experience: 'Six blacks were to be hanged that Thursday morning at dawn. Since lights-out the previous evening we had heard singing coming from the 100 or so blacks in "Beverly Hills" (the adjacent maximum-security wing). There were hymns and traditional prison songs, haunting, plaintive and never-ending. They went on steadily right through the night to keep up the courage of the doomed men. I could not sleep and stood looking through the bars towards the prison a bare 100 yards away until the first rays of dawn broke red across the hill behind it. Their families waited at the gate. The whole of our prison was quietly astir and full of an indefinable expectation. Dawn broke. The singing rose to a mighty crescendo and stopped suddenly with a triumphant "Hallelujah!" In my mind I heard the awful clang of six trapdoors dropping simultaneously. A shiver ran through me. The horror of judicial murder was a physical reality which had taken place the other side of that wall.'

As Mike was looking at a ten-year term, he naturally took what legal steps he could to free himself. Early on, he got a Durban lawyer to petition the Judge President to allow him and the men to appeal to the Appeal Court. He and Phyllis – and the lawyer – were hopeful, and even discussed bail. Then, in September 1982, a young Pretoria lawyer, Ernst Penzhorn, offered his services gratis. He worked tirelessly, but nevertheless the petition was unsuccessful.

Simultaneously, Mike was looking for opportunities to escape. 'I'm in for 10 years, so I have got to do that.' At one point, Mike was in a building squad that was working near a public road. Mike thought he would be able to somehow swing out over the road using a block-and-tackle, and someone, perhaps a son, would be there waiting on a motorbike; but the idea came to nought.

Another time, Mike became aware that the canteen for prison officers was being refurbished. All the equipment and materials had to be removed from the prison every evening, and brought back again the following morning. Mike figured he could get himself rolled up in some unlaid wall-to-wall carpeting, and leave the prison in that way. But the local 'king rat' persuaded him against it.

Meanwhile, Mike's claim that the prime minister and the cabinet did know about the planned coup, would not go away. Peter Stiff describes what happened in parliament in February 1983. Quote:

The Leader of the Opposition PFP (Progressive Federal Party) in South Africa, Dr Frederick van Zyl Slabbert, put the government under extreme pressure during a five-day parliamentary no-confidence debate. He introduced a motion that the Seychelles coup attempt illustrated the government's incompetence. 'Here,' he said, 'we have a coup planned at the level of brigadier in the SADF and where top people in the National Intelligence Service were aware of it.'

Dr Ferdi Hartzenberg, a Conservative Party frontbencher ...... suggested that although the 'cabinet' might have no knowledge, this did not preclude individual ministers from knowing. Hartzenberg looked directly at General Malan [chief of the army] across the floor of the House and asked if he had known. The general replied firmly in the negative.

Dr Hartzenberg turned to Prime Minister PW Botha. 'Did you have any prior knowledge, arising from your being the political head of the National Intelligence Service, which has been implicated through Dolinchek?'

PW Botha sat dumbly without answering. Hansard recorded unemotionally that he refused to reply.

'I receive no reply from the Prime Minister,' Dr Hartzenberg hunted on ferret-like, refusing to let go. 'He does not wish to reply? He does not wish to say yes or no?'

Dr Hartzenberg questioned him interrogatively: 'The Prime Minister says the cabinet did not know, but will not say whether he knew. The only conclusion I can draw from that is that he did know.' Unquote.[190]

As if that was not enough to vindicate what Mike had been saying all along, the *Final Report of the Truth and Reconciliation Commission*, in a subsection entitled Unconventional Military Operations, states, 'The Commission finds that the attempt to overthrow the Seychelles government was an operation undertaken by senior operatives of the NIS and the Department of Military

Intelligence, with the collusion of elements within the SADF. As such it was a violation of international law and an infringement of the sovereignty of the Seychelles government. The death of a Seychellois citizen in the operation was a gross human rights violation. For these acts, the Commission finds the following to be accountable in their capacities as heads of agencies of the state directly involved in the operation: Prime Minister PW Botha, Minister of Defence General Magnus Malan, Head of the Office of Chief of Staff Intelligence Lieutenant General PW van der Westhuizen, and the National Intelligence Service.'[191]

The UN's commission of enquiry accepted it would cost about US $1.28 million to repair and restore the airport, and that the overall loss of tourist revenue would amount to about US $16.7 million.

Meanwhile, Mike got a job as a 'tea boy' in the prison hospital, and later joined a group as a handyman-plumber. Here he worked with and got to know some of the black prisoners. Later, one of his favourite prison stories was how his 'new black friends' wanted to call him 'Sir' whereas Mike was happy to be called 'Mike'. 'In the end, they settled for a combination of "Mike" and "Sir" and called me "Sirmike", all one word. I was delighted with the prison knighthood!'

Large certificates that Mike kept show that on 3 March 1948 he became an associate member of The Institute of Chartered Accountants in England and Wales, and that on 1 January 1960 he became a fellow of the same institute. Now, in prison, he received a letter from the institute saying that as a result of his conviction, they had removed his name from their register. This went particularly hard with him.

Then, after nine months, Mike was made an A-grade prisoner which entitled him to 30 contact visits a year. Things were looking up. But Duffy was worried about Mike's naivety. He later told me Mike was 'too straight' and 'not devious enough'. So the devious Duffy set about teaching him, recalling, 'Once, the colonel had a small radio and for some reason had to hide it. Where did he hide it? Under his pillow. That was a bad place. You don't hide things under your pillow – rather hide them under <u>someone else's</u> pillow!' Duffy was street-wise, all right.

Now Mike took up the building of model sailing ships in his cell – secretly. Duffy, now nicknamed 'Gadaffi' by the warders, was at that time working as a storeman and, crafty as ever, was able to provide small pieces of wood.

'I had nothing to make the ships with except nail clippers, and this pair had a little knife that folded away, only an inch-and-a-half long. I had to have that sharpened, and Peter was able to sharpen it for me. Later, he got in among the dentist's equipment and brought me what we used to call "scimitars".' Mike gave these model sailing ships to friends; Moneta for example got a topsail schooner – with a scroll.

Duffy got a 1:300 scale, six-inch brigantine. A scroll which lived inside the base of the model is signed by Mike and dated March 1984. It says:

'The brigantine PETER DUFFY is typical of the smaller ships which traded in the Baltic in the latter half of the 19th century. She would be about 200 tonnes and perhaps 110 feet on the water line. I made the model in my cell, B2 no. 44, most evenings over a period of two months, as a form of mental therapy. Please forgive its crudity, but this I blame on too few tools and too many thumbs. Please accept it now as a mark of the very great esteem and genuine affection I feel for you; and as a modest 'thank you' for your unswerving loyalty and manly conduct during the term of our unspeakable imprisonment. Your strength of spirit carried me through many a dark day and abysmal night, and showed me:

The mind is its own place

And can make a heaven of hell

A hell of heaven.

'God will bless you my hardy Scot.'

Meanwhile, a British barrister and MP, Nicholas Fairbairn, had offered to defend the six in the Seychelles *pro deo* and came to South Africa on his way to the Seychelles to be briefed by Mike. Brooks, Carey, England and Puren were, nevertheless, found guilty of treason and sentenced to death. On a lesser charge, Sims got 10 years and Dolinchek, who had not been defended by Fairbairn, got 20 years. South Africa paid a $3 million ransom to secure the release of Dolinchek and the other five;[192] they were pardoned by René and on 23 July 1983 they returned home.

Mike hoped that the South African government might now feel less constrained, and do something to ease his plight, but it was not until April the next year (1984) that the authorities moved Mike (and Duffy) to Pietermaritzburg New Prison, some 16 km from Hilton.

As a family, we found it all distressing and we agitated behind the scenes in various ways to get Mike out. What particularly irked us was that at no point did the South African government ever say to Mike or the family privately, 'OK, so we supplied the weapons and we planned much of the coup attempt, but you must understand we have to bow to international opinion, especially regarding landing rights. You need to serve a short sentence and, if you keep your mouth shut now, we will contrive a way to release you as soon as we reasonably can. We have not thrown away the key. You will not be serving ten years.'

In March 1983, Phyllis wrote to one of the staunch Wild Geese supporters, Harry Smith, in Pittsburgh, USA: 'It now looks as if the SA government is quite prepared to sacrifice Mike and the boys to appease world opinion. We now feel that the time has arrived to ask all our members to write a letter to the South African prime minister asking for the release of the boys held in Pretoria Central Prison. They are Mike Hoare, Peter Duffy, Pieter Doorewaard, Ken Dalgliesh, Tullio Moneta, Mike Webb, Chas Goatley and Vernon Prinsloo. Your letters will have a great effect on their morale and carry a lot of weight with this government.'

Around this time, while on an internal flight to Durban, Mike's brother Ben spotted the justice minister, Kobie Coetzee, and went across and asked him to find a way to release Mike.

But none of these actions bore any fruit, not then anyway.

Now in Pietermaritzburg, Mike was put to work as a petrol-pump attendant and nurseryman. Duffy, however, was released almost immediately – leaving Mike feeling 'mortified' initially. Conditions here, however, were better than Pretoria, and Mike wrote, 'If it is possible to say I was happy in prison, then I was happy here.'

On 10 August 1984, Phyllis wrote to Smith again. 'Pmb (Pietermaritzburg prison) is a completely different ball game, all the warders etc are 100 percent behind Mike, most call him Sir, and one or two come to attention when he speaks to them, incredible. They have put Mike on the third floor all to himself, he doesn't mix with any other prisoners, and is generally not suffering but for being parted from his family and unable to make money.'

I visited Mike half-a-dozen times at the Pietermaritzburg prison, always fulfilling his standing order for ham-and-cheese rolls, Callard & Bowser butterscotch sweets, and Romany Creams biscuits. We joked about how the roles had been reversed since my boarding-school days, and always discussed our latest tactics for getting him out. I usually brought with me a book or two for him on Christopher Marlowe. We would meet in a bright ground-floor room which had a couple of wooden benches. Sometimes a warder hovered in the corridor outside, but mostly not. On one occasion, I was surprised when the warder said to me after a while, 'Let yourself out when you are finished', for the room opened onto the car park inside the prison complex.

Around this time, a senior Pietermaritzburg lawyer, Leslie Simon, offered his services gratis. As Mike was now regarded as a 'model prisoner', it was felt he could be released after serving one-third of his sentence, namely in November 1985. But even that seemed a long way off, and many people did what they could to secure an earlier release.

At one point, I wrote to the president of South Africa, PW Botha, appealing for clemency on the grounds that Mike was 65 years old. I half-expected him to reply 'You can't be serious! Just recently Mike Hoare was causing mayhem at Mahé airport with a bunch of tearaways.' But the president did not reply, not then anyway, and not as such.

In October 1984, I formed a one-man 'Free Mike Hoare Committee', found the addresses of about 30 quality newspapers around the world and produced a letter to send to them to coincide with the 20th anniversary of the Stanleyville massacre in the Congo (24 November 1984). The strategy was that they would publish the letter, and those who had benefited from, or knew of, Mike's good works in the Congo, should write to PW Botha, pleading for Mike's release. In the end, my letters did not go out on the advice of Professor SAS Strauss, a heavyweight lawyer who was now adding muscle to our attempts, also gratis.

Then Strauss asked me to get Mike to write a two-page summary of his personal role in the freeing of the 2000 nuns and priests who were being held hostage, abused and terrorised in the Congo in 1964. However, in a grim letter to me dated 24 November 1984, Mike wrote:

'The stress of prison life has sapped my brain of any constructive ability. A two-page anything is totally beyond me. This week has been the worst in the two years and four months of my imprisonment. I was seized with such depression mid-week that I honestly thought I was going to die one night. I have zero energy and find it hard to carry out my modest but intensely boring daily task. The walk up the hill to the petrol pumps leaves me gasping. I am really worried. It is not a question of going to the doctor and asking him to put me right. The cure is beyond him. It lies in myself. Bosman (author Herman Charles) went stark staring mad after four years of Pretoria Central. I imagine I am headed in the same direction. If I were a bovine type I suppose I could sit it out and emerge unscathed. But I am not. I am a typical Celt. I have marked ups and downs.'

In the end, I myself wrote the piece for Strauss, but this initiative was overtaken before it could fly.

Meanwhile, although there were people supporting Mike behind the scenes, he also had detractors. One was 'Social Democrat' whose hostile letters were published in *The Natal Mercury* in September 1984 under the headlines: Hoare's crimes were serious, and Keep him in jail. Someone calling himself Another Seychellois, wrote, 'Col Hoare is a '*mauvais*' (a bad sort) and should be kept in prison for a long time.'

Similarly, a letter signed by one Douglas Alexander appeared in

The Daily News under the headline: Wild Geese are overrated. He attacked Mike as a leader, and said, 'The Seychelles fiasco by the new breed of death-or-glory boys was in keeping with the dismal record of the original Wild Geese in the Congo.'

Rob Griffin was having none of it, however. In his response, also published in *The Daily News*, he said, 'Having known several professional adventurers and a fairly large number of military, political, business and media leaders in several countries over the past 20 years, I would rate no man higher for physical and moral courage, for inspiring and effective leadership or for the compassionate stewardship of his men.'

Mike had a lot of other supporters too. Ernest Comley wrote on 9 August 1984, in part, 'President Albert René of the Seychelles has set an example of forgiveness and understanding seldom found in world leaders, and our president might well follow this and release Mike Hoare to his wife and children. Many feel that he is being made a scapegoat and that there is a great deal of cover-up with respect to government involvement. This may or may not be so, but the crux of the matter remains that he has been punished enough and it is high time he was released.'

Others, including Mike's friend Joseph Codeghini, A Seychellois, BA Middleton (from Queensland, Australia, and a friend of Mike's from his motor-business days) and Lorenzo, wrote to the local newspapers appealing for Mike's release.

Mockler, perhaps surprisingly, also took a pro-Mike stance, saying he thought the Seychelles coup attempt was 'morally justified' and the punishment was 'disproportionate to the "crime", pitiless in view of Hoare's age ... and above all hypocritical in view of the nature and known activities of the government that is imposing it'.[193]

Then, in December 1984, a South African Press Association report was headlined: 44 prisoners pardoned by President. The report did not mention Mike, but said the prisoners would be released by the end of December after being pardoned; the prisoners had to be over 65 years of age, had to be first offenders and to have completed a quarter of their sentences. The terms seemed tailor-made for Mike.

A report in *The Natal Mercury* of 27 December said Mike 'could be released early in the new year in terms of an amnesty granted by the State President as a sign of "Christmas goodwill".' *The Daily News* of 4 January 1985 said Mike would be 'one of a group of 85 people who have been granted a release in terms of President Botha's Christmas amnesty, it was confirmed by a spokesman for the Prisons Department today'.

A quarter of Mike's term came up on 29 January 1985. The day came and went – to our consternation. Then, on 4 February, for no apparent reason, Mike was taken from the gardens where he was now working among the roses, stripped of all privileges and put in solitary confinement.

Weeks of introspection took their toll and Mike asked to see a psychiatrist. Eventually, he was allowed to spend his days constructing a model sailing ship, dedicating it to his 'two dearest American friends, Don and Elaine' (Rickard).

Duffy started talking about a grand homecoming for Mike. His idea was to arrange a helicopter to whisk Mike home from the prison grounds. There would be champagne, caviar, and cucumber sandwiches on tables with white tablecloths in the garden.

But still there was no official word, so after 90 days of solitary confinement and with no resolution in view, Mike resolved to stage a hunger strike. At his next visit from Phyllis on 5 May, he asked her to notify the press. She had a counter-proposal, however: Alistair Gilson, a lay minister at Phyllis's church, and a Christian group would begin a fast for Mike's release that evening. Mike consented to the idea.

On the afternoon of the very next day, 6 May 1985, a prison captain drove Mike home. He was free. When Phyllis phoned me with the news, she kept on exclaiming, 'It's a miracle, it's a miracle.' Not having heard about the fast, I had no idea what she meant.

I joined the celebrations at the *Old Vicarage*. The only one not there was Mikey – after finishing school he had gone to study in America under the wing of Don Rickard, and indeed Mikey had become like a son to him.

The phone at the *Old Vicarage* did not stop ringing. I screened the calls. Many were from the media, but the sentimental Mike took only one of them – from the daughter of George Clay, the journalist who had been killed on the approach to Stanleyville. I then suggested to Mike that we should hold a press conference to achieve a measure of peace.

The local Hilton Hotel kindly offered us a venue gratis, and about 30 journalists and cameramen descended. Putting on an especially cultured English accent – think Sir John Gielgud talking posh – Mike initially thanked PW Botha for the amnesty, Fairbairn for 'exerting all sorts of pressures at a very high level when he got back to Britain', René for his clemency, Phyllis and the other women, and many others.

He then entertained the media with some of his prison stories; he told the story of a 'magic moment' in his life that had given him 'tremendous joy' in prison.

'It happened, strangely enough, on the day that I was sentenced. I received a letter from America, and it said: "Dear Colonel, On the day of the Stanleyville massacre in 1964, you and some of your men and Colonel Raudstein of the US Army rescued an American family who were living on the edge of the *cité* which was overrun by rebels. You placed a small girl in the back of your truck and drove her to safety. I am that little girl. I am now 24 years of age. I have my own husband and my own family and I love them very much. Thank you for my life." That letter kept me warm in jail. It was a magic moment.'

He emphasised, however, that his 1014 days in prison had been 'measureless misery', overall. (Later, he told me he had first noticed this useful adjective in Churchill's writings.)

Mike told the media he would not be able to answer any questions, but did not say why. He concluded, 'I shall write the full story of what happened, to put the record straight. I think I owe it to my men and to my family. Looking back, I am still of the opinion my decision to abort the attempted coup was the right one. Bringing back the men was my duty at whatever cost and I am proud I did it.'

Friends and family came back to the *Old Vicarage* afterwards, and the stories flowed, in particular from the likes of Duffy, a master raconteur, and the islanders Sims, Brooks and Carey. Maud Frean was also there, and wrote a 700-word article in the *South Coast Sun* of 10 May.

Under the headline: 'Mad Mike' holds them spellbound, *The Sunday Star*[194] carried a report by Graham Ferreira, a senior journalist. He opened with the kind of facile remark that would infuriate Mike: 'Leave aside his politics, and that he kills people for money.' He then redeems himself thus: 'Listening to the world's most famous mercenary is an experience. I stood at the back of the little room crowded with reporters, cameramen, friends and mercenaries, and listened to a man who, if he had chosen to be an explorer, mountaineer, deep-sea diver or university professor, would have made as much money by selling himself. He spoke of his experiences in jail. He spoke of his band of mercenaries, of his wife and of the wives of other prisoners. He quoted poetry, joked, made tears well in the eyes of his friends and family. He is a consummate speaker: passionate, yet controlled; sincere, yet formal. You could say a lot of things about Mike Hoare, but it would take a foolish man to call him a liar.'

Soldier of Fortune magazine immediately sent a senior editor, Bill Guthrie, to Natal. Guthrie was not your typical soldier of fortune; he was in fact an intellectual who had studied widely, including archaeology and literature. He was the type who could well have known several 16th-century Norwegian dialects. As I was soon to witness, he could converse with authority on almost any humanities subject. Before he met Mike, we had lunch at The Edward. One of his first questions was, 'What sort of books does Mike read?' I told him, 'At the moment, he is studying Christopher Marlowe.' Guthrie was stunned. I realised he thought he was going to meet a 'goon'– a professional gangster.

Guthrie had a number of meetings with Mike, and wrote about his encounters in the January 1986 issue, saying: 'I hadn't expected a Renaissance man. We discussed religious writers, Greek history, medieval English drama, kayaking, sailing, motorcycling across Africa, the writings of Mohandas K Gandhi and, of course, mercenary soldiering. But the best time was a long South African winter afternoon spent in the sunlit study while Hoare told what he had done in the Seychelles.

'Then he brought out a bottle, and we drank and talked about – believe it or not – early English language and Christopher Marlowe's poetry. Hoare had memorised long tracts of Marlowe's verse, and spoke professionally and eloquently of Renaissance poets. He quoted freely from criticism and scholarship. Had Col Hoare been Dr Hoare, he would have been the best drama professor I had met.'[195]

I was in that sunlit study and I saw how Mike rose to the occasion. When he realised he was in the company of a man who had memorised the whole of the *Encyclopaedia Britannica* or whatever it was, by the age of 10, or whatever it was, Mike began engaging with Guthrie on a tricky aspect of Shakespeare's *King Lear*. The ensuing discussion took an hour, and covered the fields of religion, literature, history, politics, art, and so on. Mike was in his element. This was a classic example of something I had seen Mike do on occasion: engage at a high intellectual level with someone new on their subject. It never failed to make a huge impression.

On 5 June I signed a contract with *Soldier of Fortune* to supply 10 000 words and 40 photographs. The deal was worth $5000. I then spent several days with Mike, recording our interviews on cassette tape. The article and photographs were published in the issues of November and December 1985, and January 1986.

Meanwhile, Mike had been widely quoted in the press as saying that he had 'hung up his guns'. Mike put it like this at the time: 'I have not made a conscious decision on this one. (But bear in mind) my style of leadership is a personal one. I like to actually physically lead the men – this is very unusual, I mean can you imagine a colonel of a regular unit going on patrol? But I am not like that. It's essential for a leader to show he is prepared to do everything he is asking his men to do, to share their dangers. So to that extent, my days of active leadership in the field are probably over.'

As the euphoria of being 'out' subsided, Mike turned his attention to generating some funds. An offer came in almost immediately from the Circle Century Club, a group of macho types who met from time to time to have a drink too many, and listen to a topical speaker.

The unusual thing about this club was that the speaker was expected to use foul language, really foul language. As we know, Mike did not swear, but he accepted the terms because he needed the money – which was exceptionally good. My recording of the speech reveals that Mike bowed to their wishes once or twice. It is also worth noting that Mike did not regard the word 'bloody' as a swear word, and used it all the time; in fact, it was his standard adjective for banks, literary agents, certain British publishers, the Australian accent, the Labour Party in Britain, Belgian soldiers in the Congo and anyone who incurred his wrath.

Several hundred men turned up at the club after work on 18 May 1985. Mike gave them a fast-paced blow-by-blow description of the involvement of the NIS and what happened at Mahé airport. He revealed that he had arranged with the head of the Seychelles resistance that airport customs would be manned on the day of their arrival by resistance members; bringing the weapons in holdalls would be a 'calculated risk', he said. He touched on the trial, and told some risqué prison stories that he knew would amuse the bawdy audience; for example, he related how 'one chap came and told me about a bloke who was selling his arse for a "cutty" – four slices of bread. I said, That's disgusting! The chap said, You're damned right it is, the usual price is six slices.'

Then Mike accepted an invitation, on an honorary basis, to address the student body at the University of Pretoria, an Afrikaans institution. Why? 'There was a group among them who relished the thought of being rebels – they revered the fighters in their history. They stirred my Irish blood.'

Said Mike, 'The audience was enormous, by the left! Grim-faced professors, too. I said, "It is a pleasure to be here, especially as one rebel speaking to another", and there was a great hurrah.'

He gave a formal and thought-provoking address to about 1300 students, speaking commandingly for about 40 minutes.

The *Pretoria News* the next day, 5 June 1985, headlined the story: SA can learn from experiences of Belgian Congo – Mike

Hoare. In part, the article says, 'He told the students of some of his experiences in the Congo, but steered clear of the Seychelles debacle, and drew parallels between the Congo in the 1960s and South Africa now. Four years before the independence of the Belgian colony, a Brussels academic, AJ van Bilsen, presented a paper, "A 30-year plan for the emancipation of Belgian Africa", which was a timetable for independence.'

Mike was offering for the students' consideration a type of Van Bilsen plan as a way to take South Africa beyond apartheid. It was a continuation of his speech at the Elangeni Hotel in 1975. In particular, he put forward the possible merits of a federal system to cope with the diversity of people in South Africa, and the benefits of raising a bourgeois class.

He concluded on a high note. 'Guard your fatherland. Stand firm. Be fair. Use the tools of free enterprise. Lead wisely.' And, 'I pray we may never know the horrors and futility of war in this country.'

A book on the whole Seychelles affair was likely to be another source of revenue, Mike thought, and he wasted no time in getting started. We shared the cost of a personal computer (something that had only recently come onto the home market) and he mastered word processing quickly.

It took him only 90 days to write the 85 000 words. He dedicated the book to Phyllis 'and all those loyal women who stand by their men when things go wrong'. His literary agent, David Bolt, sold the book by auction to Bantam Press in London; it was published in 1986. 'The best I ever did out of a book was (an advance against royalties of) £12 500 for *The Seychelles Affair*. And $5000 for the paperback which was done in America.' Mike always maintained, however, there was 'no money in books for authors'.

On 27 October 1985, a *Sunday Times* report said a 'hard-up' Mike had advertised his house for sale in *Soldier of Fortune* magazine. The advertisement had described the cellar as being tested to hold over two million rounds of ammunition, the report said. But what really annoyed Mike and earned that newspaper his undying enmity was the headline: 'Ammo dump' for sale.

Later that year, a friend of mine, the literary agent Betty Crompton Lomax who played a leading role in the South African Writers' Circle, invited Mike to address their meeting on 4 December in the Durban city centre. In his opening remarks, he paid tribute to two members who had written several times to the newspapers, calling for his release. One was Ernest Comley, and the other was a great friend of Mike's, the Italian restaurateur Joseph Codeghini whom Mike described as the 'doyen of the literati' and as the 'poet of Piacenza'.

Initially, Mike shared his knowledge of book publishing with the large group of writers, touching on a wide range of topics including literary agents, advances, rejection slips, serialisation, subsidiary rights, writers' egos, etc. He said he had always been guided in his writing by the phrase 'Euphony, brevity and simplicity' which he thought might have come from Somerset Maugham. He also encouraged them, quoting his 'great friend' George Calpin; 'George wrote the most beautiful Swinburnian prose, peerless stuff, and one day he told me a real truth. He said, "If you are determined to write, remember this: when you are faced with that sheet of blank paper, unknown forces will come to your aid." And that is true. Where do those phrases come from? Somebody is helping you ...'

He then turned on the charm and told some prison stories to the rapt audience. He said that learning beautiful lines of poetry helped remove him from his sordid surroundings. 'I learned two, three thousand lines, mostly from my favourite poet, Marlowe. This got me into trouble ...'

Early one day, Mike decided to memorise the passage from *Doctor Faustus* that begins, 'Was this the face that launched a thousand ships?' and wrote the lines on the back of an envelope, forgetting that this was totally forbidden. On his way to his work that day, he was stopped and searched by a large-size warder, and the piece of paper was found.

Warder: You write this rubbish?

Mike: No, sir. Wish I had. As a matter of fact, those lines were written 400 years ago.

The warder looked at the paper suspiciously, held it up to the light, looked at Mike and said, 'You don't fool me, *ou kêrel*. These lines was written about half-an-hour ago ...'

Mike also related how he had got Phyllis to buy a portable radio for one of his black workmates in the plumbing section, James. In return, James and three of his friends offered to sing for Mike. Came the day, James 'took up a piece of half-inch pipe, unthreaded, and gave them the downbeat. They began to sing. It was the most beautiful sound I have ever heard. Great heavens, I was listening to a four-part arrangement of *The Lord is my Shepherd*, sung as a madrigal, with each successive phrase sung on the back of the other, floating out through the bars.' Mike was moved to tears, he said, by the contrast between that 'harsh and cruel place' and the beautiful singing, and turned away ...

The audience got the full Mike Hoare treatment that night – there was hardly a dry eye in the place by the time he had finished.

Mike hardly talked about the coup bid and its aftermath – he lived in the present and the future, in the realm of plans and projects, of schemes and dreams, not past failures. If you did ask him about it, he would say a few words and smoothly change the subject.

He was, however, quoted in *The Natal Mercury* of 21 August (probably 1986, as the story is datelined London where he had gone for the launch of his book *The Seychelles Affair*), as saying, 'I regret the failure but not the attempted coup. I still feel better to have tried than not to have tried at all. There are times when I have regrets, but the principles remain the same – namely, it was anti-communist, an attempt to stem the encroachment of Marxism in Africa.'

The article continues, 'Asked if he would return to being a mercenary soldier, Col Hoare said anybody fervently anti-communist would have to consider if the cause was worthy and viable, and if he was fit enough to do it. But he would not consider making another coup attempt in the Seychelles, he said.'

In the same article, he talks with bitterness about how the South African government had treated him. 'I had the feeling that because of their involvement they should perhaps have treated us differently. I am not saying they should not have sent us to prison, but we were treated as rapists and murderers and child molesters, exactly the same.'

An article in *The Natal Mercury* of 14 July 1986, attributed to Sapa-AP and datelined Paris, starts 'Col Mike Hoare said yesterday South Africa double-crossed him by sponsoring his assault on the Seychelles in 1981, then jailing him when it collapsed.'

To the end, Mike could not accept that he had hijacked the Air India plane as such, and he thought subsequent events indicated that if it was a hijack, it was certainly an unconventional one.

In 1994, when Duffy, always the livewire humourist, heard that one of the air hostesses who had been on the Boeing 707 was coming to Durban, he somehow managed to pose as a chauffeur, fetched her from her beachfront hotel and drove her to a restaurant where she was to have lunch with a group of people. When they arrived at the restaurant, he asked her if she could see Duffy. She looked around, but could not see him, she said. Then he took off his chauffeur's hat, and she responded, 'Goodness gracious, I've been hijacked again!'

Twenty-five years after the 'hijacking', Duffy arranged to meet the pilot of the plane, Captain Saxena, in Bombay, India. According to the *Sunday Tribune* of 15 October 2006, in an article headlined: Indian plane captain meets his hijacker, they greeted each other like old friends and embraced. Furthermore, the accompanying photograph shows them toasting each other with, you guessed it, mugs of beer and lots of froth!

Duffy is quoted as saying, 'I was really surprised to be given such a warm, welcoming reception. I already have had lunch with the captain's family and they are taking me out for supper tonight.'

Duffy later told me that meeting the captain had given him closure, and that he felt he had been able to right some wrongs in Bombay. There were 32 media people at the meeting in Saxena's spacious flat, including six TV cameramen, he said.

On 17 October 2006, Mike wrote in reaction, 'This visit of Peter's is extremely important to us. I don't know how or why he managed to arrange it. I sincerely hope he tried to get Saxena to admit that we took him and his plane full of passengers out of danger at his suggestion.'

Duffy also told me that on Christmas Day 2009 Saxena rang him to wish him a happy Christmas.

And that is where the Seychelles saga ended for Mike. It is, however, tragic to note that in November 1985, Gerard Hoarau was assassinated in a London street, near his home, by a gunman acting with an accomplice. Neither has ever been arrested.

14. The Pilgrim

'We treasured the thought of the cleansing march, the hardship which must absolve us of our various misdoings in some mysterious way.' – Mike Hoare

In 1986, Mike undertook a pilgrimage, probably as a form of penance for what he called his 'misdoings', but no doubt also because he loved walking and because it would be a bit of an adventure, maybe even a spiritual adventure.

Drawing on what Mike wrote later[196], the pilgrimage idea was born in a serendipitous moment. One day, while cleaning the lavatories in 'jug', as he would call prison, Mike found a newspaper cutting hidden behind one of the pans. It was from *The Times* of 21 August 1982 and a feature article by Rob Neillands carried the headline: On the road of cockleshell pilgrims. The article was about a pilgrimage to one of Catholicism's most holy sites, the cathedral at Santiago de Compostela, in Galicia, north-west Spain, a journey on foot of at least 700 miles from a starting point in France.

According to the legend, the remains of James, the son of Zebedee and a prominent disciple of Jesus, were buried where the cathedral now stands. Called the 'Way of St James', the route has been trodden for more than a thousand years; in 1986 only about 1800 pilgrims/walkers are estimated to have completed the *camino* to Santiago, whereas in 2016 the number was about 278 000.

The idea of doing the pilgrimage inspired Mike even though he was not a Catholic – he had been raised a Protestant, if anything, he said. He managed to somehow lay hold of a book on the subject, and he enrolled two fellow inmates. 'We treasured the thought of the cleansing march, the hardship which must absolve us of our various misdoings in some mysterious way and we began to plan such a pilgrimage against the day when we might be released from prison. Of course we knew deep in our hearts it was only an exercise in fantasy, but none of us would admit it. It kept us going. At that moment I was facing a term of ten years ...'

Now free, and since one of the prison pals had committed suicide and the other was back inside, it fell upon Mike to fulfil the dream. Indeed, he said the pilgrimage had become 'a compulsory journey, something I had to do if I wanted to rest peacefully hereafter'. Later Phyllis told Mikey that Mike had made a covenant in prison with God: were he to be released early, he would do the pilgrimage in a spirit of penitence and gratitude.

And so, early in 1986, Mike dug out the maps and started making plans for a family pilgrimage. He rented out the *Old Vicarage* and flew to London in May, lodging with his sister June who had the top two floors of 15 Harley Street in the West End; his mother, now in her nineties, was also living with June by this time. He bought a Leyland Highwayman campervan and Phyllis arrived from South Africa. Mikey and Simon, who were now both at university in America, flew in. The walkers all bought Meindl boots, started getting fit, and in early June drove to their starting point in south-central France.

Carrying only water and a packed lunch, the three 'boys' walked the well-marked '*Chemin de St Jacques de Compostelle*', passing through pretty countryside and picturesque villages, and fending off attentive dogs. Mike later wrote, 'Walk began at Le Puy-en-Velay. We reached Conques in eight days covering 202 km *à pied.* Really most enjoyable.'

But it was Phyllis's efforts that made it possible. Every day, she would navigate the back roads to an agreed campsite, set up camp for the night and prepare the evening meal. Then in early July she fell ill and they all returned to London to get treatment for her.

Mike used the unexpected opportunity to meet Mark Barty-King, the founder of Bantam Press and something of a legend in publishing, to discuss the publicity campaign for *The Seychelles Affair*; the upshot was that Mike agreed to return to London in mid-August for the launch. Mike also learned the book would be launched in South Africa in the September, but declined an interview on *Prime Time*, the South African show-it-all television programme, saying he would be in the wilds of Spain at that time, completing the walk.

The family returned to Conques at the end of July and continued to walk the sacred way, but now, to avoid the worst of the severe heat, they were obliged to start very early and finish for the day before lunch. This slowed progress down and took some of the shine off the walk.

Mikey recounts a memory thus: 'One especially gruelling day, Simon, Dad and I collapsed by a fast-flowing river to escape the heat. It was well over 30°C in the shade, and we were parched, our legs and feet aching from the 25-km-a-day marches we had been averaging the past two months.

'As a rare treat, Dad had sprung for a bottle of chilled milk and a woven basket of succulent black cherries. The arrangement he offered was that we'd share the milk and cherries equally, but rank – hath-ing its privileges – he would start. Like cats round the dining table, we followed as he raised the beaded bottle of milk and began to drink. As the bottle rose ever higher, and with no signs of him slowing, Simon and I began to panic. "Dad," we yelled, "you said we'd share the milk! A third each, you said ..." Wiping his chin he responded: "And I plan on doing just that. Thing is, my third's at the bottom!"'

In due course, they sojourned at the medieval town of Moissac – which was to feature in their lives again – where Mike relished the stories of historical characters who had graced the area: The Black Prince, Wellington, and Roland. By mid-August they had reached St-Jean-Pied-de-Port and from there crossed over the Pyrenees mountains into Spain, descending to Roncesvalles, and thence to Pamplona. They had covered some 500 miles on foot, and had to call it a day.

Now it was time for what Mike called a 'private pilgrimage'

to the nearby French coastal town of St-Jean-de-Luz. It was here that EW Hornung, the well-known English writer who created the character of Raffles, was buried. Hornung was one of Mike's childhood heroes.

Raffles is a charming and debonair Englishman – and also a cat burglar who can quote Keats while cracking a safe. He was educated at a public school, captained the first eleven and is now a resourceful and cunning spin bowler. He is daring, athletic, has experience with women, and is prepared to lie or worse if necessary. He is a sympathetic villain.

Mike eventually found the grave. He later wrote a sublime paragraph which reveals how he saw himself: 'I often wonder if Hornung lived long enough to know of the unique position he held in English literature. To be able to create a fictional character with whom generations of readers could identify, and grow to love, even though his hero was a gentleman crook, has secured for him a hallowed place in the hearts of very many of us, romantics, lovers of cricket, of good manners and the England of the late Victorian period.'

Mike flew to London on 18 August and spent four days promoting *The Seychelles Affair*. A full itinerary included an appearance on BBC Television, press interviews, and a day of publicity in Dublin. He also sold the paperback rights to the book to Corgi, for publication in August 1987.

The family arrived on 23 August and soon the boys left to continue their studies at Baylor University in Waco, Texas. The Seychelles book was published in South Africa at the end of October, and Phyllis returned to South Africa in the November. Mike remained at June's.

Now, in early December 1986, Mike wrote to say he was considering a trip to Darjeeling, India, or possibly Ireland. Or he might rent a cottage in Wales to apply himself to his writing. But in the end, he decided to finish the pilgrimage, winter or not.

On 8 December he wrote in a letter to me, 'The pilgrimage has come to mean something very important in my life and I shall not rest until I have completed it. Cannot explain in a letter.'

Later he wrote: 'In mid-December, I went back to Pamplona in Spain where we had left off. I began the walk again even though temperatures had plummeted and my first day of 24 km was walked mostly in the rain. Worse than that, everything was shut, and the hotels were boarded up. In one place I knocked on the door of a home and asked for accommodation; the woman took me in and was only too pleased to do so. But you don't want that at the end of a long day's walk. I even went to the police once to look for a referral.

'There are no tracks, as in France, and one is confined to the main road – which left me at the mercy of large trucks and bad drivers. A few kilometres from Logrono, a huge lorry with trailer came so close as to cause me to fall down the bank – not so pleasant with a 20-pound (9kg) pack.

'Then, in Logrono I met a bloke who said, "Please, I beg of you, do not go on, you will get killed; from here on the truck drivers are the worst in the world, they don't move, they just go straight." And, the hotelkeeper there told me I would not be able to do the last 80 miles of the pilgrimage because snow had already fallen. I realised trying to walk at that time of year was a stupid thing to do, and decided to hurl it in.'

15. *The Francophile*

With 12 people at the table, there were usually several conversations going on at once, but as soon as they heard Mike say, for example, 'So I told the prison warder to go and ....' all conversations stopped and all heads turned toward him. And then the stories flowed.

Early in 1987, still at June's in London, Mike decided to go to America to both visit the boys in Texas and his old pal Rickard in Colorado. Then, on 19 January, he wrote, 'I have run into a snag at the US embassy with my application for a visa. They require all sorts of things from the Supreme Court regarding my sentence.'

Thus, Mike returned to Natal in February 1987. After an unsettled period, he and Phyllis moved back to the *Old Vicarage* in Hilton. Ever trying to distance himself from his mercenary soldiering background, and always entrepreneurial, he hit on the idea of offering courses for would-be bookkeepers. They did not catch on.

Early in 1988 Mike sold the *Old Vicarage*, moved to Pennington on the South Coast, and kept himself busy turning the bookkeeping material into a manual.

He wrote to say his mother had died in her sleep on the night of 20/21 February 1988 and that it would 'regrettably not be possible' for him or Ben to attend the funeral of this 'great personality' with a 'sometimes difficult artistic temperament'. She was 94 years of age and had spent most of her last two decades with June, her youngest. However, Mike and Phyllis went to London in May, did a barge trip with friends on a canal in France and toyed with the idea of buying a barge; they returned in July to a rented house in Hayfields, Pietermaritzburg.

In December 1985, Mike had started writing up the story of his involvement in Katanga and the search for Donaldson and MacKay. He now polished it and sold the 57 000-word story as *The Road to Kalamata – A Congo Mercenary's Personal Memoir* to Lexington Books in America, and according to the contract dated 29 August 1988, the advance was $5000. Two years later, Lexington sold the 'television and motion picture rights' to Avocet Productions.

On the back cover the former US ambassador to the Congo, 1963-1966, G McMurtrie Godley, says, 'The scene is accurately and vividly described.'

Bill Guthrie, PhD, the former executive editor at *Soldier of Fortune* magazine, says, 'Mike Hoare .... is the twentieth century's most famous mercenary soldier and, believe it or not, the most literate, witty, touching writer on this dark and strange subject. *The Road to Kalamata* is comedy, chronicle, confession and murder mystery. It is also the last word on the war for the Congo, as it was fought, by one who fought.'

Peter Worthington, editor of the *Ottawa Sun*, said, 'As well as an eloquent, colourful writer and storyteller, Hoare is a thinking soldier.'

The book was published in May 1989. *Soldier of Fortune* magazine says in its June 1989 issue, 'Readers looking for a shoot-'em-up in which ill-disciplined, wild-eyed merc-devils mercilessly crush African savages won't find it here. Rather Mike Hoare is a thinker, an officer and a gentleman from the old school with deep respect for military tradition and discipline.' The reviewer also refers to Mike as a 'ruthless taskmaster' who used a 'velvet-glove/iron-fist approach' to his men.

The book was published in the UK by Cooper on 9 November 1989.

In November 1988 Mike and Phyllis moved to a flat in downtown Pietermaritzburg and during this period Mike started working on a book of short stories about mercenary soldiering in the Congo. Initially, he called it *The Light at Faradje* after one of the best stories, later changing the title of the book to *Warriors for the Working-day*, and later to *Congo Warriors*.

And now, four unsettled years after his release from prison, Mike was making plans to move back to England. The fact is, even after 40 years, he had not become South African in any way; he had not learned more than about ten words of Afrikaans or Zulu, he had not become a South African citizen or voted in any elections, he did not like biltong or rusks, and he had not adopted the sport-and-braaivleis lifestyle – in fact he detested braais, usually describing them as 'eating burned meat in the dark'. Anglo-centric to the core, he stubbornly regarded everything British as best …

Was it the close proximity, both in time and space, to the Pietermaritzburg prison? Was it the heavy presence of the unapologetic government that had jailed him? Did he fear, as apartheid began to be dismantled and the country began to Africanise, that white people's standards would not survive? Or was it simply that Mikey and Simon were at university in America, and in England Mike and Phyllis would be a lot closer to them?

Probably for all these reasons, on 29 November 1989 Mike and Phyllis left South Africa for London, having sold their furniture, appliances, etc. They spent most of the winter with June who was now living at 39 Montagu Square, also in the West End of London. Mike and Phyllis also drove through France to Spain with a view to settling in San Sebastian or even in St-Jean-de-Luz.

Mike was always happiest when working on a project, and that winter completed writing the 21 stories in *Warriors* and dedicated the book to Colonel EAS (Paddy) Brett DSO MC TD, RTR. According to a contract dated 7 May 1990, Hale paid an advance of £2000 and published the book as *Congo Warriors*. Hale also said they would bring out a paperback edition of *Congo Mercenary*.

In 1989, before the book was sold, one of the stories, *The Committee Men*, was published in the June issue of *Soldier of Fortune* magazine; it was accompanied by a bio-piece that described Mike as 'legendary' and 'educated, thoughtful and idealistic'. *Soldier of Fortune* published the article again in 2008. Mike and I also felt that the last story in the book, *The Light at Faradje*, had movie potential, and Mike submitted a part of that story for inclusion on the KwaZulu-Natal Literary Tourism website in 2008.

In the same winter (1989/90), he also worked on a 30-minute 150-slide audio-visual presentation on the disaster in the delta. In a letter dated 21 March 1990, he said, 'My plan is to show it as part of a lecture entitled *A Spirit of Adventure*. The possibilities for school audiences appear good and there should be a reasonable living in the venture.'

On 14 May 1990 Mike wrote asking advice, saying, 'I am studying the possibilities of making a living out of magazine articles, for instance travelling the new trans-Africa highway from Algiers to Lagos.' Then on 4 June he wrote, 'I am working on another chapter to my book on bookkeeping which Hale are showing an interest in.'

Around this time, an advertisement appeared that had Mike's name on it: 'Chateau to let'. It got better – he could do a certain amount of work as part-payment of the rent. The chateau was not a castle – it was more of a manor house which had been semi-fortified. Set in spacious grounds, the house and outbuildings formed three sides around a grass quadrangle; the fourth side overlooked a valley of vineyards, and on a distant hilltop was Lauzerte, a fortified town dating back to 1241. The chateau had seven bedrooms, most with bathroom en suite, and it dominated the village of Miramont-de-Quercy in south-west France. The village was Mike's kind of place: tiny, boasting only a few homes, a post office within walking distance, and a restaurant. The locals called the chateau *La Maison Rose* as it was painted pink. Mike and Phyllis rented a wing of the chateau from the owners, Jimmy and Mary Huizinga, and helped them supervise the restoration of the chateau.

Mike and Phyllis then drove back to London, staying at Montagu Square again. That December, Mike gave his first public showing of the audio-visual, now called *Mokoro*. He wrote to me saying, 'The people were genuinely thrilled with the show and never wanted it to end. Small audience, therefore small cheque, but a beginning.' In 1993, Phyllis took the show to America and gave a number of presentations. Mike was talented at this sort of script work, and the show always moved audiences, many to tears.

Mike spent the winter of 1990/91 writing a book detailing some of his non-military adventures in Africa. With the working title *A Spirit of Adventure*, it was as near to a biography as he was to get. Hale and Bantam and two other publishers rejected it.

In early 1991, Mike dreamed up another money-making scheme: he was going to hire a villa in Spain and run classes for people who wanted to learn English. He ran the idea by me as I had had experience in that business. I could not understand how a 'legend in his own lunchtime', as Mike sometimes jokingly referred to himself, should have to resort to such small-time schemes. Over and over. Get on the public-speaking circuit, I advised him, you will enjoy it and you will really make some money. But he would not, most likely because, as always, he wanted to distance himself from the mercenary image which had created the legend.

Then Huizinga came up with a suggestion that included payment for Mike's services, and in addition Mike was fed up with England; it was not the England he had known in his younger days, he said, what with wheel-clamping, new taxes, and too many foreigners. Miramont was to serve as a home base for Mike and Phyllis for the next 14 years.

Then Sir John Baring, a member of the Barings banking family and about to become chairman of BP, and his wife Lady Sarah, a relative of Mary Huizinga by marriage and a Churchill, bought the chateau. Mike became their go-to man.

'It was a strange position. The job was humble, but Lord John and Lady Sally (the Ashburtons) always invited me to meet their friends. I got an insight into the British aristocracy that few people would ever get. It was intriguing.' The well-mannered Mike had nothing but admiration for the well-mannered British aristocracy.

Phyllis once told me that the guests always somehow knew in advance who Mike was, and were always keen to meet him and to hear his stories. But their British diffidence got in the way, she said, and they never knew how to get him talking. Mike was well aware of the situation and, feigning nonchalance, enjoyed stringing the guests along. With 12 people at the table, there were usually several conversations going on at once, but as soon as they heard

Mike say, for example, 'So I told the prison warder to go and ....' all conversations stopped and all heads turned toward him. And then the stories flowed.

Mike loved France and almost everything about it. He once wrote, 'We enjoy living here in France, very basic and low key but entirely stress-free.' Once he wrote, 'The emotional French, how I love them'. Indeed he loved them, to the extent that, when the French were playing the Irish at rugby, he would shout for the French!

Early on, Mike received a telephone call from Youichiro Kawai, the US agent for Namikishobo, a Japanese publishing house who were publishing *Congo Warriors* in Japanese in April 1992. Mike declined to see him, but, he said, when a large sum was mentioned, he agreed. His initial reticence may also have had something to do with his almost life-long antipathy toward the Japanese, and his reluctance to buy anything Japanese as a protest against them, saying, 'Those of us who fought in Burma can never forgive the Japs their unbelievable cruelty to our men taken prisoner at Singapore in 1942.'

While he was living in Pietermaritzburg in 1988/89, Mike had resumed the model ship-building he started in prison. Now he went back to it, buying a kit of the *Astrolabe*, a full-rigged 14-gun warship of the French navy (1812). About a metre long, it took him two years to complete.

One day in 1996, a fax arrived for me. The news was startling. Mike had rented a chalet in the Swiss Alps for the forthcoming winter, and was inviting immediate family to visit for a few weeks. Just get there, and I'll take care of the rest, was his attitude.

My wife, Terry, and I, and our children, Shannon (three-and-a-half years old) and Sean (12 months old) arrived at Geneva airport just before Christmas. Grandpa was there to meet us in his Citroën. As we drove to the chalet in canton Vaud, he explained how it had all come about.

A British lawyer had written to him at Miramont saying, 'I have a client who is extremely wealthy; he wants to meet you and ask your advice. He is prepared to pay you $2000 literally for an hour, and longer than that pro rata. Please treat this seriously. He is not a gangster, he's not going to ask you to do this that or the other, he wants genuine advice.' Lord John begged Mike not to go, saying it had the makings of a disaster, a possible kidnapping, or worse. Mike was not to be deterred, however, and they met at the Holiday Inn in nearby Toulouse.

'I arrive and go in; he is a nondescript man, short, my age or older, trappings of money, highly educated, false name. I said, "What are we going to talk about?" He hedged around the subject for 20 minutes, and we talked about everything. I couldn't figure him out, but he was not a military man. Then I picked on any subject and started talking about the Seychelles affair. I said the root cause of the failure of the Seychelles affair could be put down to one thing: failure on the part of the commander to know his men. Which is true. I said that in any action, if the commander does not know his men, it will not succeed. They will have no respect for him, is one aspect. Mere discipline will only get you so far. There comes a moment when you will want them to do something which they will do because they know you. If they don't know you, you are nobody to them, you're a number.

'Whatever it was he wanted to know, this was the turning point. He said, "That answers it all." I asked if he was thinking of doing something of this nature. He declined to comment on that.' They talked for one-and-a-half hours and the fee paid for the rental of the Swiss chalet for five months.

On arrival at the chalet, *Les Planards*, we noted it was typical Mike – on a lonely hillside outside a tiny village. And, for once, not a post office in sight. In this case the village was Rossinière, near Chateau d'Oex, the hot-air ballooning centre of Switzerland. With deep snow all around, it was pure chocolate box.

Gerry, with her husband Pasquale d'Adamo, and their young children Amrit and Amar, motored up from their home in Vasto, near Pescara, Italy.

For several weeks we spent our time doing the family-reunion routine: cooking and eating together, trying out restaurants, sightseeing, open-air skating in Gstaad, skiing, short hikes, tobogganing and so on. Mike, now in the role of *grand-père*, would dutifully read stories to all the little 'uns in the early evening as they gathered around the fireplace in their pyjamas.

One day as Mike and I drove away from the chalet, we stopped on the track to engage with one of our Swiss neighbours. Something about Mike's manner had the man confused, and eventually when Mike admitted to being Irish, not English, the man finally understood, exclaiming, *'Mais voilà! Vous n'avez pas l'air Anglais.'* Mike's apparent lack of an English air became a source of great amusement between us over subsequent years.

Towards the end of the holiday, I offered as a thank-you gift to Mike, the best thing I could think of: a ride through the mountains in a hot-air balloon. He was genuinely horrified at the idea, proclaiming himself 'a devout coward in the air'. Indeed, I had heard him claim this many times before, usually followed by, 'I prefer *terraferma* – the more firmer, the less terror.'

And so it was that, for a bit of fun, we family members conjured up an imaginary 'gift' for Mike which would consist of everything he 'could not abide' rolled into one: he would go in a hot-air balloon, listening to loud pop music, eating an ice-cream on a stick and a dunked biscuit and a range of 'finger foods', while undergoing a surgical procedure conducted by a foul-mouthed, cigarette-smoking, bad-mannered, long-haired (male) doctor wearing strong after-shave lotion and flip-flop sandals.

Meanwhile, Mike was all too aware that at Miramont they were living in so-called Cathar country – the Cathars were a Christian sect who lived in the area in the Middle Ages. Researching the Cathars became Mike's project and his passion. He assembled a library in English and French on the subject, and he visited many of the sites. He was particularly interested in the historical aspects of the Cathars and the military aspects of the associated crusades.

Mike was a good correspondent and we wrote to each other regularly. On 3 May 2002, in a flippant mood, I dashed off a few satirical words about the upcoming French elections, including both a dig at Mike's tendencies and also references to our in-jokes, and faxed him the following:

Dear Dad

I thought you would be interested in this piece in *The Mercury* today. Have typed it out rather than posting, as it is current:

It is well known that former Durban resident Mike Hoare, the famous soldier of fortune and right-winger, has been lying low in France these last ten years. That he has been living in a village not far from his French counterpart Bob Denard, and also near the French Foreign Legion's HQ, has given cause for concern among observers, but so far has come to nought.

What is not so well known is that he is the man behind and largely responsible for the extraordinary new-found popularity of presidential candidate Monsieur Jean-Marie Le Pen, and has in fact been campaigning for him throughout the south-west of France.

Said Mike in a telephone interview, 'Listen man, this is rugby country. Around here we don't tolerate liberal pinkos. This campaign has required me to travel extensively throughout the region, drumming up support. And actually, at the same time – and please don't put this in – I have also been doing some research into my passion, the Cathar movement of the 12th and 13th centuries; they lived in this region you know; and I am also supposed to be writing a novel about them, a sort of historical novel, but I keep getting side-tracked.'

Asked about working for the famous Le Pen, Mike said, 'He's a damned fine bloke, you could even say Le Pen is mightier than the other chap. I refer to him as "His Nibs". And he's much better than those Belgian soldiers I suffered in the Congo who used to go around in shorts so short that their balls used to hang out – but please don't put that in either.'

Said his son Chris, 39, the talented yet modest Durban journalist, 'I haven't heard from Dad for weeks, and when that happens I know he is up to something. At times like this, I usually scan the papers for coups in the Comores and places like that, just in case. Anyway, compared to some of his past exploits, we as a family are not too concerned about this relatively harmless activity.'

Asked for comment, Le Pen said, 'Marc is a good man. I have deployed him in the south-west where he fits in well. Sectarianism is strong in the whole region, below the surface of course, and I am of the opinion that it goes back to the Cathar movement.'

Mike made conscious efforts to keep his brain working in his old age by reading, researching, writing, doing crosswords, model-building, travelling, etc, as we have seen, and by, for example, reading heavyweight magazines like *The Economist*, to which he subscribed. But, he said, 'I ceased taking *The Economist* (in 2001) after they referred to my unit in the Congo as a "rag-tag army".'

Later, he said 'Lord John' had sent him a 'conciliatory piece' that had appeared in *The Economist* of 16 February 2002.

The article was entitled: 'Why is the government planning to regulate mercenaries?' It started off surprisingly inaccurately: 'Colonel "Mad Mike" Hoare, an ex-paratrooper, entered popular culture as a byword for mayhem for his exploits in the Congo and South Africa in the mid-1970s.'

But Mike was more interested in a subsequent paragraph: 'Successive British governments have kept the mercenaries at arm's length. Now, however, the foreign secretary, Jack Straw, has decided that mercenaries are, in fact, rather a good thing. They have therefore, in true New Labour fashion, been re-branded as "private military companies" (PMCs).'

During his sojourn in France, Mike visited South Africa in March 1995, February/March 1998, end 2001-early 2002, and September 2004-January 2005. During these visits he would stay with us, as well as Tim, his wife Pat and their son Justice, in Cape Town. His impeccable manners made him the least demanding houseguest.

On one occasion, when Betty heard that Mike was visiting, she asked to see him. They sat together on a couch in our lounge talking amicably, and I suspect, making their peace. When Betty, now known as Radha, said she wanted to show him the ashram that she had been closely associated with for three decades, he agreed – on condition that it could be done in an hour or so – and they went.

Later, when Betty died in 2003, Mike was grief-stricken, somewhat to my surprise.

He was not interested in socialising at all, but when it happened he thoroughly enjoyed himself and was usually the life and soul of the party. He always enjoyed the company of two of his pals, Peter Duffy and Rob Griffin. There is no doubt about it, Duffy had gone to great lengths to make life in prison more comfortable for the naive Mike, and in so doing, they had forged a close friendship. Mike used to say Duffy had a special place in his heart.

Griffin, a volunteer with Mike in the Congo in 1965, joined *The Natal Mercury* in 1982, where I was also working. He knew his Shakespeare, loved books, was building a 17-metre Wharram catamaran, had a sense of humour as large as his adventurous spirit, and had Africa in his soul; clearly, Griffin and Mike had a lot in common. They became great friends.

Get-togethers with Duffy and Griffin tended to always end in the same way: very late, and around the dining table with a bottle of Ballantine's whisky telling stories .... And then, his tongue sufficiently loosened, Mike would recite a poem or some Shakespeare.

His classic party piece was the recitation from memory of *The coming of the Magi* by TS Eliot, and in February 2006 he recited the whole poem after lunch to those present, including me, Phyllis, her cousin Eileen Busch, and Eileen's niece, Janine Ungerer. Mike's measured pace and evocative tone created a 'magic moment' for all of us present.

Early in 2004, after 14 years in Miramont, Mike gave notice to the Ashburtons. It was the longest period he had ever spent in one place in his life. But before leaving France, he decided to have a hernia attended to, and then something else and something else. It turns out, not surprisingly, he had been putting off having his various ailments seen to.

Indeed, he would never see a doctor unless the situation was desperate, and sometimes his Irish blood would prompt him to say: 'Why go to a doctor? He will only find something wrong with you.' He even resisted simple medication like eye drops. Not so aspirins

– there was nothing that two aspirins could not fix, he would always say. That, and plenty of rest. 'Let the body heal itself.'

Now, to make matters worse, Phyllis's mother became seriously unwell, and Phyllis had to go to Fort Collins, USA, to look after her. On his discharge from hospital in the September, a somewhat frail Mike decided to fly to South Africa to convalesce with us. I drove to Johannesburg to meet him. No sooner had we checked into our hotel than, right out of the blue, he formalised something we had been discussing for months, saying, 'If anyone is going to write my biography, it should be you.'

He spent more than four months with us during which time, now as biographer-to-be, I was able to observe his behaviour close-up. I was amazed at his extraordinary health, especially as he knew nothing about nutrition. His favourite everyday foods were sausages, ham, potatoes and eggs. Or curried anything, the fiercer the better.

If someone was going out somewhere, he would invariably opt to go along. On one occasion, soon after his arrival, Terry invited Mike to join her on a shopping trip to the nearby hypermarket. There, Mike bought three large boxes of chocolates 'for Barbara de Gale and a couple of other friends' that he was going to look up. A week later, Terry found the three now empty boxes in his bedroom .... He was crazy about chocolate – and, like a small boy, would never share his stash. Ever.

My abiding memory of him is that he was polite and good natured, and certainly not mad in any way. He would never refuse a request outright; rather, he would say, 'not right now', 'perhaps later' or 'maybe tomorrow'. If I offered to make him some tea, he would always reply: 'only if you are making it for yourself'. He always seemed to be on hand to carry heavy trays, endearing himself forever to Terry.

His long-term memory was excellent; he could remember dates and especially monetary amounts from 50 or more years previously. His mind was as sharp as ever, and he had the time to pursue another long-time interest, world affairs; he listened to the BBC news on his short-wave radio avidly, watched Sky TV, and read the newspapers. He reprised the role of 'Africa watcher'.

One of the things that had irked Mike during his later life was being declared *persona non grata* in America as a result of his hijacking conviction and jail sentence. Apart from the slight, there were practical considerations. For many years, both Mikey and Simon were living permanently in America and he was unable to visit them. Similarly, he was unable to visit his great friend Don Rickard, though they did spend more than two weeks together at various five-star resorts in Mexico in 1993.

Mike felt the ban was unreasonable as he had furthered the American cause considerably in the Congo, and had they not said, 'We need you today. You may need us one day.' He tried to get it shifted, and later recollected how he was advised not to take the request any further as 'the firm' had no 'corporate memory'.

Mike, however, was determined to get the ban lifted and in 2003 composed a letter which he sent for comment to Rickard who replied, 'I like the wording and the tone of your draft (but) I think you are too modest by half. Overstatement is as foreign to you as Falun Gong, but I would like to see some of your premises punched up a bit; *Videlicet*: your role in the Congo was much more significant than "associated with", etc. It was, quite simply the fulcrum on which the Chinese/Cuban/Soviet designs were winkled out of Central Africa. The Seychelles affair was another pre-emptive move against Soviet expansion in that theater. You were found innocent, and then tried AGAIN, to satisfy the liberal jackals around the world. In any event, you paid a terrible price, and the whole matter is now 20 years gone.'[197]

Then, it so happened that Larry Devlin ('he was the CIA man in Leo who had cultivated Mobutu'), now retired, started spending summers in nearby Lauzerte. Larry and Mike became good friends, visiting each other's homes and deriving much pleasure from their conversations. Mike described Larry as a 'great personality' and Larry adored Mike, but he was unable to move the ban.

Even in March 2005, Mike was still trying to clear his name with the Americans and asked me to find out from Pretoria what the exact terms of his release from prison had been. Was he, for example, actually pardoned? He reasoned that if he had been pardoned, the

Americans might be more understanding than if he had simply been one of many who had received an amnesty.

In November 2004, Gran died; she was 96. In 2005 Mike and Phyllis rented a small flat in Doussard, a village near Lake Annecy, in eastern France. Mikey, a pilot with a major airline, and his partner Bettie Ruitenbeek, were living nearby. Despite the magnificent setting, Mike never warmed to the area – too flashy.

In February 2006, after a tragedy, Mike and Phyllis came to South Africa to give support to Tim and Pat in Cape Town. Mike also came to Durban for a week.

Throughout his life, he preferred to do his work early in the day when his mind was fresh, and so it was that we spent every morning in my office doing recorded interviews.

I also asked him about his will. 'What will?' he said. I was speechless. He agreed to draft a will within a week, but a year later he had not done so. Six months further on, now aged 88, he told me one day in a rather confident tone that he had now made a will – and it was on his computer in case anyone ever needed it! Strange bloke, awkward bloke, difficult bloke, stubborn bloke, perverse bloke, I thought, for the umpteenth time. Why can't you do what normal people do, and have a normal printed will which is properly signed, dated and witnessed?!

In 2006, Mike proposed a publishing project with me. He authorised me to publish a slim volume in the name of my consultancy, Partners in Publishing. It would consist of two stories from his *A Spirit of Adventure* manuscript, with photographs. The first story was about his search in 1958 for the lost city of the Kalahari, and the second described the disaster in the Okavango Delta in 1963 (both summarised earlier here). The book is called *Mokoro – A cry for help!*

Our plan was to 'test the water'; if it sold well, we could publish some of his other stories; but what I really wanted was that a movie mogul would turn it into a film.

One reviewer, Niki Moore, said, 'This is a man with "Adventure" as his middle name. The book captivated me from the start. One can consume it in a sitting – which is a good thing as it is hard to put down. Mike writes in a galloping, eye-witness-type style with flashes of droll humour.'

Another reviewer, Graham Linscott, in his daily column as The Idler in *The Mercury*, said, 'Mokoro is actually a very serious slim volume which ... fills in another detail of this enigmatic figure who has become part of the mythology of post-independence Africa yet absolutely fails to match the stereotype of the mercenary soldier.'[198]

Meanwhile, in mid-2007, acting as Mike's literary agent, I received a phone call from Peder Lund, the owner of Paladin Press, a specialist 'action books' publishing house in America; he wanted to republish Mike's four military books. The advance against royalties was $6000 and Mike had to write a substantial new foreword or epilogue for each book. During the course of 2008, Paladin reprinted *The Road to Kalamata, Congo Mercenary, Congo Warriors,* and *The Seychelles Affair* and described Mike as the '20th century's most famous mercenary and one of its most eloquent storytellers'.

Around 2005, I became aware of a website that billed itself an 'online clearing-house for information about Colonel Thomas Michael Hoare', run by a helpful character named Mike Harris. He would forward requests and messages of all sorts to me; many were from people looking for the father they never knew who had been a mercenary in the Congo, but they were also from admirers, students, military people, filmmakers, journalists, even academics, who wanted to correspond with Mike. Mike could never remember the 'lost-father' mercenaries, saying 'normally I can remember (only) those who were remarkably brave or remarkably troublesome', and almost never replied personally to approaches.

In early 2008, Mike turned *A Spirit of Adventure* into an African travelogue, adding a chapter on the filming of *The Wild Geese*, and his Ufiti adventure. He called it *Ten Tales out of Africa*, and we sent it to several local publishers.

Meanwhile, Mike had been scheming quietly about yet another book – to be called *In Loco Parentis*. In some notes dated 5 June 2008, Mike wrote, 'It will give young readers the sort of advice they should normally receive from their parents; it will be a collection of light-hearted essays, beginning with Polonius's speech from *Hamlet*

(Act 3, Scene 2, lines 59 to 81)' and the same speech 'transposed into good colloquial English'. Mike listed the beginnings of about 50 topic ideas, one of which was: 'Good manners [brings success with girls quicker than anything else].' The idea remained on Mike's agenda but it never got further than that, thankfully. Mike had many talents, but parenting was not one of them.

Meanwhile, Phyllis's health had been deteriorating. As a child she had had rheumatic fever – which can be linked to heart-valve damage – and indeed she had had major heart surgery during her life. In 2008 she was admitted to hospital in Annecy for two long spells. She died in hospital on 7 February 2009. She and Mike had been married for nearly 48 years.

Mike had seen the end was near and took it bravely. A funeral service was held in nearby Faverges. Mike later reflected 'that love is steadfast even after death has parted us from our loved ones', and concluded, 'It made me wonder, do we meet again? I like to think we do.'

Phyllis's body was buried at a cemetery in Doussard. Mike ordered a Celtic rock 'just like Richard Burton's' to mark the grave, engraved just like Burton's, with: Phyllis Hoare, 1937 – 2009.

Gerry later spent ten days with Mike, covering the period of his 90th birthday even though he hated birthdays and would happily have ignored this one in particular. Shortly thereafter, Mike paid his second visit to Gerry in Vasto. By now, they were really close, and Mike never stopped singing her praises.

On 29 May 2009, aged 90 and too forgetful to look after himself, Mike flew out to Durban. His brother Ben had died in October 2000, and had recalled in his last letter to Mike how 'the wheels came off' in the family when in 1930 their mother's mental health started deteriorating; by 1937 'she was lucky not to have been locked up in a loony bin', he said. Sister June died in February 2007.

Almost all of Mike's contemporaries were no longer alive, to his knowledge. 'I'm the last one left,' he would sometimes say.

16. The Old Soldier

We would sometimes tease him that he was causing more havoc
with the TV remote than he ever did with his Colt 45. – Son, Chris

W e were able to offer Mike a large separate room with bathroom
en suite. The sea and city views from his space were out of
this world, but by now he had cataracts in both eyes and could not
appreciate the vista; but he would not have the cataract operations –
he did not believe in 'interfering' with the body.

As a house guest, Mike continued to be very much the old
soldier, always charming and never needing anything except a glass,
sometimes two, of his Scottish 'medicine' before dinner. And lots of
tea and biscuits. And chocolate.

For the first few years, he was preoccupied with his various
published and unpublished books, reading almost nothing else. He
would work intensely at his laptop from breakfast till dinner, bar a
short siesta, seven days a week.

He also made a conscious effort to keep his mind active, both
to combat the unspoken grief and to remain sharp. This involved
completing a cryptic crossword every day – and reciting lines he
had memorised from Shakespeare.

Mike was 90-plus, but, with his unique way of looking at things,
did not see himself as old. For example, I took him to a formal
presentation entitled 'Shakespeare's Women' at the local branch of
The Shakespeare Society of Southern Africa, and although he was

the oldest person there by about ten years, he said he found the people 'too old'. He found the talk 'very good, but nothing new'.

His general health was perfect – but he did get confused about arrangements, people, keys, etc, and over the coming years his short-term memory declined from poor to non-existent. We would sometimes tease him that he was causing more havoc with the TV remote than he ever did with his Colt 45. But on the other hand, he surprised us with his agility both at table tennis and in learning the latest dance moves from his grandchildren.

One advantage of his memory failure was that we could share the same old jokes at regular intervals, and he would laugh and laugh. Indeed, our home was mostly full of laughter when he was with us.

One Sunday, we drove to the Spioenkop battlefield in northern KwaZulu-Natal and did a self-guided walk. Mike was mainly interested in which regiments had been there, and no doubt wondered where exactly Sgt Badcock had fought.

Soon, Tim and I took over the running of his financial affairs, which were somewhat in disarray. He was receiving a smallish British pension and had several modest investments. Although he was now into his nineties, it was with reluctance that he agreed to have a proper will and I employed a lawyer to draw it up. I was appointed executor, and the administrator of any benefits accruing from his books. He also granted me royalty-free licence to use his copyrighted material.

In March 2010, Paladin Press published the *Ten Tales* book as *Mike Hoare's Adventures in Africa*. The advance paid was $3000. Paladin also agreed to republish *Three Years with 'Sylvia'* – and to add a photo credit which Mike had overlooked for the Hale edition. I now crafted the credit, Mike approved it, and it said: 'An orange must go to my son Chris who took most of the photographs in this book.'

Also in 2010, while with Tim and Pat in Cape Town where Tim had his own professional recording business, Sun Studios, Tim recorded Mike reading his book on the Cathars, now called *The Cathar Story*, and added some of his own music between chapters. Tim had artwork done and put the CD on sale.

Then, a tragedy involving Brigid, Ben and Imelda's youngest daughter. Writing as Bree O'Mara, Brigid had won the 2007 Citizen Book Prize for her hilarious novel, *Home Affairs*, and was on her way to London to find a publisher for the sequel, *Nigel Watson, Superhero*. She was on board the Afriqiyah Airways aeroplane that crashed at Tripoli, Libya, on 12 May 2010, killing all but one of the 104 people on board. The cause of the accident was later announced as pilot error.

In 2003, Bree contacted Mike saying she had been 'directly and specifically commissioned' by a London publisher to write a 'military biography' on Mike, and would he please assist? He had apparently already told her 'there is nothing so dead to me as the past' and that biographies were of no interest to him. Mike did not assist Bree, but an obituary in *The Times* of 14 May 2010 said she had written an unpublished account of his (Mike's) adventures in the Congo.

Meanwhile, Mike continued polishing the manuscript of *The Cathar Story*, which ran to about 70 000 words. After months of this, I asked him what he was actually doing. He replied, with a twinkle, 'I am putting back the commas that I took out yesterday.'

Through fictitious characters and individuals who actually lived at that time, Mike described the Cathar beliefs and lifestyle – the so-called heresy; the rest of the book is historical and includes the *denouement* at Montségur and the Albigensian crusade organised by Pope Innocent 3 to stamp the Cathars out! It is interesting to note that mercenary soldiers played a role at that time, and by mentioning them in the book many times, Mike may have wanted, albeit in a small way, to lend perspective to the mercenary cause.

Eventually, in mid-2012, Tim edited the book, and I laid it out and had 40 copies printed with black mock-leather covers and a new title in gold foil: *The Last Days of the Cathars*. It had taken Mike more than 15 years of serious study and his 'magnum opus' gave him great satisfaction in his old age.

I would receive emails for Mike from fans and journalists around the world, but he had long put the Congo and the Seychelles behind him, and was never interested in any form of correspondence or interviews. In early 2012 however, as an exception, Mike gave a long interview to Linda Devereux (née Taylor), whom he had rescued as a little girl from a mission station at Yakusu in the Congo, and who was writing a PhD; she travelled from Canberra, Australia, to Cape Town for the meeting.

In 2012, he dug out the 'prison notebook' in which he had neatly written about 60 poems or quotations, mainly from Shakespeare. Tim recorded Mike reading about 30 pieces, played some of his own music to go between the readings, and produced a batch of CDs. Mike enjoyed listening to the readings immensely.

As Grandpa, he loved talking to family on Skype, especially Simon and his wife Lisa in Idaho, USA – and watching the musical and other antics of their four little girls.

Mike did not believe in war medals and had never actually received any World War 2 medals. 'My experience in the British Army was that the awarding of medals tended to upset more men than it pleased, apart from those given for outstanding personal bravery in the face of the enemy.'

However, in early 2012 I heard from a collector of medals, Marco Gollino, in Durban. He assisted me to apply for Mike's war medals from the Ministry of Defence Medal Office in the UK, and in due course a small parcel arrived. At a little ceremony on his 93rd birthday, Mike opened the package which contained the 1939-45 Star, Burma Star, Defence Medal and War Medal 1939-45.

Mike later received the valuable Territorial Army 'Efficiency' medal. Engraved on its rim was the wording:

'P/189576 MAJ T M B HOARE RAC' (Royal Armoured Corps).

During these years in South Africa, spent between us in Durban, and Tim and Pat in Cape Town, Mike's physical health was robust. The only medication he took regularly was for an underactive thyroid. But then, after the publication of his Cathar book in 2012, Mike slowed down a lot and by 2018 he could mostly be found dozing in the sunshine, dipping into one of the books he had written, doing crosswords, reading poetry and the Bible … and fading away.

Glossary

ab initio	from the beginning
à pied	on foot
ag	oh
apartheid	the political system in South Africa which separated different races
ashram	Hindu retreat centre
avec	with
biltong	strips of dried meat, a traditional delicacy
braai	barbecue
braaivleis	barbecue
camino	path
cité	here, cité refers to a rebel-held slum area of Stanleyville
condottieri	mercenary leaders in Italy centuries ago
dagga	dried cannabis or marijuana leaves
denouement	the final resolution
disselboom	central longitudinal shaft of a trailer or wagon
douceur	in this case, a financial sweetener
force de frappe	strike force
grand-père	*grandfather*
hardegat	hard arsed, tough
jeunesse	young Congolese rebel fighters
kraal	hutted rural village
middelmannetjie	the hump between the wheel ruts of a sandy track
mai	water
métier	trade
mielie	maize
Morena	a term of respect, somewhere between Mr and Sir
mokoro	dugout canoe or pirogue
ou kêrel	old chap
panga	long knife with a broad blade, for hacking through thick bush

Acknowledgements

In researching and writing this biography, I was assisted by scores of people, many of them in distant lands. I acknowledge you all with my thanks, in particular:

My brother Tim, for sharing his insights and observations, and more
My sister Gerry, for sharing gems brought to light by her outstanding memory
Rob Griffin, that amusing man, for his warm-hearted friendship (now so dreadfully missed) and for sharing his reminiscences
Peter Duffy, for his many kindnesses to us all
Leif Hellström, who generously shared his vast knowledge of mercenaries in the Congo, and certain archive material
John and Gill Yelland, for their readily given permission to summarise John's unpublished *Kalahari and I* and his unpublished *Abominable Ufiti*, and to use some of his sketches and photographs
Peder Lund, my 'uncle' in the publishing business, for his generosity
Eric Bridge, for his friendship, photographs and newspaper cuttings
Bob Houcke for permission to use his photographs
Nigel Osborn, for his unstinting assistance
Many Congo warriors, in particular Basil Borradaile, Russell Richardson, Gary Michell, Flemming Kerstein, Ian Yule, Eddie McCabe, Laurie Kaplan and Tom Courtney, for sharing their experiences
Roy Reed, thank you Boet, for your professional assistance with the photographs
Pat Hoare, for her collection of newspaper cuttings on the Seychelles saga
John Vigor, for his description of the second Ngamiland expedition
Yagil Henkin, for information from the Rhodesian Archives
Tony Earnshaw, for articles on the filming of *The Wild Geese*
Susan Williams, for her assistance in sourcing archival material
Euan Lloyd and Ros Kernot, Bob Sims, Mikey Hoare, Ralph Labuschagne, Neill Hunt and Sue, Mary Alexander, Asbjørn Halvorsen, Derek Roger, Terry Aspinall, Jacques Mathen, Dave Brown, Chris James, Judy Bowland, Thomas O'Hare and the many others who kindly helped in their own ways, especially those who so readily gave permission for their copyright material to be used.

Bibliography

Alexander, David. *Sani Pass – Riding the Dragon*. Durban: Self-published, 1992.

Augustijnen, Sven. *Spectres*. Brussels: ASA Publishers, 2011.

Baker, Colin. *Wild Goose – The Life and Death of Hugh van Oppen*. Cardiff: Mpemba Books, 2002.

Brooks, Aubrey. *Death Row in Paradise*. Bloomington, USA: Xlibris Corporation, 2013.

Butcher, Tim. *Blood River, A Journey to Africa's Broken Heart*. London: Vintage Books, 2008.

Spencer Chapman, Freddie. *Living Dangerously*. Leicester: Ulverscroft, Leicester – large print edition. First published by Chatto and Windus, London, 1953.

Clarke, SJG. *The Congo Mercenary – A History and Analysis*. Johannesburg: The South African Institute of International Affairs, 1968.

Colvin, Ian. *The Rise and Fall of Moise Tshombe*. London: Leslie Frewin, 1968.

Devlin, Larry. *Chief of Station, Congo*. New York: PublicAffairs™, 2007.

Fergusson, Bernard. *Beyond the Chindwin*. London: St James's Library, Collins, 1945.

Fergusson, Bernard. *The Wild Green Earth*. London: St James's Library, Collins, 1946.

Frost, David. *David Frost – an autobiography*, Part 1. London: HarperCollinsPublishers, 1993.

Germani, Hans. *White Soldiers in Black Africa*. Cape Town: Nasionale Boekhandel Beperk, 1966.

Grant-Whyte, Harry. *Between Life and Death*. Pietermaritzburg: Shuter and Shooter, 1976.

Hoare, Mike. *Congo Mercenary*. London: Robert Hale, 1967, and Boulder, USA: Paladin Press, 2008.

Hoare, Mike. *The Road to Kalamata*. Lexington, USA: Lexington Books, 1989, and Boulder, USA: Paladin Press, 2008.

Hoare, Mike. *The Seychelles Affair*. London: Transworld Publishers Ltd, 1986, and Boulder, USA: Paladin Press, 2008.

Hoare, Mike. *Congo Warriors*. London: Robert Hale, 1991, and Boulder, USA: Paladin Press, 2008.

Hoare, Mike. *Three Years with Sylvia*. London: Robert Hale, 1977, and Boulder, USA: Paladin Press, 2010.

Hoare, Mike. *Mike Hoare's Adventures in Africa*. Boulder, USA: Paladin Press, 2010.

Hoare, Mike. *Mokoro - A cry for help!* Durban: Partners in Publishing, 2007.

Hoare, Mike. *The Last Days of the Cathars*. Durban: Mike Hoare Books, 2012.

Hoare, Mike. *A Spirit of Adventure*. Unpublished, 1997.

Hellström, Leif. *Les Affreux: Mercenaries and Volunteers in the Congo, 1960-1967*. Sweden, 2007.

Hempstone, Smith. *Katanga Report*. London: Faber & Faber, 1962.

Hornung, EW. *Raffles: The Amateur Cracksman*. Bath: Lythway Press, 1976. First published 1899.

Hotchner, AE. *Papa Hemingway, a personal memoir*. London: Weidenfeld and Nicolson, 1966.

Hudson, Andrew. *Congo Unravelled – Military Operations from Independence to the Mercenary Revolt 1960-68*. Solihull, England: Helion & Company Limited; and Pinetown, South Africa: 30° South Publishers (Pty) Ltd, 2012.

Jones, JDF. *Storyteller, The Many Lives of Laurens van der Post*. London: John Murray, 2001.

Junor, Penny. *Burton, The Man Behind the Myth*. Bath: Chivers Press, 1986, by arrangement with Sidgwick & Jackson Limited, 1985.

Keegan, John. *A History of Warfare*. London: Random House, 1993.

Linscott, Graham. *Ricochets, from Gordonstoun to Africa's wars; the life of mercenary soldier Peter Duffy*. Durban: Nomapix (Pty) Ltd, 2017.

Nelson Mandela. *Long Walk to Freedom*. London: Little, Brown and Company, 1994.

Mockler, Anthony. *The New Mercenaries*. London: Sidgwick & Jackson, 1985.

Munnion, Chris. *Banana Sunday – Datelines from Africa*. Johannesburg: William Waterman Publications, 1993.

Paton, Alan. Introduced and edited by Hermann Wittenberg. *Lost City of the Kalahari*. Pietermaritzburg: University of KwaZulu-Natal Press, 2005.

Puren, Colonel Jerry as told to Brian Pottinger. *Mercenary Commander*. Johannesburg: Galago Publishing, 1986.

Reed, David. *111 Days in Stanleyville*. London: Collins, 1966.

Roseveare, Dr Helen. *Doctor among Congo rebels*. London: Lutterworth Press, 1965.

Scarr, Deryck. *Seychelles since 1770*. London: C Hurst & Co, 2000.

Smith, Ivan. *Mad dog killers – The story of a Congo mercenary*. Solihull, UK: Helion & Company, 1987, and Pinetown, South Africa: 30° South Publishers, 2012.

Stiff, Peter. *Warfare by Other Means*. Johannesburg: Galago Publishing, 2001.

Venter, Al J. *War Dog – Fighting other peoples' wars*. Havertown, Pa, USA: Casemate, 2003.

Villafana, Frank R. *Cold War in the Congo*. New Brunswick, USA: Transaction Publishers, 2009.

Weinberg, Samantha. *The Last of the Pirates – The Search for Bob Denard*. London: Jonathan Cape, 1994.

Appendix A

Who were the Wild Geese in history?

Mike Hoare came up with the name 'Wild Geese' for the men of 5 Commando to differentiate them from the mercenaries known as *Les Affreux*. In time, the Wild Geese wore a patch on the right shoulder which said 5 Commando in red, above a blue flying goose.

Mike took the name from 'the noblest mercenary soldiers who ever offered their swords for reward and their hearts for an ideal, the 'Wild Geese' of the 18th century.'

Mike wrote: 'It was 1691 and the time of the October moon. General Sarsfield's Irish troops, withdrawing from the siege of Limerick, made their weary way down the banks of the Shannon river. Exile under the French flag and service in the army of Louis XIV was preferable to a life under the English yoke.

'Overhead, the autumn skies grew black with the wings of a thousand birds, eager and strident, crying the coming of a hard winter. The defeated soldiers looked up and saw their meaning. Thereafter they called themselves the Wild Geese.

'Such were the vanguard of the innumerable Irish soldiers who sought fame and fortune as mercenary soldiers in continental armies during the course of the next two centuries.

'They fought in every great conflict from those days until the Great War. During the Anglo-Boer War they sent two brigades to fight for the Boers.'

Appendix B

In 1967 Mike Hoare devised a plan to rehabilitate the Congo and left a copy of it at the British Embassy in Leopoldville. It is reproduced below:

Outline of a plan to encourage the economy of the North-East and Eastern Congo and to free the Congo government from threats of internal and external coups.

General
- Phase out 5 and 6 Commandos and replace by 1 October 1967 with a force of well trained, well disciplined and loyal men. (The mercenary type must go.)
- The force will provide an elite unit of 80 men, highly mobile and ready for action anywhere in the Congo.
- The force will provide a specialist intelligence unit, within and without the country.

Personnel
- All men must be in possession of a skill – either artisan or professional.
- They must speak (or learn) Swahili or French.
- Must swear an oath of allegiance to the President of the Congo.
- Must contract to serve for not less than two years.
- Should be encouraged to bring their wives and families to the Congo after an initial proving period.

Organisation
- The force must have a firm base, preferably in the Eastern Congo, e.g. Bukavu, with its own hospital etc.
- The force will be sub-divided into areas of the Congo to establish permanent stations.
- The mobile unit will be stationed at base under the direct control of the Commander.
- The whole force should be under the direction of the President, assisted perhaps by the Minister of Defence and Minister of Security.

Role
- Active and energetic patrolling, liaison with chiefs, farmers and businessmen; establishing an atmosphere of peace and security.
- Assisting in all aspects of civil administration making good use of their artisan and professional skills.
- Collecting information.
- Preparing for, at a later stage, the establishment of a great TOURIST industry.

Appendix C

Mike Hoare was usually described, *inter alia,* as a 'brilliant leader'. Published below is *A Lecture on Man Management and Leadership* as it first appeared as an appendix in *Congo Mercenary*.

Every man under your command is a separate entity. Every man under your command is different. Each one has his own personality, his own background, his own likes and dislikes, troubles and fears. There is no general pattern. Your first step in man management will be in trying to understand in what way each of your men is different and what makes him tick.

The first thing you will discover is that every man has a name and prefers to be called by it. Nobody likes to be spoken to as 'Hey, you!', or worse still, as 'Hey, you with the square head'. We live in the age of the personality cult. The world of commerce has already appreciated this fact to its advantage. Is it not heart-warming to be greeted by your name by the head waiter at your favourite restaurant? Makes you feel a little important, does it not? Begin therefore, by learning the name of every man under your command. It pays dividends. A man's reaction is not, as you might suppose, surprise that you should know his name – it goes much deeper than that; he feels that you have gone to some trouble to learn it; he feels you care; he is no longer a number – now he is an entity. This is the basis of man management, the ability to care.

You will find the study of men to be an absorbing task. You will be astounded that you understand some of your men so easily. You appear to be on the same wavelength as it were. They know at once what you are talking about or trying to say, almost instinctively. Others, on the other hand, always seem to be difficult and contrary, express totally different opinions from yours and you find it difficult to communicate with them. This does not necessarily mean that you are right and they are wrong. To understand these soldiers you will need to know their minds, their backgrounds, and why they adopt certain attitudes. Some men are even more difficult and are what I call 'prickly pears', hornery cusses who just refuse to be understood. Frequently these men are tough and independent. A weak leader will accept that they are awkward and will avoid them altogether or give in to them whenever their paths cross. This is an error. You must recognise strength in personality, even if it makes your life a little harder. So often I have found these 'prickly pears' to be the ones who are still in there fighting when all others have fled – for the basic reason that they are obstinate and will not give in. These are priceless qualities in a soldier which must be encouraged, rather than weakend.

Be careful that you do not confuse the 'prickly pear', who is a pearl without a price, with the man who is truly impossible. There used to be a saying in the

British Army that there were no bad men, only bad leaders. This is a large slice of baloney. Think back to the beginnings of 5 Commando for some examples. We began with some of the most incredible soldiers of all time. What can you do with a confirmed junkie? How can you lead a habitual drunkard. My advice is – don't even try. Your duty as a commander begins and ends by recognising them quickly and getting them out of your unit before they do any damage.

You will notice that men respond willingly to some leaders and not to others. If you make a study of the methods of the successful ones, you will find that they invariably have confidence in themselves, show enthusiasm even for the most menial tasks, have a sense of humour, and are proficient at soldiering. A lot depends on the way you go about things. Tone of voice, for instance, is most important. One tone, which you will use when you are 'on duty', will indicate to your men – they will know you just as well as you know them – that you mean business, no fooling, get on with the job, lads. Be the same every day, not easy going and playful one day and hard as nails the next. This confuses the men, understandably.

The bedrock of man management, however, is discipline. Nothing is more certain than that you will obtain the best results with your men if you insist on a high standard of discipline. You will soon find that your men, all men, prefer to be lead firmly with discipline. It results in fairer treatment for one thing and every man knows what to expect and where he stands. Once you have decided on your standard of discipline – and this is really a matter to suit your personality and may vary from 'iron hand' tactics, to the other end of the scale where you merely insist that you your orders are carried out – you must apply the golden rule of consistency. My advice in this regard is to take no chances and to be 'regimental'. Be hard, but fair. Strangely enough, men take a pride in being treated hard. Let your men know that when you are 'on parade', you are very much 'on parade'. Off parade, you can perhaps relax a little. This will depend on the strength of your personality. But watch it. More man management problems arise off duty than on. It is totally impossible to spend a night drinking with your men and yet expect them to answer your commands the next day. Familiarity breeds contempt. Human nature works that way and, whilst some of your men will appreciate the difference between off duty and on, there will always be a few who will wreck the thing for you on the parade ground.

With regard to familiarity, should you use Christian names? On parade definitely not. Off parade, everything will depend on the circumstances. I do not think, however, that an occasion can ever arise where your juniors should address you by your Christian name. And whilst on this subject – make no favourites. This leads to endless discontent and can be as hard on the man favoured, as it is unfair on the others. Keep your relationship formal.

Man management is, I think you will agree, something which we can all learn. We do not have to be greatly gifted to do it. But how do we become leaders of men? We become leaders of men, in the first instance, by showing that we are worthy of being followed. Men will only follow a man they respect. Let us study how we can earn the respect which will turn us into leaders.

We begin with self-discipline. Let me give you an example. The rules, which are laid down for your men, must be obeyed equally by you, regardless of the privileges which may go with your rank. If PT parade is at 06:00 hours, then you should appear on it and not be lying in bed, encouraging your men from the warmth of your blankets. Your personal behaviour will come under the closest scrutiny. Men have an inbred desire to respect their leader and excessive self-indulgence will wreck that ideal. No man will follow a booze artist – except perhaps into a pub – no matter what excellent company he may be. This does not mean that you must been puritanical, but your standard of personal behaviour must be above average.

Next will come a thorough knowledge of your job. Anything you ask your men to do, you must be capable of doing yourself, from marching 50 miles in full equipment to stripping a machine gun. You must be technically superior in all facets of soldiering. You must be as fit, if not fitter than your men. You must demonstrate to your men that you 'know your stuff'. This will impart confidence which in its turn, will instil a sense of respect and build up your powers of leadership.

Let me stress the great importance of being able to communicate with your men. The best way to impress your personality on your men is by frequent talks and discussions. You must practise the art of public speaking and develop a facility for getting your message across clearly and concisely. You must learn to instruct, for teaching will be one of your main occupations as a leader.

There are many rewards attached to leadership but the friendship of your men is not one of them. Leadership is, generally speaking, a lonely task. It has to be so. It is impossible for a good leader to be chummy with his men and yet subject them to his orders, many of which will be unpopular, even harsh. The comradeship of men in the ranks is a warm and a rewarding feeling, a rare sensation known only to soldiers who have roughed it and braved battle together. Many men recognise this and stay in the ranks, preferring comradeship to the joy of command which is a different thing altogether. I mention this, so that you will be warned against the cardinal error of trying to curry favour with your men or seeking popularity. It never works. The best you can hope for is the respect of your men and this can be a considerable reward in itself.

Now let me deal with two aspects of leadership in practice. Firstly, a good leader is one who cares for his men. On active service, the average soldier is usually completely reliant on his leaders for a variety of things, from the supply of food to ammunition. The good leader looks after the welfare and comfort of his troops. He sees they are billeted reasonably, have blankets and food, and receive their share of any creature comforts which are available. He ensures that guard rosters are arranged fairly and that 'willing horses' are not given too great a burden to carry. The health of his men and their morale must be his constant anxiety.

He does not nurse them, but makes himself available at all times to help them care for themselves and represents their case at higher levels whenever necessary. He cares about them.

Imagine that you are riding along in convoy and suddenly you run into an ambush. Bullets flying everywhere and confusion and panic grip the column. This is the 'moment of truth' for you as a leader. Every man will look to you for leadership. In this moment you will stand or fall in their eyes. How will you react? My advice to you is simply this. Anticipate every situation which can arise in battle, and think about your reaction to it well in advance. The split second which you gain can be decisive. As soon as trouble strikes, shout out an order. It matters little what it is, so long as you let your men know you are in command. 'Take cover!', for instance – obvious enough and something which they will do in any event, but the fact that you have reacted to the situation and given an order, is a relief to your men. Instinctively, every man will obey. Your next order is eagerly awaited. Go on and on lead firmly. Do not let your men flounder around, wondering if they should take the initiative, something they have heard so much about. Invariably this leads them into trouble. This is your job. You must lead. You must tell them what to do.

Finally, let me say something about that powerful emotion, 'sympathy'. Watch out for it. It has no place on the battlefield. A stern, even a harsh word to a wounded man, will often induce in him a fighting spirit, which will react to his own advantage. I have seen many a man die from an overdose of sympathy. Sympathy no matter how well meant, must be carefully controlled on the field of battle. In the Casualty Station it may be different.

Let me recap. To manage your men well you must know them. You must know them intimately, beginning with their names and ending with their private histories. This is the very core of man management. To lead men you must gain their respect. To do this, you will have to show them you are worthy of it. You must, at the same time, be as fit as any of them and technically better than all of them. This way you will impart confidence. Finally, to lead conclusively in battle, you must show yourself to be their leader when the crunch comes. In the moment of truth, when they look to you for leadership, you must not fail them.

Let me end by saying that a leader is only as good as the sum of his men; but let me also assure you that a good leader can raise this sum to the power of ten, by caring for his men, setting a good example, and leading with a firm hand.

Endnotes

1   Unpublished manuscript: *A Spirit of Adventure* by Mike Hoare, p. 88
2   Letter from Mike's father Thommie to his mother Elizabeth, 29 March 1923
3   British Army war record. Folio 81
4   British Army war record. Folio 81
5   British Army war record. Folio 69
6   Unpublished manuscript: *A Spirit of Adventure* by Mike Hoare, p. 103-104
7   British Army war record. Folio 63
8   British Army war record. Folio 51
9   Unpublished manuscript: *A Spirit of Adventure* by Mike Hoare, p. 15-16
10 British Army war record. Folio 51
11 Unpublished manuscript: *A Spirit of Adventure* by Mike Hoare, p. 17
12 British Army war record. Folio 63 & 80
13 British Army war record. Folio 61
14 British Army war record. Folio 79
15 British Army war record. Folio 79
16 British Army war record. Folio 77, 51, 63
17 British Army war record. Folio 51 & 12
18 British Army war record. Folio 51 & 12
19 British Army war record. Folio 1
20 *Dekho!*, published by The Burma Star Association, 34 Grosvenor Gardens, London SW1W 0DH, Summer 2009
21 British Army war record. Folio 58
22 Bernard Fergusson, *Beyond the Chindwin*, p. 20
23 British Army war record. Folio 58
24 British Army war record. Folio 51
25 https://en.wikipedia.org/wiki/St._Andrew%27s_College,_Grahamstown
26 F Spencer Chapman, *Living Dangerously*, p. 11
27 Mike Hoare, *Mike Hoare's Adventures in Africa*, Chapter 1
28 David Alexander, *Sani Pass – Riding the Dragon*, p. 111-126
29 Mike Hoare, *Mike Hoare's Adventures* in Africa, Chapters 2-5
30 JDF Jones, *Storyteller*, p. 220, 222, 215
31 Mike Hoare, *Mokoro – A cry for help!*, Chapter 1
32 *The Star*, 23 July 1959
33 Undated email from Don Rickard to Mike Hoare
34 Veronica Roodt, *The Shell Tourist Travel and Field Guide of Botswana*, Shell Oil Botswana, 2008.
35 Andrew Hudson, *Congo Unravelled*, Chapters 1-3
36 Andrew Hudson, *Congo Unravelled*, Chapter 4
37 Leif Hellström, *Les Affreux: Mercenaries and Volunteers in the Congo*, 1960-1967, p. 67 and 46
38 Larry Devlin, *Chief of Station, Congo*, pp. 48, 62, 95
39 Emmanuel Gerard, an expert on the Lumumba Commission, a parliamentary investigation commission set up by the Belgian government, writing in *Spectres*, Sven Augustijnen, p. 140

40 Letter: C Huyghe and R Russell-Cargill to Col JM Crèvecoeur, 1 March 1961 pp. 1-4
41 Letter: C Huyghe and R Russell-Cargill to Col JM Crèvecoeur, 1 March 1961 p. 1
42 *Rand Daily Mail*, 29 April 1961
43 Letters from Nigel Osborn to author, 22 April 2012 and 23 April 2016
44 Letters from Nigel Osborn to author, 22 April 2012 and 23 April 2016
45 UN Security Council Resolution 161
46 Document titled 'Compagnie S.A. (Effectifs approximatifs)' by Major R Faulques
47 From Captain TM Hoare to Etat Major, 24 June 1961
48 Report by Major R Faulques, 25 May 1961
49 UN report to the Secretary-General from his acting special representative in the Congo concerning the interrogation of 30 mercenaries apprehended in Kabalo on 7 April 1961. 14 April 1961
50 Letter from Nigel Osborn to author, 25 April 2012
51 Letter from Nigel Osborn, 23 April 2012
52 ©Col Jerry Puren as told to Brian Pottinger, Mercenary Commander, Galago Publishing (Pty) Ltd. p. 27
53 ©Col Jerry Puren as told to Brian Pottinger, *Mercenary Commander*, Galago Publishing (Pty) Ltd. p. 27
54 Undated report entitled 'Situation from 6 May to 17 June 1961'
55 Second weekly progress report as of 24 June 1961 from ONUC special military mission to Katanga, p. 3 read with Annex VII p. 1
56 Conversation with Mike Hoare 9 May 2012
57 http://www.mercenary-wars.net/congo/first-recruiter.html, Letter 3
58 Harry Grant-Whyte, *Between Life and Death*, p. 63 & 65
59 In 1962, South African mines produced 25,5 million fine ounces of gold, which was 68,5% of the world's output, excluding the USSR. And 10 million pounds (avoirdupois) of uranium oxide – Chamber of Mines of South Africa.
60 Nelson Mandela, *Long Walk to Freedom*, p. 272
61 Nelson Mandela, *Long Walk to Freedom*, p. 189, 293, 294
62 *Sunday Times* 110th Anniversary Special Report, p. 4
63 *Sunday Tribune*
64 Nelson Mandela, *Long Walk to Freedom*, pp. 302, 306-7
65 *Sunday Times*, London, 15 May 2016
66 Nelson Mandela, *Long Walk to Freedom*, dust-cover front inside flap and p. 347
67 Christopher Munnion, *Banana Sunday*, p. 143-4
68 Ian Colvin, *The Rise and Fall of Moise Tshombe*, p. 140, p. 177
69 Ian Colvin, *The Rise and Fall of Moise Tshombe*, p. 158
70 Article written by Mike Hoare, *Sunday Times*, 13 December 1964
71 Ian Colvin, *The Rise and Fall of Moise Tshombe*, p. 217
72 SJG Clarke, *The Congo Mercenary*, p. 39
73 ©Col Jerry Puren as told to Brian Pottinger, *Mercenary Commander*, Galago Publishing (Pty) Ltd. p. 15 & 185
74 Leif Hellström, *Les Affreux – Mercenaries and Volunteers in the Congo*, 1960-1967, p. 74
75 Telegram from the US Department of State to the American embassy in Leopoldville, 10 August 1964
76 Conversation with Mike Hoare, 17 March 2012
77 David Reed, *111 Days in Stanleyville*, p. 118

78 Ian Colvin, *The Rise and Fall of Moise Tshombe*, p. 186
79 *The Star*, 14 September 1964
80 FO 371/181705, 4 Jan 1965
81 SJG Clarke, *The Congo Mercenary*, p. 13
82 *Sunday Tribune*, 13 September 1964
83 Andrew Hudson, *Congo Unravelled*, p. 8
84 The Recapture of Albertville: A Case History, CIA Sitrep, 4 September 1964, p. 1
85 The Recapture of Albertville: A Case History, CIA Sitrep, 4 September 1964, p. 1
86 Christopher Munnion, *Banana Sunday*, p. 112 and p. 317
87 The Recapture of Albertville: A Case History, CIA Sitrep, 4 September 1964, p. 4
88 David Reed, *111 Days in Stanleyville*, p. 124
89 Mike Hoare, *The Road to Kalamata*, p. 8
90 Ivan Smith, *Mad dog killers*, p. 38
91 Ian Colvin, *The Rise and Fall of Moise Tshombe*, p. 186
92 CIA memorandum: The Congo Situation, 10 September 1964, p. 1
93 Ivan Smith, *Mad dog killers*, p. 72
94 Jeffrey H Michaels (2012): *Breaking the Rules: The CIA and Counterinsurgency in the Congo 1964–1965*, International Journal of Intelligence and Counter Intelligence, 25:1, p. 144-5
95 Lyndon B. Johnson Library, Records of the CIA, Stanleyville Debriefing Reports, Document LBJ/A/DDP-7, Col. Knut Raudstein debrief.
96 Ivan Smith, *Mad dog killers*, p. 128
97 Chris Munnion, *Banana Sunday*, p 148, 317
98 Helen Roseveare, *Doctor among Congo rebels*, p. 100
99 Hans Germani, *White Soldiers in Black Africa*, p. 42
100 Hans Germani, *White Soldiers in Black Africa*, p. 43
101 Hans Germani, *White Soldiers in Black Africa*, p. 54
102 Hans Germani, *White Soldiers in Black Africa*, p. 53
103 Hans Germani, *White Soldiers in Black Africa*, p. 55
104 Anthony Mockler, *The New Mercenaries*, p. vii
105 http://www.bbc.co.uk/radio3/johntusainterview/mccullin_transcript.shtml
106 http://www.maturetimes.co.uk/leisure-and-lifestyle/entertainment/films/4459-joyce-glasser-reviews-.html
107 Larry Devlin, *Chief of Station, Congo*. pp. 165, 228, 229
108 The *Sunday Tribune*, 14 February 1965
109 The *Sunday Tribune*, 14 February 1965
110 The *Sunday Tribune*, 14 February 1965
111 AE Hotchner, *Papa Hemingway, a personal memoir*, p. xiii
112 Hans Germani, *White Soldiers in Black Africa*, p. 92-93
113 Hans Germani, *White Soldiers in Black Africa*, p. 61
114 Hans Germani, *White Soldiers in Black Africa*, p. 24
115 The President's Daily Brief by the CIA, 17 March 1965. p. 6 http://www.foia.cia.gov/sites/default/files/document_conversions/1827265/DOC_0005967576.pdf
116 DO 216/55, 26 & 29 March 1965
117 http://www.rjridsdill.com/CSL/StoryTCSJ.html
118 DO 216/55, 4 May 1965
119 Frank R Villafana, *Cold War in the Congo*, p. 151

120 Ian Colvin, *The Rise and Fall of Moise Tshombe*, p. 219
121 Ian Colvin, *The Rise and Fall of Moise Tshombe*, p. 218-9
122 Leif Hellström, *Les Affreux – Mercenaries and Volunteers in the Congo*, 1960-1967, p. 90
123 Hans Germani, *White Soldiers in Black Africa*, p. 127
124 Anthony Mockler, *The New Mercenaries*, p. 56
125 Colin Baker, Wild Goose: *The life and death of Hugh van Oppen*, p. 202-3, 216
126 Colin Baker, Wild Goose: *The life and death of Hugh van Oppen*, p. 215
127 Ian Colvin, *The Rise and Fall of Moise Tshombe*, p. 224
128 Colin Baker, *Wild Goose: The life and death of Hugh van Oppen*, p. 217
129 David Frost, *David Frost – An autobiography*, Part One, p. 215
130 David Frost, *David Frost – An autobiography*, Part One, p. 216
131 Undated
132 David Frost, *David Frost – An autobiography*, Part One, p. 216
133 Ian Colvin, *The Rise and Fall of Moise Tshombe*, p. 224
134 Ian Colvin, *The Rise and Fall of Moise Tshombe*, p. 222
135 FCO 25/091, 17 March 1967
136 SJG Clarke, *The Congo Mercenary*, p. 73
137 SJG Clarke, *The Congo Mercenary*, p. 72
138 Leif Hellström, *Les Affreux – Mercenaries and Volunteers in the Congo*, 1960-1967, p. 75
139 Mike Hoare in an article of 1420 words titled *Biafra*, 3 June 2005
140 *The Times*, 1 December 1967
141 *The Star*, 25 November 1967
142 Letter to Jock Roger dated 21 August 1970, written at 12 Grace Ave, Westville, Natal.
143 Email from Neill Hunt to author, February 2010
144 Email from Sue to author
145 NZPA, undated
146 *The Star*, 23 November 1974
147 Graham Linscott, *Ricochets, From Gordonstoun to Africa's wars*, p. 137
148 Rhodesian Army Archives, Box 2001/086/227
149 Rhodesian Army Archives, Box 2001/086/141
150 https://en.wikipedia.org/wiki/Tim_Spicer
151 https://en.wikipedia.org/wiki/Private_military_company
152 Mike Hoare, *Three Years with 'Sylvia'*, Chapter 11
153 *SA Outdoor Life*, December 1963 and January 1964
154 Asbjørn Halvorsen, grandson of Emanuel Moen, email 13 September 2016
155 Mike Hoare, *Mike Hoare's Adventures in Africa*, Chapter 7
156 Mike Hoare, *Mike Hoare's Adventures in Africa*, Chapter 8
157 A reference to the then elderly Sir Francis Chichester, who had recently sailed singlehandedly around the world to great acclaim.
158 Mike Hoare, *Three Years with 'Sylvia'*, p. 70
159 Mike Hoare, *Three Years with 'Sylvia'*, p. 130-150 & 171-179
160 https://en.wikipedia.org/wiki/Lord_Richard_Cecil
161 *The Wild Geese*, DVD, Severin
162 Email from Sally Carney to author, 24 May 2017.
163 Email from Euan Lloyd via Ros Kernot, his daughter, to author; 22 July 2015
164 Penny Junor, Burton, *The Man Behind the Myth*, p. 279 & p. 282

165 Mike Hoare, *Mike Hoare's Adventures in Africa*, p. 134-135
166 Anthony Mockler, *The New Mercenaries*, p. 267
167 12-18 February, 1979
168 20 November, 1978
169 *Sunday Express*, 17 December 1978
170 Unpublished manuscript: *A Spirit of Adventure* by Mike Hoare, p. 102
171 Mike Hoare, *The Seychelles Affair*
172 David Alexander, *Sani Pass – Riding the Dragon*, p. 113
173 Report of the Security Council Commission of Inquiry established under Resolution 496 (1981), 15 March 1982, Annex VI, p. 18
174 ©Peter Stiff, *Warfare By Other Means*, Galago Publishing (1999) (Pty) Ltd, p. 23
175 ©Peter Stiff, *Warfare By Other Means*, Galago Publishing (1999) (Pty) Ltd, p. 36
176 Stan Standish-White, *From the Seychelles to the Single Cells*, p. 1, 2
177 Aubrey Brooks, *Death Row in Paradise*, p. 21
178 ©Peter Stiff, *Warfare By Other Means*, Galago Publishing (1999) (Pty) Ltd, p. 37
179 Stan Standish-White, *From the Seychelles to the Single Cells*, p. 4
180 Report of the Security Council Commission of Inquiry established under Resolution 496 (1981), 15 March 1982, Annex VI, p. 28
181 ©Col Jerry Puren as told to Brian Pottinger, Mercenary Commander, Galago Publishing (Pty) Ltd. p. 379
182 ©Col Jerry Puren as told to Brian Pottinger, *Mercenary Commander*, Galago Publishing (Pty) Ltd. p. 341
183 Stan Standish-White, *From the Seychelles to the Single Cells*, p. 11
184 Report of the Security Council Commission of Inquiry established under Resolution 496 (1981), 15 March 1982, Annex VI, p. 36, p. 32, p. 21
185 Judgment in the Supreme Court of South Africa, Case No. CC 13/82, 27 July 1982, The State v Thomas Michael Bernard Hoare and 42 others, p. 3958
186 Judgment in the Supreme Court of South Africa, Case No. CC 13/82, 27 July 1982, The State v Thomas Michael Bernard Hoare and 42 others, p. 3963
187 Judgment in the Supreme Court of South Africa, Case No. CC 13/82, 27 July 1982, The State v Thomas Michael Bernard Hoare and 42 others, p. 3905
188 *The Times*, 29 July 1982
189 https://en.wikipedia.org/wiki/Capital_punishment_in_South_Africa
190 ©Peter Stiff, *Warfare By Other Means*, Galago Publishing (1999) (Pty) Ltd, p. 68, 69
191 http://sabctrc.saha.org.za/reports/volume2/chapter2/subsection44.htm p. 160
192 TRC Final Report, Vol 2, Chapter 2, Subsection 44, Paragraph 497c http://sabctrc.saha.org.za/reports/volume2/chapter2/subsection44.htm
193 Anthony Mockler, *The New Mercenaries*, p. 354, 355
194 12 May 1985
195 Bill Guthrie, *Soldier of Fortune*, January 1986, p. 46
196 Unpublished manuscript: *A Spirit of Adventure* by Mike Hoare, Chapter 8
197 Email from Don Rickard to Mike Hoare, probably 2003
198 29 October 2008

Index